explorer

GW00601025

Fiona Dunlop

AA Publishing

Written by Fiona Dunlop
Original photography by Jim Holmes
Edited, designed and produced by AA Publishing
Maps © The Automobile Association 1998

The contents of this publication are believed correct at the time of printing. Nevertheless, the publishers cannot be held responsible for any errors or omissions or for changes in the details given in this guide or for the consequences of any reliance on the information provided by the same. Assessments of attractions, hotels, restaurants and so forth are based upon the author's own personal experience and, therefore, descriptions given in this guide necessarily contain an element of subjective opinion which may not reflect the publishers' opinion or dictate a reader's own experiences on another occasion. We have tried to ensure accuracy in this guide, but things do change and we would be grateful if readers would advise us of any inaccuracies they may encounter.

A CIP catalogue record for this book is available from the British Library.

ISBN 0 7495 1615 1
Published by AA Publishing (a trading name of Automobile Association Developments Limited, whose registered office is Norfolk House, Priestley Road, Basingstoke, Hampshire RG24 9NY. Registered number 1878835).

Colour separation by Fotographics Ltd
Printed and bound in Italy by Printer Trento srl

Cover (front): Woman in boat on the Mekong River at dusk
Page 2: Boat tour of Ha Long Bay
Page 3: Dragon dance near the Opera House, Hanoi
Page 4: Resting cyclo driver, Hanoi
Page 5(a): Workers head home at Hoa Lu
Page 5(b): Ba Be National Park
Pages 6/7: Landscape of rice fields and mountains near Lai Chau
Page 6 (b): Buildings in old Hanoi
Page 8: Duck herding
Page 9: Boy at the Le Dynasty graves near Lam Son, Thanh Hoa

Titles in the Explorer series...
Australia • Boston & New England • Britain
Brittany • California • Caribbean • China • Costa Rica
Crete • Cyprus • Egypt • Florence & Tuscany
Florida France • Germany • Greek Islands • Hawaii
Indonesia • Ireland • Israel • Italy • Japan • London
Mexico • Moscow & St Petersburg • New York
New Zealand • Paris • Portugal • Prague • Provence
Rome • San Francisco • Scotland • Singapore & Malaysia
South Africa • Spain • Thailand • Turkey • Venice
Vietnam

AA World Travel Guides publish nearly 300 guidebooks to a full range of cities, countries and regions across the world. Find out more about AA Publishing and the wide range of services the AA provides by visiting our Web site at www.theaa.co.uk.

How to use this book

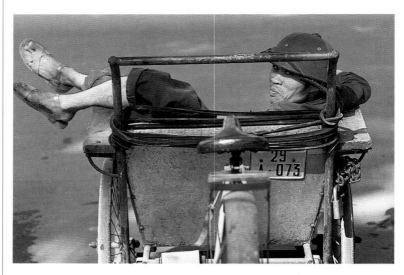

This book is divided into five main sections:

❑ Section 1: *Vietnam Is*
discusses aspects of life and living today, from ecology to handicrafts

❑ Section 2: *Vietnam Was*
places the country in its historical context and explores past events whose influences are still felt

❑ Section 3: *A to Z Section*
covers places to visit, arranged by region, with suggested walks. Within this section fall the Focus-on articles, which consider a variety of topics in greater detail

❑ Section 4: *Travel Facts*
contains the strictly practical information that is vital for a successful trip

❑ Section 5: *Hotels and Restaurants*
lists recommended establishments in Vietnam, giving a brief résumé of what they offer

How to use the star rating
Most places described in this book have been given a separate rating:

▶▶▶ Do not miss

▶▶ Highly recommended

▶ Worth seeing

Not essential viewing

Map references
To make the location of a particular place easier to find, every main entry in this book is given a map reference, such as 53C2. The first number (53) indicates the page on which the map can be found; the letter (C) and the second number (2) pinpoint the square in which the main entry is located. The maps on the inside front and inside back covers are referred to as IFC and IBC respectively.

Contents

Quick reference

This quick-reference guide highlights the elements of the book you will use most often: the maps; the introductory features; the Focus-on articles; the walks and the drives.

Map Country distinguishing signs

On some maps, international distinguishing signs have been used to indicate countries close to Vietnam. Thus:

CN = China
LAO = Laos (Lao Peoples Dem Rep)
T = Thailand
K = Cambodia

For a glossary of Vietnamese terms used on the maps, see page 243.

My Vietnam by Fiona Dunlop

My arrival in Saigon threw back in my face all the visual clichés that I had amassed over the years. Fresh from my home base in Paris where the Vietnamese community keeps a high profile, from Tran Anh Hung's film *Cyclo*, from Duong Thu Huong's novels, and distinctly less fresh after a flight that clearly revealed seemingly idyllic paddy-fields and waterways far below, I had a jumble of preconceptions desperate to find a pattern. Add to this distant memories of TV footage and press photos depicting the horrors of the Vietnam War, and you have high contrast. Two months later, exhausted after covering the country from top to bottom on motor bikes or in clapped-out buses, the pattern was still frustratingly absent.

Yet my trip was packed with images that could only be Vietnamese. Where else would you see an immaculate old gentleman being chauffeur-driven in an ancient 2CV, resprayed in silver? Or a woman farmer with pink plastic curlers peeping out from under a coolie hat? A man taking his pig for an evening walk? Or the quiet acceptance of a Buddhist monk recounting the years of tragedy? And landscape after sweeping landscape that leaves your camera lens itching?

Finally, I realised that Vietnam is about the present, about transcending the past and forging the future. This dinosaur of Marxist-Leninist rhetoric, now letting chinks of free-market economy lighten the gloom, follows its own determined path. It is tough, poor, hard-working, ambitious – and, of course, beautiful. The Vietnamese can be charm itself, inquisitive, highly informed, gentle, or downright rude, obsessed by stockpiling dong or, preferably, dollars. But the sense of equality is there, together with an extraordinary capacity for survival.

While they rediscover their identity, buried for decades under the dust of war and Communist dogma, people like you and me can only observe without fully comprehending. It makes a unique destination; annoying, exhilarating, always stimulating and ever enigmatic.

Fiona Dunlop has a taste for the tropics and a fascination for developing countries that she has exploited to the full in writing AA Explorer books on Singapore & Malaysia, Mexico, Indonesia, Costa Rica and India (forthcoming). Before her total immersion in journalism she worked in the arts from her Paris base, later penning Explorer Paris and contributing to numerous art, interior design magazines and newspapers. She now lives in London. For this guide, she rattled around cities in rickshaws, burned incense in pagodas, braved the Cambodian jungle and dived in the South China Sea to present an honest insight into Vietnam's people, places and practicalities.

VIETNAM IS

■ **The classic images of Vietnam – sampans, lotus-ponds, monkey-bridges, Ha Long Bay, paddy-fields, water-buffaloes, deserted beaches, boat-people and coolie rainhats – are all connected with water, the lifeblood of a less-than-tranquil country that is now struggling to emulate its more prosperous neighbours.** ■

Few other countries can claim such a close association with water, an omnipresent element that washes over 3,000km of coastline, and meanders along thousands of canals, ditches, arroyos and two major rivers, altogether totalling over 44,000km in length. Torrential rains and typhoons regularly flood the natural waterways, while Vietnam's rice economy would not exist without this aquatic abundance. Meanwhile, sampans float gently down the rivers and fishermen ply the ocean waves. Across the plains stretch endless patchworks of paddy-fields, while high in the mountains thundering waterfalls create impressive spectacles. Without water, the quintessential images of this visually harmonious land would evaporate.

Out of the fire True to the spirit of *yin* and *yang*, water is the complement of fire. After several decades of an infernoesque hell provoked by guns, mines, bombs and napalm, closely followed by economic misery under a misguidedly authoritarian regime, Vietnam is now raising its head to look at the outside world. At the same time, this outstandingly beautiful land is opening its doors and pockets to foreigners, doing its utmost to smooth the path through a country that is still licking its war wounds. Visitors to Vietnam cannot fail to be frustrated by the lack of infrastructure, but this is part and parcel of the spell cast by its idyllic pastoral scenes, rural activities and archaic farming methods. For the Vietnamese, however, these mean one thing only: hard work. Yet the word 'impossible' does not exist in Vietnamese, and the indomitable spirit of the people, coupled with a national talent for resourcefulness, augurs well for reconstruction.

Geographic switchback Early civilisations were all linked to water, from Funan in the Mekong Delta to the Lac Viet of the Red River Delta and the Chams, who moonlighted as pirates around the South China Sea. Vietnam's curving white coastline edges a land that varies in breadth from just 50km at its centre to

The 15,000sq km of the Red River Delta undergoes severe flooding during the monsoon

Wet rice cultivation remains the backbone of Vietnam's rural economy

600km along the northern border. Laos, Cambodia and China embrace this S-shape, which is washed to the east by the turquoise waves of the South China Sea and twists into the Gulf of Thailand in the south-west. Scattered across the ocean are several archipelagos that await tourist development but currently offer a few Robinson-Crusoe hide-aways. Inland, the spinal column of the Truong Son mountains delineates the northern and western borders, ending abruptly 100km or so north of Ho Chi Minh City (Saigon), where the flat Mekong Delta takes over. It is at these higher altitudes that some 53 minority ethnic groups live, some more comfortably than others but almost all with distinctive and fascinating lifestyles.

Lotus revival Moving into more esoteric spheres, the aquatic link continues. Buddhism has made a strong comeback since obligatory atheism was relaxed, and refur-bished pagodas once more throng with worshippers kowtowing in

clouds of incense. To the fore stands Quan Am, the Goddess of Mercy, borne on a lotus. This flower, symbol of Buddhist purity, grows out of the muddy depths of countless ponds and lakes to unfold in the sunlight. Some would identify this as a premonition of Vietnam's future. According to the tenets of *feng shui* (geomancy), water brings luck and prosperity, but for the moment at least, over 90 per cent of the Vietnamese population is still waiting.

❏   The Vietnamese word for 'country' (*dat-nuoc*) translates literally as 'land-water'. The legend surrounding the country's genesis involves a fight between two dragons, both so intent on obtaining a sacred pearl that their intertwined bodies fell into the South China Sea to form this sinuous land. Yet another legend relates the origins of the Viets, descendants of the fairy, Au Co, and the Dragon King, Lac Long, in a symbolic marriage between land and sea.   ❏

■ **Reunified in 1975, North and South Vietnam are now ostensibly following the same economic and political path. Yet deep historical and cultural divisions are not reconciled overnight, and government policies tend to exacerbate new problems. As a result, Vietnam is becoming a nation of conflicting goals.** ■

To all intents and purposes, Vietnam is a united nation of 76 million people with its administrative heart in Hanoi and its commercial pulse in Ho Chi Minh City. Apart from the minorities, all speak the same language and all share the same hopes. But do they? There remains a profound division between North and South, as well as a rapidly expanding gap between the rural poor and *nouveau riche* city-slickers, and between those who can profit from back-handers and those who cannot. The recent relaxing of control that came with *doi moi* (open-door policy) in one of the world's last bastions of Marxist-Leninism is highlighting rifts that may prove deeply corrosive.

Traditional ao dai *(tunic and pants) adapt effortlessly to motor bikes*

Antecedents From its three original kingdoms, the northernmost of these ruled by the Chinese for 1,000 years, Vietnam evolved into two cleanly divided halves that lasted over two centuries. When the French arrived the country was again broken into three separate protectorates (Tonkin, Annam and Cochinchina), before resuming the North–South division in 1954. Today, as the more prosperous and extrovert South champs at the bit, raring to vie with its peers in Thailand and Hong Kong, much of the North remains confused by the contradictions between 40-odd years of strict communist diktats and the recent opening to Western values and systems.

North versus South Hanoi may hold the reins, but it is Saigon (Ho Chi

Minh City) that provides the fuel. Although Hanoi's hardliners almost fatally reorganised much of Saigon's industrial base post-1975, this dynamic port has made a spectacular comeback. One-third of Vietnam's GDP and a similar proportion of its central-government revenues come from Saigon's textile factories, shrimp-processing plants and other businesses. The city is also the uncontested capital of Vietnam's burgeoning oil and gas industry, which generates most of the nation's export income. Flourishing rice yields in the Mekong Delta create incomes that are double those of the North's Red River Delta, English-language and computing schools in Saigon attract thousands of ambitious young Southerners, and astute ethnic Chinese businessmen operate from their base in the city's Cholon district. Yet government posts are occupied by Northerners – whether they be local police or post-office officials – thereby creating widespread resentment. Northerners regard Southerners as soft, undisciplined and rich, while, looking north, the Southerners see cold, unsophisticated and humourless disciplinarians.

Restrictions Concern about these potentially disruptive divisions played a covert role at the 1996 Party Congress, reflected in an increase in representation of officials from the army and from the Interior Ministry in the Politburo, the 19-member inner 'Cabinet'. Confronted with a long national history of rebelliousness, central government is wary of too many liberties, and in numerous towns public-address systems spout propaganda from dawn to dusk. Press freedom is limited, as is the Internet (controlled along the lines of the Singaporian model), while books, films and videos undergo strict censorship or, in some cases, suppression.

Resourceful as ever, the Southerners have created black markets to sell photocopied books or under-the-counter videos smuggled across the border from Thailand.

Since doi moi *opened Vietnam's doors, East meets West amicably*

Imbalances Today, economic momentum is leaving much of the rural population out on a limb and is creating an even more glaring fracture. With a per capita income of US$280, Vietnam ranks with Bangladesh as one of the world's poorest nations, but top wage-earners make up to 40 times as much as the lowest. Government officials, teachers and doctors earn a mere US$50 per month, an unrealistic salary that generates corrupt practices among the former and moonlighting among the professionals. This in turn means that schoolchildren whose parents can afford private lessons are the ones who pass exams, and that medical care is at its best when paid for on a private basis.

Today, over 20 years after reunification, perhaps the only generalised attitude is one that recognises the useless sacrifices and futility of the Vietnam War.

The entrepreneurial spirit flourishes

■ **As Vietnam drags itself through a confusingly slow transition from a Marxist-Leninist state-controlled economy to a free-market one, international finance institutions are watching. Initial euphoric optimism now fluctuates as the party stalls youthful ambitions and clings to the heavy-handed old ways.** ■

At reunification in 1975, party leader Le Duan promised a television and a refrigerator in every home within a decade. Over 20 years later, this is far from the case, and the rural population is at the receiving end of all the economic woes: Ho Chi Minh City-dwellers earn up to three times the national average, while 90 per cent of the official poor live in the country-side. However, the face of Vietnam has changed profoundly since the mid-1980s, and few can predict whether or not the country will join the ubiquitous Asian tiger economies. In the words of the much-revered General Giap, architect of Vietnam's military victories, 'Before we launched a war against foreign aggressors. Today we must launch a war against poverty.'

Opening doors *Doi moi* ('open-door' policy) was officially instigated at the 6th Party Congress in 1986, and although it temporarily sent inflation into an upward spiral (by 1988 it had soared to 100 per cent) by cutting state subsidies, it permitted private enterprise, reduced centralised government and liberalised foreign investment. First at the door were Vietnam's Asian neighbours, eager to profit from a young, well-educated and low-paid workforce. Until then, all foreign investment had come from Eastern Bloc countries (notably the Soviet Union), but soon a stream of joint ventures with Taiwan, South Korea, Japan, Hong Kong and Singapore began bidding for oil, manufacturing and tourism slices of the emerging economic cake. Foreign interest increased in the 1990s, crowned by the lifting of the US embargo in 1994 and Vietnam's adhesion to ASEAN, the Southeast Asian economic forum, in 1995. With annual economic growth now averaging 8 per cent, inflation at under 10 per cent and international aid flowing in, Vietnam's future should be rosy. But is it?

Handicaps Joint ventures are beset by obstacles. Bureaucracy, ever-changing regulations, licensing restrictions and endemic corruption at every level

The influential Vladimir Ilyich Lenin in 1922

14

Official propaganda attempts to boost socialist values – a losing battle in today's world?

emigrated under the UN's Orderly Departures Programme. Those that have prospered reinvest in their native country or, at a lesser level, support their impoverished relatives back home. Educated *Viet Kieu*, often graduates of business or law schools, have so far favoured small-scale investments in trade, tourism, manufacturing and real estate. Much of the entrepreneurial dynamism of Ho Chi Minh City stems from their input, overlapping with the work of ethnic Chinese who, since the 1980s reforms, have resumed their pivotal financial role. Yet despite these external influences, Vietnam seems doggedly set on an independent – and still unpredictable – path.

❑   From 1972 to 1992 Vietnam's population increased by 20 million. Today, some 60 per cent of the country's population is aged under 25.   ❑

French Catholicism watches over market innovations in Hanoi

are proving to be frustrating and costly handicaps, while Vietnam's basic infrastructure remains limited. Many had high expectations of the 1996 8th Party Congress, a critical barometer of the nation's direction for the next five years. However, it proved anticlimatic as the same trio of ageing leaders (Party Leader Do Muoi, aged 79, President Le Duc Anh, 75, and Prime Minister Vo Van Kiet, 73) was re-elected and a tighter grip put on the party in an attempt to stem corruption, deflect the reformist branch and control potential social disorder. Another outcome was the instigation of a campaign aimed at stamping out the 'negative social evils' of Western values and lifestyles – not quite but almost a replay of the late-1970s ideological campaign that saw the arrest of anyone wearing bell-bottomed trousers. It seems that Vietnam's 'mandarins' want to direct the pace and orientation of the economy themselves, without being dictated to by foreigners and at the same time keeping the lid on any dissent.

Viet Kieu An added boost to the economy has come from the esti-mated 2.5 million *Viet Kieu* (overseas Vietnamese), about half of whom live in the US. Most were refugees of the post-1975 period, while others

■ **As is the case in other Southeast Asian countries, Vietnam's tropical hardwoods have been a prime target for logging companies. But this is only one factor in the immense environmental jigsaw that confronts this impoverished and war-ravaged nation.** ■

Vietnam's post-war ecological inheritance of vast swathes of defoliated hills and bomb craters are just the beginning of the story. About 2,000sq km of land are deforested annually and only about 1,600sq km are reafforested, leaving a shortfall that is not best filled with the soil-destructive eucalyptus that has been propagated so extensively in recent years. Environmental consciousness is a luxury that the average peasant (80 per cent of the population), intent on finding firewood or on clearing land for subsistence agriculture, may not be aware of and in any case cannot afford. Meanwhile, shrimp farms of the Mekong Delta, coffee

❏ 'Crickets chirped feebly. Nothing was like it used to be. The insecticides the farmers used had depopulated the countryside just as the bombs had killed something in our souls, the divine inspiration that had once filled our lives.'
From *Novel Without a Name* by Duong Thu Huong (1995). ❏

plantations in the Central Highlands and timber companies in the North are more concerned with immediate profits than ecology. As a result, the country's ecological balance is being dangerously tilted, and side-effects such as soil erosion, silted-up rivers and polluted water supplies are compounding the problems.

New thinking Although environmental legislation kicked off in 1994, lack of resources and commitment meant that it was rarely enforced. Serious government concern was reconfirmed in 1996 with the projected establishment of the Vietnam Business Council for Sustainable Development, a watchdog and advisory body representing industry, government, the UN Development Fund and the Worldwide Fund for Nature. With Vietnam on the brink of expanding industrialisation and able to learn from the mistakes of its neighbours, the council may be just in time. Or is it?

Going, going, gone Forest cover in Vietnam has been waning steadily for centuries, cleared for paddy-fields

Slash-and-burn farming (top) and bombs (left) have left their marks

Peddling hardwood logs – a common but illicit practice

and, in colonial times, rubber and coffee plantations. In 1943, 44 per cent of the land was forested; by 1976, following the 'ecocide' of US chemical warfare (see page 204), this had dropped to 29 per cent. Today, an estimated 16 per cent remains, of which only about half is primary tropical forest, although this still harbours some 15,000 plant species. The creation of 87 national parks has partly stemmed the deforestation tide, but these are both limited and difficult to patrol. Equally problematic are controls over slash-and-burn farming carried out by ethnic minorities in remote mountainous areas; in the past, resettlement programmes have been used, but are the motives for these environmental or political control? In addition, accidental forest fires remain an unpredictable, highly destructive hazard.

Endangered Tigers, elephants, rhinoceroses, leopards, deer, bears and monkeys once roamed freely throughout Vietnam's inland areas, and although there remain 400 species of mammals, 300 species of reptiles, 1,000 species of birds and the same of fish, their numbers and varieties are rapidly declining. Poaching is a major problem, whether of species for export to

❑ The incense powder of joss-sticks is made from the bark of the *boi loi* tree and the stick itself from bamboo. It is estimated that 1cu m of *boi loi* is needed to produce 25kg of bark, so the billions of joss-sticks burned annually are another less obvious cause of deforestation. ❑

Hong Kong (such as the gastronomic delicacy of tigers' testicles or traditional medicines such as rhinoceros horns) or more common species heading straight for the Vietnamese peasant's pot.

During the war, many Viet Cong survived their jungle existence by hunting, an impossibility today as large mammals are confined to small pockets of primary forest. The Asian elephant now numbers 250–300, about a quarter of the total that existed in the 1970s. Half their decline is thought to be due to poaching for ivory, meat and leather, and half due to shooting by farmers in an effort to prevent the animals' destructiveness. Elephant reserves are now being set up and a total ban declared on their hunting. However, it will be a long time before the average Vietnamese, whether fisherman or farmer, has either the time or the desire to be concerned with environmental problems.

■ **After years of persecution and suppression under the strict communist regime, religion has made a resounding comeback, and nowhere is this more apparent than in the country's incense-filled pagodas. The three beliefs of Buddhism, Taoism and Confucianism compose Vietnam's spiritual base, creating a ritualistic system that overflows into social and political life.** ■

Animism and Hinduism were joined in Vietnam by Buddhism in the 2nd century AD, but it was not until the 11th century that it became the official state religion. From then until the 14th century, *chua* (pagodas) proliferated through the Chinese-ruled North and numerous emperors were educated in Buddhist monasteries. In the South, Theravada Buddhism (the Lesser Vehicle school) arrived directly with Indian monks, but it was Mahayana Buddhism (the Greater Vehicle school) that eventually came to dominate Vietnam after arriving via China.

Tripartite worship Mahayana Buddhism was then fused with the philosophies of Taoism and Confucianism to form Tam Giao, the 'triple religion', now the belief of over 70 per cent of the population. Domestic ancestor shrines (Confucian) and spirit altars (Taoist) thus coexist alongside pagodas with their hundreds of Bodhisattvas,

although the Khmer temples of the Mekong Delta remain faithful to the more purist Theravada Buddhism. During the years of strict communist rule religion went into retreat, but since 1989 *chua* and *dinh* (community assembly halls) have been dramatically revived.

Bodhisattvas rule At the basis of Mahayana Buddhism is the ideal of the Bodhisattva, striving for earthly perfection and helping others on the path without aiming to achieve nirvana, the state of non-being and Buddhahood perceived by Theravada Buddhists as the ultimate escape from the cycle of reincarnation. Gautama Buddha is regarded as just one of countless manifestations in a vast pantheon that includes Quan Am (the Goddess of Mercy and of Mother and Child), A Di Da (Buddha of the Past), Sakyamuni (the historical Buddha) and Di Lac (Buddha of the Future). In pagodas, these central figures are often surrounded by *arhat* (saints) and Avalokitsvara (a Bodhisattva seen as the saviour of Mahayana Buddhism), as well as funerary tablets dedicated to monks buried in stupas near by.

Taoism The popular form of Buddhism that developed among Vietnam's rural population was marked by the adoption of Taoist spirits and gods. *Tao*, meaning the 'path' or 'original principle', is a complex metaphysical system based on the dualism of the cosmos (*yin* and *yang*, heaven and earth, sun and moon) as

Hanoi's Van Mieu sees offerings ranging from Tiger beer to mangoes

related by Lao Tse, a 6th-century BC Chinese philosopher. Its basis is that a person's fate is predetermined, and that happiness comes through contemplation, asceticism and maintaining the balance.

In Vietnam the enigmatic abstractions of this philosophy are overtaken by its more tangible deities, representing the forces of nature, a logical extension of early Vietnamese animism. Ruling the endless spirits, genies and demons is the Jade Emperor (Ngoc Hoang), while the Eight Immortals

(seven men and one woman who drank the elixir of immortality) have become 27, the majority of these now women. Four Venerated Mothers (of Heaven, Earth, Water and Forest) rule the cardinal points and protect rice-fields, helped by a host of assistant deities. Taoist and Buddhist altars often stand side by side in Vietnamese pagodas, their spiritual beliefs supplemented by the social ethics of Confucianism.

Confucianism The teachings of this virtual contemporary of Lao Tse aimed to restore basic virtues to Chinese society, and as such were never

intended as a religion. Like Taoism, much of this philosophy depended on a respect for the status quo. This brought the cult of ancestor worship, along with the goal of determining one's own destiny (the opposite of Taoism) through moral perfection and knowledge. The crux of Confucianism lies in the Three Bonds, these demanding loyalty of government to the emperor, obedience of children to parents and submission of wives to husbands. Although its hierarchical code was apparently incompatible with Communism, the importance of social and family obligations set this philosophy aside from the egocentric ambitions of bourgeois capitalism (see also panel on page 63).

(see also panel on page 63).

Top to bottom: incense sticks and coils, paper token offerings, and a roadside shrine

■ **Vietnam's numerous ethnic minorities together form a fascinating tapestry of ancient Asian cultures that lies hidden beneath the surface of that of the dominant Viets. For centuries these peoples have been migrating from southern China to join the existing minorities of Chams and Khmers in Vietnam.** ■

About 88 per cent of Vietnam's 74 million people are Viets, also called Kinh, who dominate the socio-politico-economic life of the cities, deltas and coastal plains. However, up in the highlands of the Centre or the North there is a wealth of 53 different minorities, all of whom have their own languages, identities and customs. Relations between majority and minorities have wavered over the centuries, but in many cases geographical isolation has prevented any Viet cultural interference and left ethnic groups remarkably untouched. Today, government policies veer towards integration and the days of semi-autonomy are over.

❏ Minorities now have proportional representation in the National Assembly, and President Le Duc Anh himself, elected in 1992, is of Montagnard origin. ❏

Hoa The largest minority group, numbering nearly a million, is the Hoa (ethnic Chinese). This mainly urban, southern minority underwent endless miseries post-1975, the result being that they deserted the country in their hundreds of thousands as boat-people. Traditional Chinese business acumen, secret societies and congregations (according to their ancestors' province of origin) have done little to improve the Hoa's social acceptance, while Vietnam's historic mistrust of its northerly neighbour has often led to government persecution. With Vietnam's recent open-door policy, the Hoa have become better appreciated for their commercial input, and

many Chinese *Viet Kieu* (overseas Vietnamese) are returning to become a major economic force once again.

Montagnards A fabulous patchwork of 53 ethnic groups peppers the highlands of the Centre and North, some accounting for over a million people and others consisting of barely a hundred. In total there are 8–9 million minority people. Their generic label, Montagnards, meaning 'mountain-dwellers', was applied by the French colonists and is still used in preference to *Moi*, a pejorative Vietnamese word meaning 'savages' that is now largely redundant. Linguistically, the Montagnards fall into three main groups: the Austro-Asians, speaking Mon-Khmer languages; the Malayo-Polynesians; and the Sino-Tibetans. However, each minority has its own language, and sub-groups have developed startling variations in costume or in vernacular architecture (see also pages 84–5 and 142–3). As all were nomadic, there is an overlap between those groups inhabiting the Centre and the North.

Ambivalent future Over the years the status of ethnic groups within the nation has fluctuated under the influence of Catholic and Protestant missionaries or the wars with the French and Americans. Minorities of the lower central areas were more accessible and as a result have undergone greater integration, whether through having worked on plantations, missionary education, being recruited by the French or US armies, or through government policies. This has produced an ambivalent situation that on paper appears to be making positive

socio-economic efforts but in reality is destroying traditions, motivation and self-respect. Elders who had French educations and were brought up as devout Christians now find themselves out on a limb, while poverty prevents the younger generation from attending the few schools. For centuries minorities have existed largely on slash-and-burn farming, an environmental no-no that is now being countered by government moves to gather former nomadic farmers in lowland settlements. This two-sided coin offers on the one hand better education (including a university for minorities in Buon Ma Thuot), medical facilities and farming potential, but on the other an erosion of traditions and identity.

Top: just a few faces from Vietnam's 53 ethnic minorities

Hands off In the remote northern mountains it is a slightly different story. Less affected by colonialism and supportive of the North Vietnamese cause, certain minorities were granted semi-autonomy in the mid-1960s. Fiercely independent, they have brushed off outside interference, continuing to cultivate opium illegally, maintaining matriarchal systems or living astride the Chinese border to be near their peers. Growing curiosity on the part of tourists may now be the main threat to their relatively unpolluted cultures.

Stilt houses designed for rooting pigs – beneath

■ **Fireworks displays, wrestling matches, water-puppetry, water-buffalo sacrifices, human chess games and dragon-boat races pepper the Vietnamese festival calendar, making it a virtual certainty that some form of celebration will be in full swing whenever you visit the country.** ■

Vietnam's festival calendar is dominated by Tet, the quintessential public holiday that announces the lunar New Year (see pages 180–1) and the reign of a new zodiac sign. This movable feast falls between 19 January and 20 February in the Western calendar and officially lasts three days, but in reality it spills riotously over a week. From this new moon there is a lunar countdown to hundreds of pagoda, village-spirit, historic and agricultural festivals, all perfect excuses to cook special cakes, burn more joss-sticks, make temple pilgrimages or join in the festive throngs. Village festivals usually take place in the spring after the harvest or rice-transplanting. Each is celebrated differently, from buffalo-fighting to song contests revolving round the pagoda or *dinh* (village assembly hall). Similarly, minorities have their own festivities and extraordinary customs.

Fervent worshippers at the Den Ngoc Son (Jade Mountain Temple) festival in Hanoi

Military prowess It is hard to forget Vietnam's long history of resistance and victories over foreign invaders as, even a millennium later, heroic generals and major battles are celebrated (although not always on a national scale). The legendary names of Tran Hung Dao, Le Loi, the Trung sisters and Quang Trung all come alive during their respective festivals, while Dien Bien Phu (victory over the French on 7 May 1954) and Liberation of the South (30 April 1975) are reminders of more recent triumphs. Politically charged festivals peak on 19 May when Ho Chi Minh's birthday is officially commemorated.

Dead revival More esoteric in nature are Buddhist festivals such as Vu Lan (Wandering Souls, 15th day of the seventh lunar month), when families make offerings at the graves of deceased relatives and at specially prepared domestic altars for the forgotten dead. Top of the offerings list are *tam sinh,* the three living creatures (fish, meat and shrimp), and *ngu qua,* five kinds of fruit. Ancestors again receive special attention at Thanh Minh (5th day of the third lunar month), a day devoted to appeasing the dead by cleaning and painting graves, and, in extreme cases – for example, if the family has not had much luck of late – exhuming a coffin to move it to a more auspicious site. More focused, although not as formally celebrated as in the past, is Phat Dan or Buddha's birthday (8th day of fourth lunar month), when pagodas are filled with lanterns and evening processions celebrate his attainment of nirvana. In some regions there is a ritual setting-free of caged doves, which are then judged for best flight patterns and altitude.

Celebrations extend to the burning of specially made paper figures

Nature worship This agricultural country pays equal attention to the changing seasons, celebrating Tet Doan Ngo, the summer solstice (5th day of the fifth lunar month) to harmonise the complementary *yin* and *yang* principles of nature, a Taoist practice that sees brightly painted dragon-boats and offerings made to the God of Death. Autumn harvest brings Tet Trung Thu (15th day of the eighth lunar month), a full-moon celebration devoted to children, who parade with candles, lanterns and toys while gorging themselves on sticky-rice moon-cakes. Less widespread is the double-nine festival marking the transition from autumn to winter (9th day of the ninth lunar month), when kites take to the skies.

Idiosyncracies Apart from the above there are countless local festivals that re-enact legends, make buffalo sacrifices or organise singing or wrestling contests. In certain pago-das of the North, a ritualistic chess game is performed with costumed human 'pieces', while minority mountain-dwellers reserve one day a year for reliving youthful romances in the company of their ex. Fertility celebrations peak in the festivities of Ken, mainly practised in the Red River Delta. Wooden symbols of the phallus (*non*) and the female organ (*nuong*) are paraded, danced with, suspended from branches and finally thrown to the crowd to bring luck in love and life.

Festivals fire the gastronomic imagination

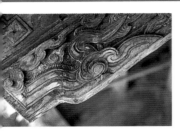

■ **From simple thatched dwellings with woven bamboo walls to precarious-looking post-modern concrete structures and fast-ageing Soviet-built apartment blocks, Vietnamese domestic architecture roller-coasters through the styles and centuries. In radical contrast are the decorative eaves and carved rafters of the country's stunning ancient pagodas.** ■

As you travel from one end of Vietnam to the other you are faced with an array of architectural styles moulded by diverse climatic and cultural influences. However, Chinese characteristics in the North and Khmer in the South become obsolete when it comes to urban architecture. This is the domain of solid French colonial styles, from neo-classical to art deco, or of 1960s and 1970s apartment blocks designed by Soviets for their cheapness and functionalism. More whimsical are the 1980s and 1990s 'post-modern' concrete matchboxes that bristle with arches, columns and balustrades, while the most colourful are the houses of Vietnam's central coast, painted in contrasting lavender, saffron-yellow and turquoise.

❑ The remarkable attributes of bamboo have made it a favourite for domestic architecture throughout tropical Southeast Asia. Fast-growing, waterproof, insectproof, flexible and resistant, it makes an economical though relatively short-lived material. After splitting lengthwise, the bamboo cane can even be plaited into walls that provide natural ventilation. ❑

Pre-colonial Before the French arrived, a Vietnamese architectural style was only visible in imperial palaces, citadels, pagodas and *dinh* (village assembly halls). Dominating both town and countryside were simple shacks, tiled in the North and thatched with palm leaves in the South, and with walls of packed earth or woven bamboo. The only exceptions to this rule were Hoi An's elaborate Chinese houses and the Malayo-Polynesian stilt-houses adopted by highland minorities. Although bricks had been made from the clay of the deltas since the early centuries AD, these were generally only used for religious and administrative buildings, and in any case were abandoned in favour of carved wood when the Chinese model became the adopted style for Buddhist pagodas.

Eaves point heaven-wards at the Tay Phuong Pagoda outside Hanoi

Gallic pretensions With the French came the grandiose stuccoed and colonnaded government buildings of Hanoi and Saigon, laid out according to clear urban patterns and adapted to local climates with

24

throughout Hanoi's Hai Ba Trung district, where some 400 examples survive.

Spiritual retreats In pagodas and *dinh*, with their floors of packed mud, rows of wooden columns were used to support heavy, elaborately sweeping roofs. Nails were unheard of and timber was joined by shafts, dowels or wooden pegs, making for extreme flexibility within the structure. Carvings, fretwork and lacquering embellished some interior features, while the corners of tiled roofs could swing skywards to culminate in ornate carvings. Multi-storeyed towers (*thap*), popular in the 11th–13th centuries, or bell-shaped burial stupas stood outside the main temple. Walled *quan* (Taoist temples) and *dinh*

Hai Phong's French neo-classical theatre disappears behind another ode to Ho

Villagers opt for stilt-houses in the Central Highlands

shutters and verandas. Minor Hanoi officials lived in turn-of-the-century villas reminiscent of Normandy, with steep tiled roofs and wooden beams, a style that also came to dominate the hill-stations of Da Lat and Sa Pa. The last architectural influence imported by the French was art deco, a style still seen in 30 per cent of Hanoi's old buildings. This style also occasionally incorporated local features: the British Ambassador's residence at 13 Phan Chu Trinh is a prime example of typical art deco symmetry crowned by an oriental tiled roof. Four Vietnamese architects trained at the former Indochina Art College, and their purist 1930s style spread to Emperor Bao Dai's villas in Da Lat, Vung Tau and Do Son, as well as

complexes devoted to village spirits provide striking variations in design, the latter often raised on piles. Religious architecture changes again in the Khmer pagodas of the Mekong Delta, where extravagantly winged roofs, cremation towers, brightly painted stupas, murals and intricate floral paintings create a total decorative unity.

■ A fabulous wealth of handmade *objets* awaits visitors to Vietnam, some faithful replicas of centuries-old forms and others more recent evolutions in style and technique. But whatever the finished piece, the country's artisans display dexterity, patience and, once again, a will to survive. ■

Hanoi, Hue and Ho Chi Minh City are the three main craft centres, their needs often supporting the livelihoods of entire outlying villages. Lacquerware, ceramics, embroidery, inlay, carving, masks and silverware swamp the tourist shops, while the domestic market demands basketware, coolie hats and endless bamboo utensils. Interesting textiles are the domain of the minorities, whether sophisticated Cham weavings or the colourful embroideries of the northern highlanders.

Lacquer Originally brought from China several centuries ago, the laborious lacquer technique is now being overtaken by mass-produced synthetic finishes that obtain an equally high sheen and are used to coat a vast array of decorative containers. The original basic resin comes from the Japanese tree *Rhus vernicifera*, which grows prolifically in the North. The resin is applied successively up to 12 times to impeccably sanded and polished wood (in the past, top-quality pieces could be coated 200 times), incorporates

❏ Although ivory and tortoiseshell items are unfortunately widely available, this industry is ecologically damaging and so should not be supported. ❏

eggshell, gold-dust and/or mother-of-pearl inlay, and needs a week to dry out between coats. The result is a densely coloured, smooth and lustrous surface, traditionally only in black, red, yellow and brown but now extending to a rainbow of colours.

❏ Since the mid-18th century, mother-of-pearl from oyster and mollusc shells has been finely chiselled, polished and cut for use as inlays in lacquered objects, wooden furniture or screens, usually in the form of animal and plant designs. ❏

Ceramics Vietnamese pottery dates back to the neolithic period, but yet again it was the Chinese who introduced more advanced glazing techniques so that by the 11th century Dai Viet was producing ceramics of great sophistication. Emperors and mandarins patronised the busy kilns of the Red River Delta and Thanh Hoa province, while Buddhist pagodas stimulated a new demand for statues and ritual objects. Roof-tiles, glazed bricks and monochrome objects in ivory-white, jade-green and brown glazes became popular during the

Vietnamese dexterity extends to the weaving of fish-traps (top) and painstaking lacquerwork (left)

The art of woodcarving is taught from an early age

extensively with delightful scenes of farmers, villages, kite-flyers, birds, dragons and flowers. Designs are often specific to the function of the cloth. Hanoi's old quarter once had its Hang Theu ('Embroiderers' Street', now Hang Trong), but the craft extends throughout the country, whether touted alongside superb lacework by a waterborne hawker at Hoa Lu or marginally more serenely in Ho Chi Minh City's prolific silk shops.

❑ A recurring symbol in this country of outdoor workers is the classic conical coolie hat, which can be snapped up at any market for under US50¢. Woven from translucent young palm leaves, its up-market versions (notable in Hue) incorporate cut-out motifs between the layers, embroidery and even poems. Chin-ribbons vary from coquettish velvet to basic cotton. Countless alternative headgear is also on sale, sometimes producing surreal sights – a fisherman in a frilly raffia sun-hat? ❑

Tran Dynasty (1225–1400). In the following two centuries ornamentation became richer and cobalt-blue appeared from China; this created the renowned blue and white ceramics that proliferated in 19th-century Hue.

Today's main ceramics centres are Hue, Bat Trang and Tho Ha villages near Hanoi, Ho Chi Minh City, Song Be province and Bien Hoa.

Woodcarving Vietnam's rich tropical forests provided woodcarvers with a glorious array of ironwood, ebony, mahogany, teak and rosewood, all prime materials for carving into the beautiful religious icons, rafters and pillars that filled the pagodas and *dinh*. These, together with the remarkably carved Chinese homes of Hoi An, offer a vision of a craft that has now been adapted to produce more functional items. A spin-off of wood products are the colourful woodcuts illustrating Vietnamese legends that are sold during Tet (see panel on page 79).

Embroidery This skilled craft, exclusive to women, has been successfully adapted to the tourist market. Table-linen, silk shirts and kimonos are embroidered

Embroidery remains the woman's domain

■ **Folk-tales, harsh realism, ghosts and social comment all have their place in Vietnamese literature, an art form that has evolved over the centuries from an oral tradition to Chinese-influenced classical poetry and, in the 20th century, to Western-inspired novels.** ■

Melancholy could be said to be the overriding theme and irony the tone that link Vietnam's contemporary literature with its early poetry. Chinese themes and language dominated until the 10th century, but with independence and the development of *chu nom* (a written language using Chinese characters to express Vietnamese sounds), more national expressions developed although form still obeyed strict syntax. Radical change finally came in the early 20th century with the

The yen to learn takes form in endless pavement bookstalls

generalised adoption of *quoc ngu* (Alexandre de Rhodes' transcription of spoken Vietnamese into a Romanised script) and the spread of French. Today, a strong literary output is nurtured by the Writers' Union, although expression continues to be tightly controlled by censorship and repression.

Classics Vietnam's first great poet was Nguyen Trai (1380–1442), the gifted adviser to the military hero Le Loi. His *chu nom* poetry glorified popular national characteristics, although he was also skilled at writing in classical Chinese, the language used for official documents and academic literature. Adaptation of Chinese themes continued into the 18th century with the celebrated *Lament of the Warrior's Wife* and the *Complaint of the Royal Concubine*, the former an anti-war poem and the latter a nostalgic feminine account of the passing of the years that has since been reinterpreted as having an anti-feudal message. Above all, it was the epic *Tale of Kieu* by Nguyen Du (1765–1820) that marked the pre-colonial period. Every Vietnamese knows a few verses of the 3,000 that make up this story of the corruption of pure love by greed and power-lust.

❏ An exceptional literary figure at the turn of the 19th century was the proto-feminist poetess Ho Xuan Huong, whose subtle poems worked on two levels, often concealing erotic content while satirising pompous officialdom or celebrating free love and women's equality. ❏

Bitter-sweet and with a strong moral tone, this tale of a Vietnamese Romeo and Juliet nevertheless ends with the couple being reunited.

Contemporary writing Several contemporary Vietnamese writers are now accessible to the West in French and English translations (in itself a difficult task as the Vietnamese language operates on ambiguity and even intuitive meanings, quite the opposite to the formal logic of French). Foremost of these is Duong Thu Huong, who returned to Hanoi after spending seven youthful years on the warfront. Her four novels (including *Love-story Told Before Dawn*, 1986, *Paradise of the Blind*, 1988, and *Novel Without a Name*, 1995) interweave poignant studies of daily life with the illusions and suffering of war or the absurdities of government diktats. In 1991 she was imprisoned for her outspoken advocacy of democratic reform and human rights, but although her novels are still officially banned they continue to circulate in photocopied versions.

A writer of the same generation whose six years on the front opened his eyes to the futility and delusions inherent in the Northern cause is Bao Ninh, who published *The Sorrow of War* in 1991. Yet again, melancholy is the key word, and the book was decried by officialdom for focusing on the 'dark and utterly tragic' side of war.

Closer to the popular Vietnamese tradition of rural tales and village relationships are the short stories of Nguyen Huy Thiep, a skilled ceramicist, painter and writer who, so far, has managed to stay within the bounds of politically correct literature.

❏ Vietnam's 20th-century tribulations have inspired numerous Western writers, from the spirited, insightful travelogues of Crosbie Garstin and Norman Lewis to Graham Greene's novel of political intrigue describing the cusp of the French and US presence, *The Quiet American* (1954). Queen of them all is Marguerite Duras, whose Mekong Delta childhood coloured the emotions of *Un Barrage Contre le Pacifique* (1950) and *L'Amant* (1984). Unique are the short stories of Robert Olen Butler, an American linguist who, after serving in Vietnam, donned the Vietnamese psyche in *A Good Scent from a Strange Mountain* (1992). ❏

■ **From North to South the national dish is *pho*, a nutritious, cheap noodle-soup that is slurped down for breakfast and no doubt partly responsible for that unique Vietnamese energy. Equally omnipresent is boiled rice, doused in *nuoc mam* (fermented fish sauce) and accompanying anything from seafood to beef or snake.** ■

Positioned half-way between Chinese and Thai cooking styles, Vietnamese cuisine exploits countless fresh ingredients that vary depending on the region. MSG (monosodium glutamate), the bane of many Asian cuisines, is rarely encountered, leaving space for subtle herbal flavours or stronger chilli and garlic. The national pastime of snacking is made easy by itinerant vendors and roadside stalls, while the post-prandial floor debris of banana-leaf wrappers, prawn-shells, fish-bones, napkins and toothpicks is proof of the gusto that accompanies such indulgence. Fresh lobster, shrimps, squid and cuttlefish raise their bestial heads from the waters of the Mekong Delta to Ha Long Bay, while abundant fruit and vegetables grow in the tropical South. However, it is the North that has given Vietnam its national dish of *pho*.

Pho Huge bowls of steaming broth laced with rice-noodles, finely sliced meat, spring onions, garlic, ginger and red peppers, and spiced with mint leaves, star anise and pepper have become a daily fix for every Vietnamese. Originally from Hanoi, *pho* (pronounced 'fur') is now found throughout the country, inspiring rapturous reactions when it has simmered the

❑ Coiled white rice-noodles, eaten cold, are used in endless *bun* dishes: *bun cha* is made with grilled pork; *bun oc* includes freshwater snails; and *bun bo* is a bowl of cold noodles mixed with beansprouts, fried garlic, herbs and shredded beef, all generously doused in a vinegary chilli sauce. ❑

obligatory 12 hours without ever boiling. *Pho bo* (beef noodle-soup) is more common in the North, while *pho ga* (chicken noodle-soup) is the standard in the South; either can be at their refined best in an obscure backstreet food-stall.

On a roll Another national addiction is the fried spring-roll (*cha gio* to Southerners, *nem ran* to Northerners). Ingredients comprise variations on minced pork, crab, shrimps, mushrooms, beansprouts, onions, eggs and seasoning, all wrapped into a cylinder of transparent rice-paper and fried. Artful eating requires wrapping the rolls in fresh herbs such as mint before lifting them with chopsticks to dip in *nuoc mam* (fish sauce) and

Dried squid ready for the pot in Ho Chi Minh City

transferring them to your mouth. Westerners usually give up and use their fingers. This appetiser is then followed by a main course of fish or meat, always accompanied by generous bowls of *com* (boiled white rice).

Desserts However appreciative they may be of rice and its derivatives, the Vietnamese also have a sweet tooth that is catered for by *che*, especially common from Hue northwards. This syrupy pudding is served with shaved ice in summer and comprises extraordinary combinations of mung beans, coconut milk, dried bananas, jelly, lychees, peanuts and sesame- or lotus-seeds. Southerners love to indulge in ice-cream (*kem*) or the French legacy of crème caramel. In contrast, New Year cakes (*banh trung*) are salty mixtures of sticky rice, meat and mung beans wrapped in banana leaves.

Noodle-soup stands can be works of art (above), while taste-buds are tickled by guavas sprinkled with chilli-salt (left)

❑ The enormous lotus flower provides edible roots, seeds and leaves. Not just a delicacy, the lotus is also symbolic as it grows up from the murky depths to the light, and as such is common in Buddhist imagery. The leaves are used to wrap sticky rice sweets, the stamens are mixed with tea to impart a special scent, and the seeds are boiled into sugary *che* or glazed and eaten as candy. ❑

Drinks Tea has great ritualistic social significance, and sharing a few thimblefuls is a necessary preliminary to business negotiations, scholarly meditation or merely getting acquainted. Speciality fragrant teas are made by adding flowers to the brew, while the cheapest tea (*voi* or 'poor man's tea') is not actually tea at all. Beer-drinking is making huge inroads, with frothy *bia hoi* (draught beer) a cheap favourite at male lunches (foreign breweries are bidding madly for a stake in this burgeoning market). To finish a meal in style, however, try viperine (*ruou ran*, or 'snake liqueur'), a transparent liquor flavoured by the corpse of a small viper curled up in the bottle.

■ **Inextricably linked with songs, mime and music, traditional Vietnamese theatre is still performed by state-funded troupes even though its popularity is waning. Although all classical theatre originated in China, French influences have been absorbed into drama forms of the South.** ■

Three forms of theatre have evolved to create performances in which much of the enjoyment stems from the interaction between the actors and the public. *Cheo* (popular opera), thought to date from the 14th century when it was introduced by a Chinese actor, is preserved above all in the North. This simple synthesis of folk songs, dances and narration was traditionally performed in *dinh* (village assembly halls) with a cast of only three: a hero, a heroine and a clown, the latter the mouthpiece for satirical observations as well as enacting pure farce and acrobatics. Proverbs and popular sayings have occasionally been infiltrated by more political observations, leading to the sporadic banning of *Cheo*.

Epic rituals More stylised is *Hat Boi* or *Tuong* (court opera), a dramatic form that probably came from China in the 13th century, went underground for a long period, but was revived by the Nguyen Dynasty in Hue when texts were written down. Legends of epic heroes and heroines are performed according to set rules

with equally symbolic make-up and costumes. Interest lies in the formal gestures and songs, in the six-piece orchestra and in the audience's familiarity with some 500 classical plays. Woe betide the actor or actress who veers from the ritualistic path.

Operetta A more recent drama form is *Cai Luong* (renovated opera), which evolved in the Mekong Delta in the 1920s. French boulevard farce combines with about 20 set melodies, each one expressing a specific emotion according to the tempo at which it is played. Despite the numerous and elaborate scenes, the most stirring element for a Western observer is the audience's instant reaction to the opening bars of 'Vong Co', the popular song of sadness whose name literally means 'Nostalgia for the Past'.

Left: The pivotal clown in Cheo *is a vehicle for both satire and farce Opposite: Spiritual peace at Chua Thay*

VIETNAM WAS

■ **Vietnamese history goes back some 300,000 years, but it was in the first millennium BC that civilisations took shape, also giving rise to endless whimsical legends. These sophisticated cultures eventually formed three distinct kingdoms, all strongly influenced by India or China. ■**

Lang Son province (on the Chinese border), Hoa Binh and Thanh Hoa have so far produced Vietnam's oldest fossils and stone artefacts, these dating from 11000 BC to 3000 BC, while Sa Huynh pottery emerged around 2500 BC. By 1000 BC Bronze Age culture was reaching heights of sophistication in the idiosyncratic art of the Dong Son culture (in Thanh Hoa), whose bronze-casting techniques spread as far as Indonesia. These skills were shared with the Lac Viets of the Red River Delta, whose legendary Hung kings, seen as the founders of Vietnamese civilisation, took on greater substance when their ruler An Duong built his citadel at Co Loa (outside present-day Hanoi) in 258 BC. Soon after, the Cham and Oc Eo civilisations emerged in the Centre and South respectively.

Funan Oc Eo was the main port of Funan, an Indianised kingdom centred on the fertile Mekong Delta that lasted from the 1st to 6th centuries AD. Criss-crossed by elaborate canals that were edged with brick and wood buildings containing superbly subtle statuary, Oc Eo foreshadowed Angkor, the latter founded by the accomplished Khmers in the early 9th century. Funan's trading network put the kingdom in touch with China, Rome and, above all, India, source of

The Chams produced superlative sculptures

Brahminism, Hinduism and Buddhism. Political and religious systems were based on the Indian model, but as many of the kingdom's beautiful urban structures were made of wood, little remains of this civilisation bar its wonderful sculpture. It eventually evolved into Chenla, whose capital moved into central Cambodia.

Champa Contemporaneous with Funan, Chenla and Angkor was the maritime kingdom of Champa in Central Vietnam, which erected fabulous brick towers and filled them with remarkable statues. Sandwiched between the Chinese-controlled Viets to the north and the Khmers to the south, the piratical Chams were constantly under pressure. Over their ten-odd centuries of concentrated power they managed to beat off attacks from the Chinese, Javanese, Mongols and Khmers, finally bowing to the inevitable in 1471 when they were defeated by the Viets. Hinduism was again the dominant religion, and the decorative styles of their bas-reliefs and towering pavilion shrines

had much in common with those of India and the Khmers. Buddhism came too, leading to the erection of monasteries. The Cham cult of divine kingship resembled the Khmer god-kings, but as their kingdom was more fragmented it never attained the scale and sophistication of Angkor.

My Son, the Cham religious capital from the 4th to 13th centuries

Chinese colony In the North, the expansionist Chinese Han Dynasty made serious inroads into the region, first conquering the Lac Viet in 208 BC and then, from 111 BC, ruling northern Vietnam as a province, a state of affairs that was to last over a thousand years until AD 938. Despite this lengthy dominance – which brought systems of administration, agriculture, medicine, science, literature and philosophy – Vietnam managed to preserve its own identity, traditions and language. Ploughs, domesticated animals, and dike and irrigation systems transformed Viet society, previously dependent on hunting, fishing and slash-and-burn farming. Confucianism, Taoism and Mahayana Buddhism arrived with the Chinese, while Theravada Buddhism came with monks directly from India. The mandarin education system was introduced, bringing with it the official Chinese language and a civil and military hierarchy that was to last until the 20th century. Not least, the name An Nam ('Pacified South') was applied to this colony. Yet the Viets were no push-over: rebellions and revolts took place time and time again, whether led by the Trung Sisters or Ba Trieu, and culminated in the final victory at Bach Dang in 938 when Ngo Quyen outwitted his Chinese opponents (see box).

❏ Vietnam's military wiliness was first illustrated at Bach Dang River, when General Ngo Quyen lured a huge Chinese fleet into the estuary where he had planted an underwater network of iron-tipped stakes. The Chinese duly arrived and were impaled, half their crews drowning. The same system was employed successfully again in 1288 by Tran Hung Dao against Kublai Khan's Mongol fleet of 400 ships. ❏

Bronze-casting was perfected by the Dong Son culture c. 1000 BC

■ **The 800 momentous years following Ngo Quyen's victory were highlighted by battles against the Chinese, Mongols and Chams, renewed Chinese dominance, civil war between North and South, the arrival of European traders and missionaries, and the flowering of Vietnamese arts.** ■

Dai Viet was the name given to the newly independent state that was established by the Dinh Dynasty at Hoa Lu in 968. A period of unrest followed, with rival clans vying for control. It was finally seized by Le Dai Hanh, a Buddhist who surrounded himself with monks as advisers and did much for raising the quality of daily life. Under the Late Ly Dynasty (1009–1225) the capital moved to Thang Long (Hanoi), where a stable government backed by a large army led to renewed confidence. Irrigation in the Red River Delta expanded, and financial rewards poured into beautiful pagodas and *dinh* (community halls), palaces, citadels and Vietnam's first university, the Temple of Literature. Music, dance, water-puppetry, classical opera and wrestling all flourished. As well as repelling Chinese attacks from the north, the Ly advanced south, eventually eating into Cham territory.

Ming aggressors Following the Ly came the Tran, who distinguished themselves by implementing reforms, improving the civil service and even forming an alliance with the Chams when Kublai Khan's

❑ Alexandre de Rhodes (1591–1660) was a dynamic French Jesuit who devised *quoc ngu*, the phonetic Latinised transcription of Vietnamese still used today. In 1645 he narrowly escaped a death sentence for illegally proselytising and was expelled from Vietnam. ❑

formidable Mongol forces appeared on the doorstep in the 13th century. By the late 14th century this fruitful period dissolved into internal unrest, creating a fragile situation soon taken advantage of by the Chinese Ming, who from 1407 to 1427 re-established direct rule. Once again, however, Vietnam produced a brilliant leader, Le Loi, who spent ten years turning out the Chinese in tandem with his scholar-adviser, Nguyen Trai. Viet guerrilla tactics and psychological warfare had been born.

Overstretched Led by Le Loi, the reunited nation embarked on its golden era, a period of flourishing arts and education, social and land reforms and the creation of an advanced legal code. Inexorably, the Viets expanded, pushing the Chams back until Le Thanh Ton won a decisive victory over the southern kingdom at Vijaya in 1471.

Problems soon appeared with the impracticability of this overextended kingdom, and Late Le Dynasty authority was increasingly challenged by local clans. This evolved into a situation where a puppet emperor

Hoa Lu's temple statues witnessed Vietnam's independence from Chinese rule in the 10th century

was maintained but real power lay in the rival hands of the northern Trinh and southern Nguyen lords, whose respective control stopped at the 17th parallel, a highly prophetic division. In 1672, 50-odd years of civil war finally ended with a treaty between the Trinh and Nguyen, the latter transferring their capital to Hue.

'Foreign devils' Meanwhile, Vietnam had been permeated by European missionaries and, close on their heels, traders, all part of the play of Western powers angling for Asian profits. Portuguese Catholic missionaries had arrived in the mid-16th century, but were now joined by Japanese Jesuits, Dutch and, most importantly, French Catholics, who often acted as go-betweens for traders. By the mid-17th century, Vietnamese rulers were seeing this new religion as subversive and as eroding the Confucian respect for authority. Although many European merchants had by then moved on to more profitable pastures, the entrenched French missionaries did not hesitate to campaign for greater French political involvement in order to further their cause.

Vietnamese dynasties
- **939–65** Ngo Dynasty (capital: Co Loa)
- **968–80** Dinh Dynasty (capital: Hoa Lu)
- **980–1009** Early Le Dynasty (capital: Hoa Lu)
- **1009–1225** Late Ly Dynasty (capital: Thang Long, now Hanoi)
- **1225–1400** Tran Dynasty (capital: Thang Long)
- **1400–7** Ho Dynasty (capital: Tay Do)
- **1407–27** Chinese Ming Dynasty
- **1428–1527** Late Le Dynasty (capital: Thang Long)
- **1527–92** Mac Dynasty (capital: Thang Long)
- **1532–1788** Restored Le Dynasty (capital: Thang Long)
- **1539–1787** Northern Trinh Lords (capital: Thang Long)
- **1558–1778** Southern Nguyen Lords (capital: Hue)
- **1788–1802** Tay Son Dynasty (capitals: Hue, Saigon, Hanoi)
- **1802–1945** Nguyen Dynasty (capital: Hue)

37

Le Dynasty graves near Lam Son

■ **Continual peasant famines and subsequent discontent and rebellions culminated in a brief period of rule by the successful Tay Son, followed by Vietnam's last dynasty, the Nguyen. While the emperors were blithely designing their extravagant tombs in Hue and closing themselves to the world, French interest was sharpening.** ■

In 1771 three brothers from the village of Tay Son in Central Vietnam started gathering followers to fight against the appalling government of the Nguyen lords. Redistributing land as they went, they gradually swept south and, in 1783, captured Saigon and killed the heads of the Nguyen clan who had taken refuge there. The military genius of the brothers was Nguyen Hue, a former Buddhist monk, who then overthrew the northern Trinh and in 1788 declared himself emperor under the name Quang Trung. His next obstacle was a 200,000-strong Chinese army that was attempting to exploit the internal power struggle. Astute as ever, Quang Trung devised the first Tet offensive, routing the Chinese – who were busy celebrating at Dong Da outside Hanoi – and sending them packing. Quang Trung's sudden death in 1792 announced the premature end to his enlightened, socialistic ideals.

These jackwood statues at the Tay Phuong Pagoda west of Hanoi date from the 18th century

Le Petit Prince Meanwhile, Prince Nguyen Anh, the only survivor of the Nguyen clan, had escaped to Cambodia where he was supported by a French bishop, Pigneau de Béhaine. Desperate to regain his throne, the prince turned to France for aid and in 1784 sent his seven-year-old son with the bishop to be received at the court of Louis XVI. A treaty was signed but nothing concrete transpired, so Pigneau de Béhaine himself set about organising the financing, mercenaries and arms for a Vietnamese counter-revolt. Although the bishop died in 1799, Nguyen Anh and his French-trained men were by then on the road to victory. When he proclaimed himself Emperor Gia Long in 1802, the country was united for the first time in nearly two centuries and was renamed Viet-Nam.

Prelude Over the next few decades, the absolutist Nguyen Dynasty was to steer the country unwittingly into the hands of the French, so precipitating the tragedies of the 20th century. Already, French merchants

who had backed Nguyen Anh had obtained important commercial concessions, and Catholic missionaries were becoming increasingly self-assertive. However, it was not until 1847 that the French government intervened in Vietnam, ostensibly in response to the execution of missionaries but in reality to counterbalance the increasing financial rewards being reaped by the British in China.

Polarisation Intent on stabilising his new regime, Gia Long not only reasserted the respectful values of Confucianism but also embarked on improving the country's infrastructure. Dikes, canals, bridges and roads were built – notably the Mandarin Road that linked Hanoi, Hue and Saigon – and Vauban-style citadels crowned provincial towns. However, these public works also put pressure on the population, either through taxes or forced labour, adding further burdens to repeated drought and epidemics. All this fuelled unrest in the paddy-fields, thereby reinforcing the Nguyen emperors' defensiveness.

Ostriches Gia Long was succeeded by his son, Minh Mang, in 1920. A conservative Confucian scholar, Minh Mang became increasingly hostile to Catholicism and Western influences.

❏ The first French military intervention launched against the imperial power was at Da Nang in 1847, but it was under Napoleon III in the 1850s that the French captured Saigon, so that by 1863 they controlled the entire Mekong Delta. Cochinchina became a French colony, and in 1883 Annam (the Centre) and Tonkin (the North) were signed away as French protectorates. ❏

In the 1830s an imperial edict encouraged the persecution of Catholics, an attitude that became more prevalent under the emperors Thieu Tri (ruled 1841–7) and Tu Duc (ruled 1848–83), and that led to executions of priests and massacres of Vietnamese Catholics. Closeted in the baroque palaces of Hue's Imperial City, the Nguyen emperors had little desire for Western democratic notions of *liberté*, *égalité* and *fraternité*, or the personal salvation offered by the Catholics. This obstinacy was to be their downfall. By 1884, the entire country had been carved up by the French.

Hue's well-heeled emperors prepared for a five-star after-life as at Minh Mang's tomb

■ **Under French control, Vietnam was nominally headed by a string of puppet-emperors, some more active than others in opposing foreign rule. Classic colonial exploitation nurtured resistance, in turn provoking harsh repression. At the same time, Vietnam was being modelled into a replica of the French provinces.** ■

When France added Laos and Cambodia to its Vietnamese possessions in 1893, the Union Indochinoise was created and the die was cast until 1945. Ultimate political, administrative and military power lay in the hands of the French governor-general, while each protectorate was headed by a senior resident who acted in liaison with the administrative mandarin system. Vast improvements were made to infrastructure, including an extensive railway network, ports and irrigation and drainage systems. Education was opened up (later to the detriment of the colonisers through the creation of a nationalist intelligentsia) and medical research institutes founded. The École Française de l'Extrême Orient accomplished important excavation work at Angkor in Cambodia and My Son in Vietnam, and grandiose French villas sprang up all over the country. In the evenings the colonial community met at the Opéra, while at weekends they bathed at Cap Saint-Jacques. But all this hid the reality that was life for the Vietnamese.

Exploitation In 1875 the Banque d'Indochine was founded, the commercial enterprise that was to finance coal, tin and zinc mines, as well as rubber, tea and coffee plantations. Vast tracts of land were turned over to companies such as Michelin, whose rubber trees were tapped by hundreds of thousands of indentured workers, many of whom signed up without being able to read their contracts. All companies were guilty of imposing miserable working conditions and poor levels of pay for the hard labour of the Vietnamese. Other peasants, now landless, were forced to practise sharecropping, paying out most of their profits in rent, taxes and to Chinese intermediaries. Paul Doumer, the Governor-General from 1897 to 1902, introduced French monopolies on alcohol, tobacco, salt and opium, thereby further depriving the local population of potential revenue.

Resistance Given these conditions and Vietnam's long history of rebellions, it is no surprise that active discontent became widespread or that the guerrilla tactics developed at this time were those later perfected by the Viet Minh and the Viet Cong. One of the first to take a stand was, paradoxically, the young Emperor Ham Nghi, who led his rebel movement from the mountains for three years before he was captured by the French and exiled to Algeria in 1888. Sporadic uprisings continued, countered with harsh reprisals such as the guillotine at Hanoi's Hoa Lo Prison or torture and imprisonment in 'tiger cages' at Con Son. This did not stem the tide: ethnic minorities in the North continued to stage raids, and in 1916 Emperor Duy Tan

❏ '...I declare to every Frenchman: this rumbling that is rising from every corner of Annam, this anguish that has reunited bitterness and hate over the last few years, this can become, if you are not careful, the song of a terrible harvest.' André Malraux, in his Saigon-based newspaper, *L'Indochine Enchaînée*, 1925, subsequently shut down by the French authorities. ❏

Hanoi's opera-house (1911) crowned 20 years of frenetic urban activity by the French

supported a large-scale rebellion that resulted in his exile and the execution of hundreds of his supporters.

Ripening socialism China's first revolution, led by Sun Yat-sen, took place in 1911, and that of Russia in 1919. Socialist ideals were spreading fast, and Vietnam's new proletariat in mines, cotton-mills and plantations created fertile recruiting grounds. By the 1920s, the rise of more organised groups – above all branches of the Thanh Nien (Revolutionary Youth), created by Ho Chi Minh from Guangzhou (Canton) – increasingly threatened the colonists and culminated in 1930 with the founding of the Vietnamese Communist Party, again orchestrated by Uncle Ho. Soon after, 6,000 peasants joined a hunger march on Vinh. This organised demonstration saw the first people's assemblies or soviets, spelt specially for the Vietnamese as 'xo-viet'.

French baguettes and processed cheese have been firmly adopted

❑   Today's French heritage: baguettes; Vache qui Rit cheese; yoghurt; filter coffee; crème caramel; tailors called Veston ('jacket'), denoted by an Eiffel Tower logo; pre-World War II Peugeots and Citroëns; antiquated Renault buses; art deco furniture.   ❑

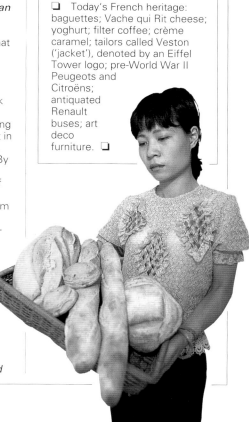

■ **The return of Ho Chi Minh to Vietnam in 1941 was the catalyst that was to forge the country's destiny. With his Viet Minh, this benevolent but astute figurehead, who had been hell-bent on his goal since the 1920s, embarked upon a single-minded eight-year struggle for independence.** ■

In September 1940 Japanese forces moved into Vietnam, soon arriving at an agreement with the French that allowed the latter to continue their administration while Japan gained full military powers. Along with forced native labour, Vietnam's tungsten, tin and rice resources were used to support Japan's war effort in the Pacific. France's collaboration was to continue until March 1945, when the Japanese, sensing the approaching end, declared Vietnam 'independent' and took over. Their brutality was meted out against a chaotic background of the worst famine in memory, claiming around a million victims.

Mastermind Meanwhile, the indefatigable Ho Chi Minh had been busy. From 1940 onwards he was flanked by two men who became his most faithful allies: Pham Van Dong, a brilliant young militant; and Vo Nguyen Giap, a formidable strategist who was to defeat both the French and the Americans. The year 1941 was decisive in devising tactics that involved the founding of the Viet Minh. This aimed to 'unite all patriots, without differences of wealth, age, sex, religion or political opinion, to work together for the liberation of our people and the salvation of our nation'. Ho's message was thus clear: his movement was above all nationalist and democratic. Training of cadres began, Ho penned brochures on guerrilla tactics and soon the first propaganda units were sent south.

Above: Pham Van Dong, Ho's trusted adviser and later prime minister
Left: General Vo Nguyen Giap, the brilliant strategist who led his peasant army to victory over both the French and the Americans

August revolution In April 1945, Ho received members of the American OSS (Office of Strategic Services, precursor to the CIA) in his cave headquarters and agreed to provide intelligence networks in exchange for US training and arming of his Viet Minh against the Japanese. Four months later Japan had surrendered, and while British forces carried out the mopping-up operations in the South and Chinese nationalists were arriving to do the same in the North, Ho pre-empted the latter, instigated a general insurrection and liberated Hanoi. In Hue, Emperor Bao Dai formally abdicated, and on 2 September 1945 Ho declared himself president of the Democratic Republic of Vietnam.

Peace and war The atavistic fear of having another massive Chinese army inside Vietnam pushed Ho to negotiate with the French. The agreement they reached recognised the new republic as a free state within the Union Française until future independence (an ambiguous clause) and anticipated elections in Cochinchina took place, and saw the return of the French army to replace Chiang Kai-shek's rampaging forces. However, as French troops returned so did their appetite, and by late 1946 Franco-Vietnamese amicability came to an end. The French bombarded the port of Hai Phong, killing 6,000 civilians, the Viet Minh attacked garrisons, and soon the country was polarised between the French-controlled towns and Viet Minh-controlled countryside. Meanwhile, General Giap had transformed his original 5,000 guerrillas into a well-armed force of 100,000 men.

First Indochina war By 1950, China and the Soviet Union were supplying arms to Ho's jungle government, while the desperate French had resurrected

Emperor Bao Dai and sought aid from the Americans. Obsessed by the spread of the Reds after the success of communist North Korea in 1948 and Mao's Chinese triumph in 1949, the US installed an economic mission in Saigon to channel in massive aid and advised the regime to form a Vietnamese army to supplement colonial forces.

Meanwhile, the Viet Minh slipped effortlessly through the paddy-fields, indoctrinating, recruiting, organising and training. A first major defeat for the French came in the Red River Delta in late 1950, but it was not until 1954, at Dien Bien Phu (see page 82), that Général Navarre was forced to bow to Giap's tactical superiority. French capitulation led to the Geneva Accords that provisionally divided Vietnam into North and South, pending elections in 1956. The stage was thus set for two more decades of war.

43

A memorial at Dien Bien Phu recalls the role of women and children

■ **From 1954 until the Tet Offensive in 1968, American involvement in Vietnam built up steadily to counter increasing Viet Cong strength. Meanwhile, the South Vietnam regime was wracked with petty jealousies, coups and corruption, which did little to further its cause.** ■

The new prime minister of South Vietnam, Ngo Dinh Diem, brought in from exile by the Americans just before the Geneva Accords, refused to sign the agreement, as did the US, and so felt free to cancel the projected elections. In their eyes, South Vietnam was a sovereign country and North Vietnam's subsequent interference was 'foreign aggression'. The Catholic Diem also turned to dealing with the South's internal chaos, nurtured by the Binh Xuyen criminal syndicate in Saigon and the private armies of the Cao Dai and Hoa Hao sects in the Mekong Delta. In late 1955 a rigged referendum left him president of the Republic of Vietnam, definitively abolishing the by then terminally debauched Emperor Bao Dai.

Repression Diem's police, headed by his neo-fascist brother Ngo Dinh Nhu, embarked on a ruthless campaign using torture and execution to uproot communist sympathisers and recalcitrant Viet Minh. Things were no better in the North: Catholics fled south and the rest of the population was subjected to brutal land reforms in order to enforce collectivisation. Anyone who owned a paddy-field was treated as a bourgeois, his home confiscated and public confessions extracted. Persecutions and 10,000 deaths ended with a governmental volte-face in 1956, when the campaign for the 'Rectification of Errors' brought back the popular Uncle Ho to initiate more subtle reforms.

Structuring resistance In 1960 the government in Hanoi created the NLF (National Liberation Front) to embody its new policy of armed resistance by guerrilla units headed by Viet Minh cadres. By the time President Kennedy started seriously intervening in 1961, the NLF numbered over 16,000 men, nearly all of them armed with weapons captured from the ineffectual Southern army. By 1962, Kennedy had increased the 600 or so US military advisers to 11,000 troops, backed up by helicopters, artillery, armoured vehicles and deadly chemicals. This increasingly formidable foe was rapidly countered by growing peasant support for the Viet Cong, who were also adept at exploiting the corruption and incompetence of the Southern commanders.

Disenchantment As American frustration with Diem grew, exacerbated by his tyrannical handling of the Buddhist crisis (see panel on page 177), so did their military supplies and men. The Strategic Hamlets Program of herding peasants into guarded settlements backfired too, as it only served to increase support for the NLF. Diem's paranoia finally proved justified when he was

US troops in the heat of battle

44

assassinated in a CIA-engineered coup in November 1963. Political turmoil was only resolved in 1965 when General Nguyen Van Thieu took over.

The real war After Kennedy's assassination, Lyndon B Johnson's administration, still led by the bullish Defense Secretary Robert McNamara, dramatically escalated involvement. The Viet Cong were mounting assaults of unprecedented force in the Mekong Delta and Centre, where they controlled most of the countryside, and were now joined by regular infantry units from the North. In response, the toll was tragic: apart from military casualties, an estimated 25,000 civilians were killed yearly and thousands of hamlets lay in ashes.

Sparked by the 1964 Tonkin Incident, an allegedly unprovoked attack on two US destroyers, the Americans started merciless bombing of the North, unleashing twice the tonnage used during World War II. By 1966, US forces had doubled to 400,000 men, and American commanders refused to believe that their superior technology and men could be beaten by the 'gooks'. Few understood the history of Vietnamese resilience or the moral strength and discipline of Northern socialist ideals.

❑   The term Viet Cong (an Americanised version of Viet Cong-san, meaning 'Communist Vietnamese') was generally used from 1960 onwards to label the guerrillas. Apart from their green pith helmets, the Viet Cong were often indistinguishable from peasants in their black *ao baba* 'pyjamas'.   ❑

The turning point came in early 1968, with General Giap's brilliantly conceived Tet Offensive (see page 181). Although Hanoi did not achieve a general insurrection, an incredible psychological blow had been dealt. World public opinion, already alerted, now turned completely against the Americans.

Smoke, fire and personal tragedy: all part of a senseless war

■ **While the North reeled under B52 bombing, its men and supplies were still filing down the Ho Chi Minh Trail. With peace negotiations under way, Nixon announced his projected withdrawal, although from 1969 to 1973 the Americans extended their target practice to include Cambodia.** ■

Pressure in the US mounted after the Tet Offensive: the opinion of the public and even military advisers shaped Johnson's decision to halt the bombing and initiate peace negotiations with the North. Discussions opened in Paris in late 1968 but were not to bring results until late 1972. Meanwhile, President Nixon started 'Vietnamisation' – gradually pulling out US troops while stepping up arms and training for the Southern army.

Psychological escapes In 1968 US forces peaked at 540,000, with South Koreans, Australians, New Zealanders, Thais and Filipinos adding a further 90,000. These vast contingents were backed up by an ambitious logistics support that flew ice-cream and beer to isolated outposts, and organised R & R (rest and recreation) on China Beach and in Hong Kong. However, among the drafted troops – many only 18 years old – morale was low. The futility of the war, the lies about body counts, 'friendly fire', fear, anger and daily confrontation with maimed or dead buddies all left profound mental scars. Drugs often became the moral props for search and destroy missions or lonely night sentries. Others turned to monstrous sadism, as at My Lai (see page 162), while still more, bored by the routine, would take pot-shots at peasants as if they were rabbits. Human atrocities became rife in a lawless situation that eroded all sense of values.

Cambodian connection For years the Viet Cong had been using Cambodia as a sanctuary and as an extension of the labyrinthine Ho Chi Minh Trail. In 1969, Nixon embarked on a policy of secret bombing over the border that contributed to the toppling of Prince Sihanouk in 1970. The war in Cambodia spread fast, with attacks by Saigon forces and massive US bombing soon followed by open American intervention, when 32,000 troops crossed the border. Anti-war protests again reacted vehemently, fuelled by the revelations of the Pentagon Papers, a leaked US government study into American involvement in Indochina. Nixon eventually withdrew, leaving the desperate Cambodian population defenceless against the rise of the Khmer Rouge (see pages 222–3 and 230).

Spring Offensive Meanwhile, Ho Chi Minh's death in September 1969 changed little, and his collective leadership carried on as before. US forces had dropped to about 70,000 when

Left: in May 1968 Hue was completely devastated
Right: Southern troops deal with the injured during the 1972 An Loc siege

46

North Vietnam launched the Spring Offensive of 1972. This conventional military attack stormed through the DMZ (Demilitarised Zone) into Quang Tri and the western mountains, and also saw troops launching assaults in the Mekong Delta. Although both sides resumed a virtual status quo, the results were unprecedented numbers of casualties and over a million refugees. In response, Nixon resumed massive bombing on Hanoi and Hai Phong in the North.

Peace accord Exhaustion had set in when Kissinger and Le Duc Tho resumed negotiations in January 1973. Finally, a ceasefire agreement was reached that the Americans forced President Thieu to accept: while US troops were completely withdrawn, Hanoi and Saigon's respective armies would remain in place pending a permanent settlement. The Americans did pull out by March, as agreed, but both the Northern and Southern armies repeatedly violated the ceasefire and war soon resumed.

Nothing had changed in Saigon's army except that, if anything, it was weaker: desertion had joined corruption and an inept command. In January 1975 the Northerners launched their final offensive, advancing effortlessly past the disintegrating Saigon forces amid a growing flood of panicking refugees. On 30 April 1975 the legendary T-54 tank crashed through the gates of Saigon's Presidential Palace. A few days earlier, Thieu had resigned and fled. South Vietnam was 'liberated' and Uncle Ho's long crusade had posthumously succeeded.

> ❏ Fatalities of the Vietnam War were an estimated 500,000 civilians, 240,000 South Vietnamese troops, 1 million North Vietnamese/Viet Cong and 58,000 Americans. ❏

■ When it awoke from its long and bloody nightmare, Vietnam was in complete shambles. The bombed North was nearly destitute, while the crater-ridden Centre was inhabited by the 'wandering souls' of the dead and the South was completely divided. Revenge, reconstruction, re-education and another war were to mark the next decade. ■

Formally reunited in July 1976, Vietnam faced a vast, confusing array of problems: millions of refugees whose villages had been destroyed, thousands of hectares of defoliated countryside and thousands more pockmarked with craters and laced with mines, an equally ravaged economy, diplomatic isolation, and, not least, a psychologically scarred and embittered population. Orphans, amputees, prostitutes, junkies and millions of illiterate unemployed were the social legacy of the South, soon brought to heel by the rigorous People's Committees that governed every town.

A week after the fall of Saigon, a reported 100,000 Southerners fled

Retribution Hanoi's heavy-handed attitude soon became clear as all top positions in the South were filled with Northern cadres, the Southern officials and intelligentsia who had supported their cause being ignored. Within a few months 300,000 South Vietnamese (mainly army officers, police and government officials) had been interned in re-education camps where they were force-fed Marxist-Leninist dogma and put to 'cleansing' manual labour. Political purges extended to thousands of businessmen, intelligentsia, Buddhist monks and Christian clergymen, all of whom were imprisoned without trial, and in 1978 escalated into the 'anti-capitalist' campaign, mainly targeting Chinese businesses and property. Meanwhile, peasants were shunted into collective farms and vast sums were squandered on unrealistic industrial projects.

Boat-people Hundreds of thousands of Southerners panicked when the red flag was raised in Saigon. Fear of political and economic reprisals sent nearly a million Vietnamese fleeing; many were ethnic Chinese, but all sailed into the unknown in atrocious circumstances. They braved the South China Sea in perilously tiny boats without navigation equipment or even charts; many sank while others were attacked by pirates, the women raped, passengers murdered and their worldly possessions (usually converted into gold or jewellery) taken.

As their numbers turned into a flood by the late 1970s, neighbouring countries such as Malaysia and Singapore started refusing entry; the lucky ones eventually reached the more accommodating Australia. Others ended up in refugee camps in Thailand, Malaysia or Hong Kong,

Above: museums graphically depict the horrors of war
Right: Amerasian children and the scrap-metal trade are further reminders of the war

from where they applied for asylum in the US, Australia and Europe. Since the late 1980s this process has been transformed into the Orderly Departure Programme run by the UN High Commission for Refugees. In 1996, 21 years after the fall of Saigon, the camps' remaining 36,000 boat-people were repatriated to Vietnam.

Third Indochinese war One problem Hanoi did not have to face immediately was the demobilisation of its massive army, at that point the fifth largest in the world. On 25 December 1978, in response to repeated raids across the border by the murderous Khmer Rouge, 100,000 Vietnamese troops invaded Cambodia. Within two weeks they had occupied Phnom Penh and replaced the fanatical Pol Pot with

❏ 'The (Vietnamese) Communist Party, with its hierarchy and ritual, has become a kind of modern counterpart of the Confucian mandarinate that governed the country before the arrival of the French.'
From *Two Cities* by Neil Sheehan (1991). ❏

their own man, who was backed by the Soviets. Chinese reactions to this affront to their protégé, Pol Pot, were not long in coming: in February 1979 their army massed on Vietnam's northern border in a much replayed historical scenario. After destroying several border towns, the Chinese were finally repelled by the indomitable Vietnamese. In Cambodia, Vietnam was drawn into a protracted war against Khmer Rouge guerrillas that only ended in 1989.

Change Military withdrawal from Cambodia coincided with a change in Hanoi's attitude, stimulated by Gorbachov's perestroika in the Soviet Union and, as the Eastern Bloc collapsed, by Vietnam's need for new financial partners. During the resultant economic chaos a new wave of boat-people set off, this time from the North, in search of more fertile pastures. But *doi moi* ('open-door' policy) was soon to change the face of the nation.

*The modernising
face of Hanoi
includes street-
lighting and
Japanese cars and
motor bikes*

HANOI

Tourist services

● Commercial & Tourist Service Center, 1 Ba Trieu (tel: 04 826 5244; fax: 04 825 6418).
● Green Bamboo Travel, 42 Nha Chung (tel: 04 826 8752; fax: 04 826 4949).
● Hanoi Tourist, 18 Ly Thuong Kiet (tel: 04 825 4209/7886; fax: 04 825 4209).
● Red River Tours, 73 Hang Bo (tel: 04 826 8427/828 7159; fax: 04 828 7159).
● Vietnamtourism, 30a Ly Thuong Kiet (tel: 04 825 5552; fax: 04 825 7583).

Endless drizzle or monsoon downpours keep the plastic mac industry booming

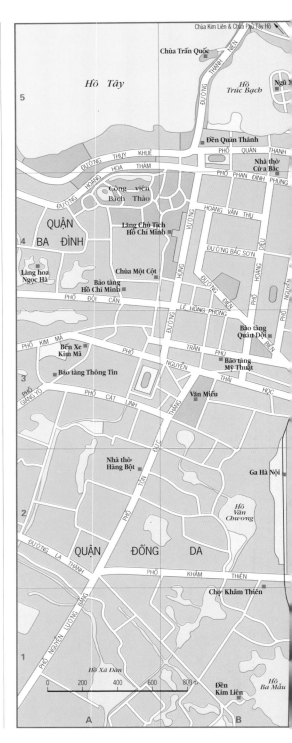

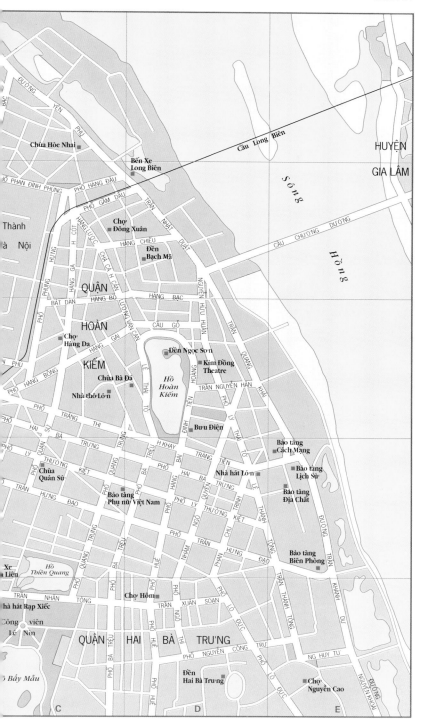

Chùa Hòe Nhai

Bến Xe Long Biên

Cầu Long Biên

HUYỆN

GIA LÂM

PHỐ PHAN ĐÌNH PHÙNG

Thành

à Nội

Chợ Đồng Xuân

Đền Bạch Mã

QUÂN

HOÀN

Chợ Hàng Da

KIẾM

Đền Ngọc Sơn

Kim Đồng Theatre

Chùa Bà Đá

Hồ Hoàn Kiếm

Nhà thờ Lớn

Bưu Điện

Bảo tàng Cách Mạng

Bảo tàng Lịch Sử

Chùa Quán Sứ

Nhà hát Lớn

Bảo tàng Địa Chất

Bảo tàng Phụ nữ Việt Nam

Bảo tàng Biên Phòng

Xe Liên

Hồ Thiền Quang

Chợ Hôm

hà hát Rạp Xiếc

Công viên Lê Nin

QUÂN   HAI   BÀ   TRƯNG

5 Bảy Mẫu

Đền Hai Bà Trưng

Chợ Nguyễn Cao

SÔNG

HỒNG

CẦU CHƯƠNG DƯƠNG

C

D

E

Hanoi (Ha Noi) Superficially beautiful but with a heart of stone, Hanoi can be a frustrating city for tourists. At the same time, it holds the key to understanding Vietnam today: progress and money are fast flowing, bringing a radical change in lifestyle to what was only recently Vietnam's most traditional city. Once caught in a time-warp somewhere between its stately colonial avenues and the animated narrow lanes of the old quarter, Hanoi is now striking out towards the 21st century, with modern developments, an expanding tourist infrastructure and a less prestigious urban sprawl. With 1.2 million inhabitants, the inner city is one of Asia's most densely populated urban centres, while shoddy apartment blocks and shacks in the suburbs now house over 2 million, a number that climbs yearly as the rural poor are drawn to the bright lights of the capital. Housing is a major problem, and nor is it free of countless scams and government scandals.

Lakes Ha Noi means 'River Exterior', a reference to the Red River, whose 100km or so of dikes embrace the city and which is also the source of numerous tributaries and Hanoi's characteristic lakes. The latter are the lungs of the city, their banks lined with pagodas and attracting picnickers and *t'ai-chi* enthusiasts, and their waters used by fishermen and courting couples in paddle-boats. Few foreign visitors will venture beyond Ho Hoan Kiem, Ho Tay and Ho Thien Quang as all the major sights are concentrated between these lakes. Hoan Kiem district wins hands down for central convenience and facilities.

Recoiling dragon

'The Dai La Citadel is situated in the middle of the country. Its location has the posture of a recoiling dragon and a crouching tiger. As regards the four directions East, West, South and North, the citadel is securely protected with mountain ranges at the back and a river in front. Its land is a vast, flat expanse on a high-level surface. The population are free from floods and prosperity is found everywhere.' Emperor Ly Thai To's words in AD 1010 on discovering Thang Long.

Hanoi's pace may be accelerating, but the past lingers on

Evolution Thang Long (Hanoi's original name) was founded in 1010 when Emperor Ly Thai To moved his court here from Hoa Lu. Despite a few gaps over the centuries, it remained the capital until 1802, when Emperor Gia Long settled in Hue. The name Ha Noi only came about in 1831, when Minh Mang established it as the capital of the northern province, but it was with the arrival of the French in 1888 that the city really developed. Their post-Haussmann urban design soon transformed the town from a ramshackle sprawl of huts clustered around local pagodas into a graceful network of tree-lined avenues and parks.

Built on the site of the old citadel, the French cantonment of yellow-stone buildings sporting shutters and pillars is now occupied by government offices, ministries and museums, while the provincial villas once inhabited by minor French officials south of Hoan Kiem Lake have been turned into embassies, banks and international offices. The ornate **Municipal Theatre** (1911) and **St Joseph's Cathedral** (1886) are still central landmarks in this area, while the 36 streets of the old quarter now see a tightly packed juxtaposition of old shophouses and new concrete.

Bombs Although seemingly left unscathed by the Vietnam War, Hanoi underwent intense B52 bombing during the infamous Christmas 1972 raids ordered by President Nixon. For 12 days bombs rained down, during which time Bach Mai Hospital received a direct hit, part of Long Bieh Bridge (built in 1902 by the French) and an adjacent residential area were flattened, and several houses in Pho Kham Thien, a road south of the railway station, were pulverised. The North Vietnamese responded in kind with anti-aircraft artillery, missiles and MiGs, but it was the worldwide public outcry that finally halted the bombs; a few weeks later the Paris Agreement was signed, signalling the American retreat.

Hanoi Hilton
Not a luxury hotel, but once a grim prison that held hundreds of American POWs during the Vietnam War, the Hanoi Hilton is now all but a distant memory. On the site of the structure, located by the junction of Hai Ba Trung and Hoa Lo, south-west of Hoan Kiem Lake, a modern commercial block has appeared. Even before the Hanoi Hilton became infamous for its torture sessions, the Hoa Lo Prison (as it was officially called) functioned under the French, who built it in 1904 as part of their barracks.

A student takes it easy in the Botanic Gardens

Climate Hanoi's radical climatic fluctuations are another tricky aspect of the city. The winter months between November and March see steady drizzle, cold winds and incipient damp that does not help the leprous appearance of the ubiquitous concrete slabs – and nor does it inspire much joy among the inhabitants. Fuel is scarce and for lesser mortals often consists of bricks made of polluting lignite dust; it is not surprising that the café society is so widespread. The rainy season gets underway as temperatures rise in May and ends in September, leaving August–October as the best period to visit, when clear skies and gentle breezes are punctuated with short showers.

Hoan Kiem Lake, the focal point of Hanoi's history

Hoan Kiem District

Hanoi's central business district has grown up around the peaceful Hoan Kiem Lake, crowned by its emblematic tortoise tower and island pagoda. Lining the lake are imposing colonial buildings that now house banks and the central post office, and these are backed up by broad peripheral avenues that are home to embassies, museums, hotels, shops and restaurants. The shady lakeside lawns, paths and benches are a favourite spot for old men playing checkers, teenage flirtations, joggers and families catching the breeze, while an army of vendors hawks trays of cakes, fruit and corn on the cob. The activity continues at night when fairy lights festooning the trees add to the lake's romantic atmosphere and attract more promenaders. North of the lake lies the labyrinthine old quarter, while several blocks south Hoan Kiem becomes Hai Ba Trung district, home to several lakes, **Lenin Park (Cong vien Le Nin)** and the **Hai Ba Trung Pagoda►** (on Dong Nhan Lake; often closed), dedicated to the Trung sisters (see page 96).

Old quarter Some 36 streets meander through Hanoi's atmospheric but confusing hub of traditional trades. The old quarter starts at the northern end of Hoan Kiem Lake, stretches north to the railway line, and is bordered to the west by Pho Phung Hung and to the east by Tran Nhat Duat. Around the perimeter stand a few relics of the old citadel, while **Dong Xuan►**, the main food market that was destroyed by fire in 1994, now lives again in a new building at the northern end. Another food market, **Hang Da**, lies on the western perimeter near the Protestant church. Central Hang Buom is home to **Den Bach Ma►►**, a pretty little 18th-century pagoda dedicated to several saints, including Long Do, the golden dragon, and Bach Ma, the white horse.

The main interest of this quarter, however, lies in the maze of human activity that revolves around Hanoi's old guilds, whether in street markets, arty cafés or specialist shops. The narrow, shady streets harbour an endless stream of flower-sellers and squatting women with baskets of produce, all set against a backdrop of stuccoed shophouses draped in laundry, plants and birdcages, and interspersed with flimsy matchbox-style constructions. Not surprisingly, the charms of the old quarter have also attracted mini-hotels, tourist cafés, tour agencies, art galleries and souvenir shops, all serviced by squads of persistent cyclos and motorbike taxis. Despite this, the 36 streets have somehow managed to preserve a unique atmosphere that has long since disappeared from most other Vietnamese towns (see also Walk on page 59).

► Ambassadors' Pagoda (Chua Quan Su) *53C2*
73 Quan Su
Open: daily. Admission: free.
This 17th-century pagoda was originally designed for the convenience of foreign Buddhist ambassadors resident in an adjoining guest-house, but was rebuilt in the 1930s to accommodate the Northern Buddhist Association and a seminary for monks and nuns. As such it is an important

The turtle, the sword and the lake
The name Hoan Kiem ('Lake of the Restored Sword') derives from a story concerning the Chinese Ming invasion in the 15th century. Countless versions include the following: Emperor Le Thai To (formerly the fisherman Le Loi) had for ten years used a magic sword in battle. On his victorious return to the capital, he was cruising on the lake when a golden turtle appeared, snatched the sword from his hand and plunged into the depths. For the emperor, this was a sign that peace had returned and that the sword was 'restored' to its guardian spirit. Five centuries later, in 1968, a gigantic turtle was found in the lake, over 2m in length, weighing 250kg and thought to be 400–500 years old. Was this the return of the legendary turtle?

cult centre, and crowds of vendors await worshippers in the outer courtyard. The lofty prayer-hall is strung with old lanterns and banners, while grey-haired, whiskered old ladies kneel and chant from prayer-books balanced on floor lecterns.

▶▶▶ History Museum (Bao tang Lich Su)   53E2

1 Pham Ngu Lao
Open: Tue–Sun 8–11.45, 1.15–4. Admission charge: cheap.

This grandiose colonial folly was built in 1926 to house the rich archaeological finds of the École Française de l'Extrême Orient, and its airy structure and original art deco chairs all add to the pleasure of a visit. Exhibits start with prehistory at the back of the ground floor, moving through history in a clockwise direction and then continuing upstairs. Unfortunately only the main captions are in English, but highlights include Dong Son tools and magnificent drums (*c.* 500 BC), 10th-century relics from Hoa Lu, a superb inscribed stela (1126) mounted on a tortoise, and, upstairs, a section of wall from a 13th-century stupa, 15th-century books and artefacts from the Lam Son culture. Enamelled bronzes from Hue and Hanoi, French watercolours and a magnificent sedan chair inlaid with gold add to the offerings.

▶▶ Jade Mountain Temple (Den Ngoc Son)   53D3

Dinh Tien Hoang
Open: daily 8–5. Admission charge: moderate.

Hanoi's picture-postcard pagoda has been sitting on an island in Hoan Kiem Lake since the Tran Dynasty (1225–1400), but underwent major transformation in 1864 when the tapering entrance tower (Thap But) was added. This was the work of the writer Nguyen Van Sieu, who also added several literary and intellectual saints to accompany Tran Hung Dao, the 13th-century Vietnamese military hero. Related to this is Dai Nghien, a carved stone designed to resemble an ink-slab and supported by three frogs, which crowns the main entrance gate. Another curiosity is a glass case containing a turtle (see panel opposite). Above all, it is the setting that makes the pagoda, much appreciated for romantic photo opportunities and by young couples who spend hours whispering to each other under the island's banyans.

57

The Ngoc Son Temple bridge is known as The Huc, meaning 'Place Touched by Morning Sunbeams'

58

Essential raingear includes the ubiquitous conical hat

▶ **Revolution Museum (Bao tang Cach Mang)** 53E2

25 Ton Dan
Open: Tue–Sun 8–11.30, 1.30–4; Sat 8–11.30. Admission charge: cheap.
This museum dates from 1959 but later expanded its collection to cover the Vietnam War. Start in the left-hand corner of the first floor to follow exhibits chronologically. Documents and old photographs illustrate French colonial repression and peasant rebellions of the 1880s, culminating in the founding of the Communist Party in 1930. In among the heavy propaganda are some interesting exhibits, including a wooden telephone used by Uncle Ho in 1951, banana-bark notebooks used by schoolchildren in the 1950s and numerous enlightening, sometimes hard-hitting photos.

▶▶ **Women's Museum (Bao tang phu nu Viet Nam)** 53C2

36 Ly Thuong Kiet
Open: Tue–Sun 8.30–11.30, 1.30–4. Admission charge: cheap.
Hanoi's latest museum, inaugurated in 1994, glorifies the role of women in Vietnamese society. The exhibits, arranged on three floors, are introduced by a statue of Quan Am, the Goddess of Mercy, and a nod to Auco, the mythical Mother of Vietnam. Exhibits range from Dong Son bracelets to rudimentary weapons used by Viet Minh women guerrillas, crafts such as silverware, lace, ceramics and inlay, and, on the top floor, traditional costumes and weavings of the Viets, Khmer, Ede, Cham, Dao and H'Mong. For once there are fully translated English captions.

Walk **Thirty-six streets**

59

This two-hour stroll through Hanoi's old quarter takes you through the heart of the traditional trade streets.

Start at **Hang Dao**, near the lake, and walk north past antique shops and watch-sellers, stopping to see the portraitist Nguyen Bao Nguyen at work at No 47, to reach **Hang Buom**. Turn right along this tree-lined street, where bottles of whisky jostle with natural elixirs containing snakes, and stop at the attractive **Den Bach Ma** on the left. At the end of the street turn left into **Dao Duy Tu**, passing an old gate-way, food-stalls and a contemporary design shop at No 28 before turning left into **Hang Chieu**. This is the specialist street for packaging: sacks, mats, bags and rope monopolise the shopfronts. It eventually becomes **Hang Ma**, where paper decorations, tinsel, lanterns, gift-wrap, kites and greetings cards create a brilliantly coloured display.

Follow **Hang Dong** to the left, where smithies hammer away as they create forged iron, while gleaming brass bells, candlesticks, incense-burners and gongs fill the shops. At **Hang Vai** turn left, stopping to buy folk-prints in a café at No 22, before entering the domain of herbalists in **Lan Ong**. Here, roots, twigs, leaves, fruits and ginseng await the needy customers.

At **Hang Can** turn right then right again into **Hang Bo**, passing a huge

Above: shops in an old guild street

banyan tree studded with joss-sticks to reach a mixture of soup-stands and stationery and clothes shops. Turn left at **Hang Thiec**, Hanoi's 'tin city', where watering-cans, sieves, trunks, pans, woks and mirrors are strung along the street. At the end turn left into **Hang Non**, stopping to see musical instruments at No 11, embroidered slippers, hats, banners and parasols at No 12, and ceremonial robes at No 4. Carry straight on to **Hang Quat** past banners, lacquerware and elaborately appliquéd costumes, before turning right down the alley of **Tu Tich**, where more wood and lacquer shops introduce the tourist shops of **Hang Gai**.

Uncle Ho

■ **Who can remain oblivious to Ho Chi Minh, the champion of Vietnamese democracy and independence? His effigy is everywhere, from his embalmed corpse in Hanoi to endless statues throughout the country, while his ideology, although much warped since his death, continues to shape the nation.** ■

Top: Ho's heavily guarded mausoleum

A real sun
'In Vietnam as in China, a legend speaks of a magic bag; when you are in great difficulty, just open the bag and you will find the solution. For revolutionaries and for the Vietnamese people, Marxist-Leninism is not only the magic bag, not only a compass, but a real sun that lights the road to final victory, to socialism and to communism.'
From *The Road that Led Me to Leninism* by Ho Chi Minh (1960).

Affectionately called Uncle Ho by his followers, Ho Chi Minh underwent several incarnations throughout his life. In 1890 he was born as Nguyen Sinh Cung, but several other pseudonyms followed, including Nguyen Ai Quoc, before he finally opted for Ho Chi Minh. Even today, nearly 30 years after his death, his life story is by no means clear, the Vietnamese Communist Party guardedly maintaining his demi-god image.

Early days Ho's early life was spent in a village in the impoverished province of Vinh, known for nurturing rebellious spirits. His mother died when he was 11 and Ho was raised by his father, a scholarly peasant-turned-teacher who became an anti-colonial militant. After attending school in Hue, Ho left for Saigon and in 1911 turned his back on Vietnam to embark as a messboy on a French steamer. For three vital years he saw the world and, between stops at African, Mediterranean and American ports, germinated his anti-colonial thesis. During his sojourn in London (1914–17), he worked in the kitchens of the Carlton Hotel while frequenting a secret Asian society and socialist groups. His political motivation now well sharpened, he moved to Paris to join 100,000 other Annamites brought in by the French to help out during World War I.

Communist International Paris in those years was an international hotbed of political radicalism, and Ho's contacts included leaders of French unions whose struggle he saw as parallel to that of his country.

Below: Ho's birthplace near Vinh

Uncle Ho

Soon a fully fledged communist and anti-colonial militant, Ho contributed articles to *L'Humanité* (the French Socialist Party newspaper), attended meetings and distributed political tracts, incurring surveillance by the secret police that prevented his return to Vietnam for over 20 years.

On realising that the only solution for the colonial oppressed lay in the 3rd Communist International, Ho moved to Moscow in 1923. Here he visited revolutionaries and spoke at the 5th Congress on the importance of peasant revolt.

On the run From Moscow, Ho continued his peregrinations to Canton (Guangzhou) to take up a hazily defined function beside Borodin within the revolutionary government. Ever since France had taken over Indochina, the southern Chinese provinces of Guangdong and Yunnan had become refuges for Vietnamese activists, and Ho was soon able to found his party: the Vietnamese Association of Revolutionary Youth. Nationalism rather than revolution was Ho's priority, with socialism projected to follow a preparatory period of 'bourgeois democracy'. In 1927, however, this little school for revolution was disrupted when Chiang Kai-shek seized power and banned the Communist Party. Ho and his lieutenants fled, he himself finally reaching Thailand in 1929 where, disguised as a monk, he indoctrinated young bonzes (Buddhist monks) with Marxist dialectics.

The year 1930 saw Ho in Hong Kong, from where he officially united splinter groups into Vietnam's Communist Party. This soon instigated peasant revolts that led to radical repression by the French and ultimately to Ho's imprisonment by the colluding British in Hong Kong. In 1933 it was announced that Nguyen Ai Quoc (Ho's pseudonym of the time) was dead. In reality, helped by a British lawyer, he had escaped and gone into hiding. The French Sûreté was only to learn of his reincarnation in 1945. Meanwhile, he had founded the Viet Minh and named himself Ho Chi Minh. The rest of his life was spent steering North Vietnam to victory (see pages 42–5).

*Top & above:
Soviet embalming
techniques keep the
national icon fresh
inside his mausoleum*

Night air
'The rose opens and the
rose
Fades without knowing
what the rose
Does. It is enough for the
perfume of a rose
To lose its way into a
prison
For the heart of the
prisoner to roar
Against all the injustices of
this world.'
From *Prison Notebook* by
Ho Chi Minh (1942).

The West Lake's Kim Lien Pagoda, renowned for its triple shingle roof

Ho Tay District

The immense 480-hectare Ho Tay (West Lake), once part of the Red River, is seeing rampant development of apartment blocks and hotels along its banks. Long gone are the royal palaces and pavilions that once edged the lake, and in their place are concrete high-rises, many designed with hypothetical armies of tourists in mind. Several historic pagodas lie between the rowing-boat centres and waterfront restaurants, while bordering the southern shore is Ba Dinh, a district monopolised by government offices in grand old French villas that stand along tree-lined avenues. Centrally placed is the unmistakable Ho Chi Minh Mausoleum complex, while further south stands the unique Temple of Literature, Van Mieu.

▶▶ Army Museum (Bao tang Quan Doi)   52B3
28a Dien Bien Phu
Open: daily 8–11.30, 1.30–4.30. Admission charge: cheap.
Appropriately located in a street named after France's decisive defeat, the Army Museum is also fronted by a statue of Lenin – at least visitors know the ideological stand. A predictable display starts outside with recent military relics (MiGs, B52s, F-111s, helicopters, mortars, artillery, tanks and weapons), while inside models of historic battles – including Dien Bien Phu – are backed up by numerous press photos of the Vietnam War; captions remain resolutely in Vietnamese. Next door is the hexagonal flag-tower, once part of the Vauban citadel built by Emperor Gia Long in the early 19th century.

▶▶ Fine Arts Museum
(Bao tang My Thuat)   52B3
66 Nguyen Thai Hoc
Open: Tue–Sun 8–12, 1–4. Admission charge: cheap.
This fine colonial building, its corridors usually deserted, stands opposite the Van Mieu complex and was converted into an art museum in 1966 to house a wide-ranging

Licking stamps
'Hanoi is an administrative town and little else. It is stuffed with a host of *fonctionnaires*, big and little, who lick stamps by day and then go home to tick off the hours to their pensions, growing enormously fat and hairy in the process... The town boasts an imposing theatre and several moving-picture houses where early experiments in cinematography are exposed nightly... Rain fell continuously. The French, in their ironic way, call this winter deluge the *crachin*, or "spitting" to distinguish it from the real rains. Should necessity drive me back to Tonking when it is really raining, I shall pack a diving-suit.' From *The Dragon and the Lotus* by Crosbie Garstin (1928).

display. Start on the top floor, where weavings, costumes, basketware, instruments and dusty old photos give interesting insights into Vietnam's minority cultures. Artefacts from early civilisations include fabulous Dong Son drums, while decorative arts from the following centuries continue through the middle floor (look out for the impressive 16th-century Quan Am, almost 3m high) to reach the less imaginative, though technically impressive, output of the 20th century – mainly silk and lacquer paintings, plus some oil paintings and sculptures.

► **Golden Lotus Pagoda (Chua Kim Lien)** *52B5*
Duong Yen Phu
Open: daily. Admission: free.
Located on a spit of land jutting into West Lake, this pagoda is reached by a dirt-track from prosperous Nghi Tam 'village', famed for its bonsai and dwarf apricot and orange trees, but now virtually swallowed up by Hanoi. The tranquil, scenic pagoda acquired the name Kim Lien ('Golden Lotus') in 1771, but it actually dates from the 13th century and was most recently restored in 1988. The triple roofs with upturned corners shelter richly carved interior beams, while the wooden entrance gate has a wealth of bas-reliefs depicting flowers and dragons.

►►► **Ho Chi Minh Museum (Bao tang Ho Chi Minh)** *52A4*
3 Ngoc Ha
Open: Tue–Sun 8–11.30, 1.30–4. Admission charge: cheap.
Looming behind the One-pillar Pagoda (see page 64) in the south-western corner of Cong Vien Bach Thao park is the most dynamically presented museum in Vietnam. The complex layout circulates on two floors, with a parallel history of world developments occupying the outer sections. This produces some bizarre juxtapositions: pop art, Picasso's *Guernica*, the Eiffel Tower, Dizzy Gillespie and Einstein are presented just a few metres from Uncle Ho's life story, his loom, cane, pith helmet, letters to luminaries, drafts of speeches and endless fascinating photos. English captions are composed in very radical-chic revolutionary terms. The building itself, in Soviet-inspired concrete, is almost a monument to an epoch.

►►► **Ho Chi Minh's Mausoleum (Lang Chu Tich Ho Chi Minh)** *52B4*
Duong Hung Vuong
Open: Tue–Thu, Sat and Sun 7.30–11am. Closed Oct–Nov. Admission charge/bag check: moderate. Visitors must first register at an office on Pho Le Hong Phong in front of the museum before circling north-east to the bag-check office. From here, they queue to be led inside the mausoleum.
Paying one's respects to Uncle Ho should be a priority for visitors to Vietnam, and the experience, accomplished in reverential silence under the immobile eyes of sphinx-like guards (are they real?), is certainly unusual. Ho Chi Minh's body lies immaculately embalmed in a glass casket, his hands and face spotlit, in the bowels of a grim, Soviet-built marble mausoleum that was inaugurated in 1975. Every year his body is flown to Russia for a 'check-up' as

Centuries of lacquer painting are covered in the Fine Arts Museum

Thus spake Confucius
The venerable Confucius (551–479 BC) was born in the state of Lu, probably of noble stock but with little time for the indolence engendered by inherited wealth. His thinking emphasised the importance of the individual working to shape his own society, and for this aim Confucius drew up a code of ethics that laid down obligations to the family, society and the state. All men were seen as having the same potential for achieving happiness, best achieved if they bettered themselves through education and acting on his principles. Little, however, was said about women. His far-reaching doctrine had a major impact on the culture, psychology and ethics of the Chinese and, by extension, on the Vietnamese.

Tripartite
'When I'm dead...divide my ashes into three and place them in three ceramic urns: one for the north, one for the centre, one for the south.'
Ho Chi Minh's (non-respected) testament.

The One-pillar Pagoda, originally designed to resemble Buddha's lotus-seat

it was a certain Dr Sergei Debor who was responsible for the embalming, initially carried out in a secret cave to escape US bombing.

On leaving the mausoleum, the next pilgrimage is to the peaceful lakeside setting of **Ho Chi Minh's house►** (*Open* daily 7–11, 1–4), where he lived and worked from 1958 until his death in 1969. The house stands on stilts and its interior can only be viewed from an outer staircase, but this gives a glimpse of the simple interior and minimal furnishings. A walk back south through the park passes the much-lauded **Chua Mot Cot (One-pillar Pagoda)**; again, interest is more academic as its fame lies in its intriguing though limited structure, perched like a stork on one pillar in a pond. It dates from 1049 but was rebuilt in 1955 following a French assault.

Vital virtue
'Virtuous and talented men are state-sustaining elements. The strength and prosperity of a state depend on its stable vitality; it becomes weaker as such vitality diminishes. That is why all the saint Emperors and clear-sighted Kings have never failed to recognise the education of men of talent and the employment of literati to develop this vitality.'
Inscription on a stela at Van Mieu, dated 1442.

► **Phu Tay Ho Pagoda (Chua Phu Tay Ho)** *52B5*
Off Duong Yen Phu
Open: daily. Admission: free.
Another out-of-the-way West Lake location (reached from the dike of Duong Yen Phu) shelters this small, ornately decorated pagoda with its serene views across the water. Its promontory position is reached via a narrow lane of food shops and stalls, so an authentic lunch could be included in the outing. One sanctuary is dedicated to Auco, the primal Mother of Vietnam, flanked by her daughters and the 18 Hung emperors of the legendary Hong Bang Dynasty.

►► **Quan Thanh Temple (Den Quan Thanh)** *52B5*
Duong Thanh Nien
Open: daily 8–5. Admission charge: cheap.
Dominating the south-western corner of the West Lake and its baby sister, Truc Bach Lake, is this temple dedicated to Tran Vu, another of Vietnam's legendary heroes who became the guardian saint of Thang Long (Hanoi). The general's statue rises nearly 4m, and is flanked by a smaller statue that commemorates the bronze-caster who accomplished this feat in 1677 and who also cast the

immense bronze bell hanging over the gate. The temple is said to date from 1010 and was restored in 1893.

▶▶▶ Temple of Literature (Van Mieu) 52B3
Quoc Tu Giam
Open: daily 9–5. Admission charge: moderate.
This rare temple dedicated to Confucius dates from 1070, when it also doubled its function to become Vietnam's first university. Proof of this are the 82 stelae (1484–1780) mounted on tortoises and inscribed with the names of 1,036 graduates. The entire 350m-long complex is divided into five courtyards, its central alley once reserved for the emperor and the side paths for mandarins. Entering from the south, a path leads through the dragon-adorned Van Mieu Gate, followed by the Dai Trung Gate. Rising in front of the third courtyard is a pavilion gateway (1805), dedicated to the Constellation of Literature, which introduces the impressive rows of stelae flanking a pond. Beyond is the fourth courtyard, with its red and gold sanctuary honouring Confucius and his disciples, and guarded by two superb bronze storks perched on tortoises. The richly carved House of Ceremonies in front occasionally stages performances of traditional music. The last court-yard once housed the university itself, later replaced by a temple dedicated to Confucius's parents, but was extensively damaged in 1947 and is now closed to the public while undergoing restoration.

▶▶ Tran Quoc Pagoda (Chua Tran Quoc) 52B5
Duong Thanh Nien
Open: daily. Admission: free.
This floating pagoda, reached via a tiny bridge, is the West Lake's version of Den Ngoc Son (see page 57). Inside, it is an atmospheric little complex, with painted stupas, two prayer-halls that contain a wealth of old statues, a lake-side garden and kiosk, and, not least, 14 stelae dating from 1639. The pagoda was rebuilt in the 15th and 19th centuries but is said to be Hanoi's oldest, as it was founded in the 6th century on another site.

Hanoi backstreet
'And I saw the roof of the shack in Hanoi where my mother lived. Sheet metal patched together with tar paper. On rainy days, the roof leaked. In the heat of summer, the acrid smell of tar was overpowering, nauseating. All around, the gutters, gurgling under slabs of cement, flowed from one house to the next. Children played in this filthy black water, sailing their little white paper boats. The few mangy patches of grass were at the foot of the wall where men drunk on too much beer came to relieve themselves... This was my street; I had grown up here.'
From *Paradise of the Blind* by Duong Thu Huong (1988).

65

One of the five courtyards leading to the Temple of Literature, once home to Vietnam's first university

Water-puppetry

■ **Dragons, tortoises, unicorns, princesses and peasants are among the lively players in Vietnamese water-puppet legends. This tradition originated in the villages of the Red River Delta but is now performed all over the country by some 20 different troupes. ■**

Top puppets

Hanoi's official Thang Long Water Puppet troupe produces three sophisticated performances nightly at the Kim Dong Theatre beside Hoan Kiem Lake (57 Dinh Tien Hoang; tel: 04 824 9494/825 5450). However, the air-conditioned theatre mainly attracts tourists, so much of the audience participation is lost. Another troupe, founded in 1956 by Uncle Ho himself, performs at the Water Puppetry House (132 Truong Chinh). The best water-puppet performances, however, take place at temple festivals, when audience feelings run high.

Devised for the pleasure and leisure of the 11th-century Ly emperors when they settled in Hanoi, water-puppetry has since become a widespread form of entertainment, ranging from simple performances during rural temple festivals to more sophisticated productions during Tet and the full-blown version backed up by a live orchestra at Hanoi's Kim Dong Theatre. Here, percussion music of cymbals, flutes, drums, xylophones and lutes accompanies one or more singers who enter into dialogue with the puppets or narrate the tale. Many smaller troupes now resort to recorded music and voices.

Culture of the earth In the old days plays were performed on lakes or ponds with spectators seated on the banks, but today most theatres erect a large tank of water, vaguely disguised by artificial foliage. Puppeteers stand in waist-high water behind a decorative screen shaped like a pagoda, manipulating the rods and pulling the strings of the puppets to make them cavort around the pool in front. The puppets themselves are sculpted wooden pieces brightly painted with waterproof lacquer and dressed according to their status: regal robes, fishermen's tunic and pants, or warriors' trappings.

Invisible puppeteers activate the rods of a host of water-acrobats

Pirouettes The stories enacted vary from short, humorous sequences (basic humour, for example, involves a peasant urinating lengthily and at an outrageous distance) to longer, more complex legends or moral tales. Originally known as *oi loi* (devils), the puppets accomplish fantastic acrobatics, often announced by bursts of firecrackers and clouds of smoke – an element much appreciated by crowds of gleeful Vietnamese children who cheer on their favourites. Battles have a high profile, while homage is paid to the rituals of tilling the soil, raising ducks or hunting frogs. Unicorns (symbolic of imperial power) play ball, while lions and phoenixes romp through their numbers, all in light-hearted and astonishingly supple fashion.

Excursions

The Red River Delta surrounding Hanoi is rife with historical interest, from ancient citadels such as Co Loa to Vietnam's oldest pagodas and temple complexes. As accommodation in the delta villages is non-existent apart from at Son Tay (see page 94), day-trips from Hanoi are the only solution.

▶   **Ba Vi National Park**   77D2

If you want to escape from the city's traffic, head into the wilds of this small national park (60km west of Hanoi), which surrounds three mountain peaks and is edged by the Da River. It was first developed by the French as a hill-resort, but all that remains of their villas are foundations and mossy walls. Despite the advantages of having a climate ranging from tropical to subtropical, Ba Vi has lost almost half of its abundant flora and fauna (once including 45 species of mammals and 5,000 plants) due to slash-and-burn farming practised by the local Muong and Dao peoples. The interest of this area extends to numerous *dinh* (community halls dedicated to guardian spirits) that are dotted around the villages, and to the island-studded **Dong Mo Lake▶**, a popular swimming and hiking spot now proudly boasting an 18-hole golf course.

Traitress

Mi Chau has gone down in history as Vietnam's first traitress. While her father, the Vietnamese king, was battling away against the Chinese general Trieu Da, she was inadvertently giving away state secrets to the attacker's son, who had become her lover. As a result of Mi Chau's betrayal, the citadel soon fell and the 1,000-year rule of China was ready to begin.

A trip to Co Loa through densely farmed landscapes (below) meets the hero of 2,200 years ago (bottom)

▶▶   **Co Loa**   77D2

Vietnam's oldest citadel and capital (16km north of Hanoi) was built by the Au Lac Kingdom (258–208 BC) and ruled by King An Duong Vuong. Three concentric rings of walls surrounded the hilltop, the outer walls forming a circumference of 8km and protected by a moat. At the centre of the 'Snail' (the meaning of Co Loa) was the palace and parade ground, while the guards' quarters lay beyond the inner walls. Today, only sections of the ramparts remain, but at 5.5m high they provide an idea of the sophisticated structure. At the entrance stand statues of King An Duong and his treacherous daughter, Mi Chau (see panel), while a well-preserved *dinh* flanked by ancient banyans stands next to a 17th-century temple that was erected on the site of the old palace. The pond in front is reputed to have alchemical properties and to be home to (what else?) a golden turtle.

77D2

▶▶▶ Pagoda Trail

West of Hanoi Three exceptional pagodas can easily be combined on a half-day trip. Closest is **Chua Tram Gian▶▶** in the village of Tien Phuong, about 28km from Hanoi via Highway 6. Founded in 1168 and substantially restored in the 17th–18th centuries, it sits high on a wooded hill in perfect harmony with the landscape. Over 150 statues people the sanctuary, one of which contains a mummified monk of uncertain vintage.

From here, a road leads about 15km north to the village of Sai Son and the **Chua Thay▶▶▶**, built in the 11th century into a limestone cliff that rises out of the paddy-fields. In front, the placid little Dragon Lake reflects the swooping tiled roofs of the **Dinh Thuy**, a temple dedicated to water-puppeteers, and two covered stone bridges named after the sun and the moon. The pagoda itself rises on three levels and receives worshippers of a triple cult: Buddha, Emperor Ly Thanh Tong and the multi-talented first chief bonze, Tu Dao Hanh (see panel). The peaceful gardens come to life with water-puppetry during the temple festival (7th day of the third lunar month).

About 10km further west, by the village of Thach That, stands **Chua Tay Phuong▶▶▶** (42km directly from Hanoi). This is the most frequently visited of the three pagodas and sits on a low hill reached by 250 steps. Founded in the 8th century, it was radically rebuilt in the 16th–17th centuries and was again restored after heavy bombing in 1954. Three consecutive buildings with richly carved double-layered roofs and ceramic ridge-poles shelter a host of remarkable life-sized carved and lacquered jackwood statues (numbering over 70), mostly dating from the 18th century.

Cult figure
Tu Dao Hanh, a chief bonze also referred to as Thay ('Master'), is reputed to have been the light behind the construction of Chua Thay. This exceptional monk set about teaching local worshippers dancing, singing and water-puppetry, and became a cult figure in all senses of the word. On his death, his bones were placed in a wooden statue inside a shrine. Legend enters here with a story of the statue rising from its pedestal like a puppet. During the same period a prince was born who later became Emperor Ly Thanh Tong, a fervent Buddhist and assumed to be a reincarnation of the singing and dancing monk.

Above: shaving a monk's head at the Thay Pagoda
Right: the Dinh Thuy, part of the temple complex, honours water-puppeteers

East of Hanoi The four pagodas to the east are dominated by **Chua But Thap▶▶▶**, located in fields near Thuan Thanh (about 30km east of the capital). Its name refers to the tapering tower, or *thap* (typical of Ly Dynasty architecture) that stands outside the 17th-century pagoda precinct. Inside, the complex is linked by galleried passages, bridges and paths. Outstanding is a nine-tiered octagonal tower that contains a 13th-century wooden prayer-wheel; stairs circling around it enable visitors to view Buddha statues on each level, these evoking his nine lives. Of the many exceptional statues in the main sanctuary, the most striking is a portrayal of Quan Am (the Goddess of Mercy) in lacquered wood inlaid with gold, her thousand eyes and arms radiating from her body (1656). She is flanked by numerous other superb *arhat* (saint) statues. Outside the walls, the bell-tower houses the Jade Emperor and the Emperor of the Heavens with their respective followers. The pagoda was extensively restored in 1991–3 with aid from the German government.

Vying for the honour of being Vietnam's oldest pagoda is **Chua Dau▶▶**, located in Khuong Tu village about 8km south of But Thap. It is thought to date from the 3rd century, when it was part of the Chinese Luy Lau citadel, but has undergone numerous transformations since then. It remains a sober construction, and is highlighted by a three-storey stupa with stone dragons, unicorns and even sheep (probably Chinese). The main sanctuary has numerous lacquered clay statues, one of which is a mummy.

Nearly 60km east of Hanoi on Highway 18 near Pha Lai is the small but significant **Chua Con Son▶**, a 15th-century pagoda devoted to the patriarchs of the bamboo forest sects that flourished on nearby Yen Tu mountain (see page 95). The pagoda's 14 stelae recount their activities and 600 steps lead up to a flat summit known as the 'chessboard of the gods'. Some 5km away is the **Den Kiep Bac▶**, dedicated to the great general Tran Hung Dao and a focal point for shamanistic rites during the shared pagoda festival on the 16th to 20th days of the eighth lunar month.

Rising on the far right is the tower that gave the But Thap Pagoda its name

Flux
'Everything changes, that is the rule, the wheel turns continuously
After the rain comes fine weather
In a split second, the universe changes its damp clothes
Across ten thousand *li*, the landscape spreads its magnifcent tapestries.

'Gentle sun…a soft breeze…a flower smiles candidly
At the top of a tree…a shining branch…
The hum of a chorus of birds.
Men and beast feel the change coming
What is more natural?
After unhappiness, here comes joy!'
From *Prison Poems* by Ho Chi Minh (1942/3).

Accommodation

Finding a bed
If you're not booked into one of Hanoi's more comfortable mid-range hotels, the best way of finding accommodation is to head for the old quarter in a rickshaw. Drivers will wait outside with your luggage while you check out the room and, if necessary, propel you on to the next hotel. They will often have their own suggestions, which can be worth investigating as new hotels are opening weekly and middlemen's commissions make no difference to your bill. Make sure you give the driver more than your initial negotiated offer if he has waited or covered extra distance. Even if you forget, he won't!

Spring brightens the old quarter

For several years following the start of *doi moi* (open-door policy), reasonably priced hotels were few and far between in Hanoi. However, the last few years have seen a spate of budget and mid-range hotels opening in the old quarter and west of Hoan Kiem Lake – precarious constructions rising on narrow plots of land over the roofs of their neighbours – while the shores of West Lake (Ho Tay) are angling for the more up-market and business clientele. Despite the growing competition, rates remain substantially higher than elsewhere in the country, and through the cold winter months heating becomes a major problem at the lower end of the range.

Staying in style Queen of them all is the **Metropole**, a turn-of-the-century landmark that has been renovated by the Sofitel chain and which sprawls in colonial splendour east of Hoan Kiem Lake. Even if you cannot afford to pay the exorbitant room rates, the bar is a relaxed place to escape from the intrigues of the Orient. Another old, central favourite is the **Dan Chu** (formerly the Hanoi Hotel), convenient for sorties to the Opera, while the rambling old **Hoa Binh** has recently undergone a major facelift and gained a modern extension. Visitors looking for a room with a sunset view should head for **Bac Do**, a medium-priced, medium-sized hotel overlooking West Lake, or group together to rent one of the colonial **Ho Tay Villas**.

Old quarter In the maze of the old quarter an expanding network of accommodation ranges from basic backpacker hostels that specialise in windowless cells to some intelligently designed mid-range hotels such as the **Hong Ngoc**, where traditional furniture, spacious rooms, works of art and excellent amenities contribute to its comforts. Right in the thick of Hang Dao is the **Thanh Binh**, a friendly art gallery-cum-hotel with a wide price range that descends as you climb. A reliable fall-back is the **Especen** group, an odd network of 11 hotels dotted around Hoan Kiem whose staff are Esperanto enthusiasts. Some rooms have seen better days but facilities are good and staff exceptionally helpful – a big bonus in Hanoi.

Another hotel epicentre lies immediately west of Hoan Kiem Lake along Hang Trong. Apart from an errant Especen, this street offers reasonable-value accommodation such as the **Hoa Long** or the more up-market **Freedom** right opposite the cathedral.

Restaurants and nightlife

As with accommodation, Hanoi lags far behind Ho Chi Minh City in terms of gastronomic offerings. Traditional *pho* or *bun bung* specialists are not lacking (Hang Da market area is well provided for), but stylish restaurants preparing reliable cuisine and giving good service remain thin on the ground. However, the situation is changing rapidly and increased competition should improve the general quality and service.

Cafés Countless travellers' cafés serving East-West medleys have sprung up in the old quarter, none of which is recommendable with one exception: **Smiling Café** in Cau Go. Far more atmospheric are the gloomy art-cafés that pepper the backstreets, where bereted painters sip endless cups of strong coffee. Try **Café Lam** (60 Nguyen Huu Huan), Hanoi's equivalent of Paris's La Rotonde; the trendy **D&B Fashion Café** (139 Trieu Viet Vuong); or, for an open-air setting and views, the overpriced, design-conscious **Au Lac** at the southern end of Hoan Kiem.

Institutions For a taste of the real thing, head for **Thit Ran** (not to be confused with *thit cho* or *thit cau*, meaning 'dog' – another speciality), a suburban restaurant that specialises in cobra dishes washed down with a glass of the reptile's blood cut with alcohol. Tamer, pricier and definitely for nostalgics is **Indochine**, an up-market classic whose colonial-style décor outdoes its Vietnamese

Ice-creams

When the winter damp changes into the hot, steaming summer, Hanoi's ice-cream parlours do a roaring trade. Most scenic but with offhand service and mediocre food is the Thuy Ta, a terrace restaurant on the north-western bank of Hoan Kiem Lake. South of the lake at 57 Trang Tien is the Bodega, where a vaguely 1950s interior acts as a backdrop to good ice-cream, coffee and cold drinks. If you fancy delicious French pastries and coffee, try Kinh Do Café at 252 Hang Bong.

Local tipples include fresh snake's blood, but bia hoi (draught beer) has more appeal

cuisine. Less pretentious is the venerable **Restaurant 202**, which offers excellent Vietnamese and French dishes (as does **Club Opéra**), while **Restaurant Bistro** is a firm Gallic favourite that attracts French tour groups. The pizzas of Hanoi's first Italian restaurant, **A Little Italian**, vie with several others now, including the popular **La Terrazza**. Meanwhile, another Hanoi landmark, **Cha Ca La Vong**, continues to sizzle its inimitable fried fish in a buzzing, upbeat atsmosphere.

Late-night pubs with loud music include the institutional **Apocalypse Now** and the **Sunset Pub** (roof of Dong Do Hotel), with snacks and live bands. After-hours coffee and cocktails are served at the **Art Café**, or you could always end the night dancing at the **Queen Bee** or **Dai Dong Centropell** nightclubs.

Shopping

Art for art's sake
Hanoi's art community is blossoming in the city's shady cafés and in a plethora of galleries where abstract and figurative works hold equal status. Charming traditional woodcuts and watercolours make easily transportable souvenirs and are sold for derisory prices, while some oil paintings are easily comparable to Western output and can be bought at a tenth of the price. Large art galleries on Trang Tien often hold group shows, allowing for comparisons, while the Red River Gallery (71a Nguyen Du), the 29 Hang Bai Gallery and the 16 Ngo Quyen all hold regular exhibitions of local artists.

Lacquerware, inlay, silk, silverware, porcelain, puppets, old and new watches, books, artworks…such are the multifarious offerings of Hanoi. The art and crafts capital of Vietnam still lives up to its name, however much it has adapted to the Western market, and the backstreets of the old quarter offer countless more functional but still unusual objects, ranging from woks to embroidered slippers. Anyone in need of reading material should head for Pho Trang Tien: street-stalls here offer photocopied books, while No 61 is the **Foreign Languages Bookshop** and No 40 the **State Bookshop**. A block south at 32 Hai Ba Trung is **Xunshaba**, the state book distributor.

Eclecticism Dong Xuan market in the north of the old quarter is Hanoi's central emporium for anything from nail-clippers to monkeys, but is now housed in a soulless custom-built edifice. For more sophisticated goods, a string of handicraft and antique shops lines Hang Khay, south of Hoan Kiem Lake, while to the north, Hang Gai is the main strip for embroidery, silk clothes, jewellery and endless gleaming lacquer objects, with a few paintings thrown in. For a wide range of up-market jewellery and antiques, try **Phuc Tin** at 80 Hang Gai, while **Hanoi Gallery** at No 101 stocks an interesting range of paintings, woodcuts and watercolours alongside porcelain and silverware. **Salon Natasha**, a tiny gallery run by an eccentric Russian woman at 30 Hang Bong, is an anomaly in Hanoi as it specialises in more conceptual pieces.

Kitted out Khaisilk at 96 Hang Gai (or with a wider choice at 121 Nguyen Thai Hoc, near Van Mieu) offers up-market silk clothes designed by a young Vietnamese designer who trained in Paris. Alternatively, there are countless tailors – including **Le Minh** at 79/111 Hang Gai (frequented by Catherine Deneuve during the filming of *Indochine*) – which offer off-the-peg or made-to-measure numbers. Shoes and luggage of all styles are the focus of Hang Dau, while a bustling street market on Gia Ngu trades such necessities as shampoo, flowers and live chickens.

Hang Gai is Hanoi's shopping mecca where tourists stock up on thimble-sized teacups or finely worked silver

Locomotion Hanoi's relative compactness makes getting around straightforward. Taxis, cyclos and motorbike taxis are readily available, your choice of transport depending on your budget. Taxis are metered (expensive), although for the 35km airport run there is a highly negotiable rate. Fares for cyclos and motorbike taxis need hard bargaining in advance (about 25–30 per cent of the asking price), but Hanoi's voracious drivers have a habit of demanding extra on arrival: you are in no way obliged to comply. If you are intending to do intense sightseeing, work out a daily or hourly rate. Bicycles can be hired from several tourist cafés and hotels in the old quarter.

Escape The railway station, **Ga Hanoi**, lies west of Hoan Kiem district at 126 Le Duan. Tickets for night trains should be bought at least one day in advance at a special foreigners' ticket office (*Open* 7.30–11.30, 1.30–3.30). Trains to Hai Phong also stop at the smaller **Ga Long Bien** by the bridge, which is more convenient if you are staying in the old quarter. Bus stations are dotted around town: **Ben Xe Kim Lien** by Thien Quang Lake serves the south; **Ben Xe Kim Ma** on Pho Kim Ma, just south of Ho Chi Minh's Mausoleum, serves the north-west; and buses east to Ha Long Bay leave from **Ben Xe Long Bien**, right by the bridge. Private transport can be hired through hotels or tour agencies: count on US$30 per day for a car or US$50 per day for a jeep, although rates increase with distance and overnight stops. Airport buses run from the Vietnam Airlines office at 1 Quang Trung, but check that their departure time corresponds to your flight check-in time, allowing an hour for the journey.

Communications Hanoi's central post office (Buu Dien), on the eastern bank of Hoan Kiem Lake, is an impressive, surprisingly efficient affair with an international section (87 Dinh Tien Hoang) devoted to calls, telexes, faxes and parcel post, and also has a DHL service. Street pay phones are virtually non-existent, so you will have to rely on your hotel for making calls.

Hanoi's cyclo-drivers may strike a hard bargain but they beat the traffic

73

Radio taxis
- City Taxi
(tel: 04 822 2222).
- Fujicab
(tel: 04 825 5452).
- Hanoi Taxi
(tel: 04 853 5252).
- PT Taxi
(tel: 04 853 3171).
- Red Taxi
(tel: 04 856 8686).

Monetary magnificence Money exchange becomes an aesthetic experience at the Vietcom Bank, presiding over the crossroads at 49 Ly Thai To. This grandiose, ritzy establishment, dating from the French colonial era, has preserved most of its art deco furnishing and fittings, and stools are even provided at counters so that customers can sit out protracted transactions. A scenic addition is the mountain of dong bricks that rises in the background.

THE NORTH

*A sickle, a conical-hat
and fresh rice paddy:
the classic image of
the northern deltas*

THE NORTH

North of the Red River, vast stretches of agricultural land rise into the foothills and mountains bordering China

The North Slashed diagonally by the Red River (Song Hong), which wends its way from Yunnan in China to the delta east of Hanoi and runs parallel to the awesome Hoang Lien mountains, the North region swings from rugged remoteness into a densely populated patchwork of paddy-fields. At the centre of this delta sits Hanoi, already a dynastic capital by the 11th century and now the hub of 20th-century government diktats (see pages 50–73). The Red River Delta is the cradle of Viet culture, and despite the carpet bombing of the Vietnam War it still harbours magnificent, if inaccessible, pagodas, temple complexes and crumbling citadels. And to the east, the region ends in the mesmerising aquatic landscapes of Ha Long Bay.

Delta diversions Some 40 per cent of the nation's population inhabits this region, largely concentrated between the dikes of the Red River Delta, where agriculture and

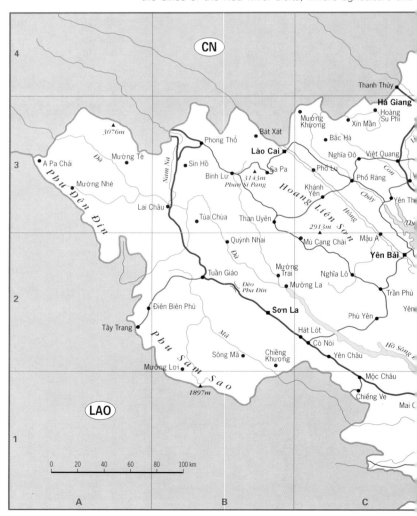

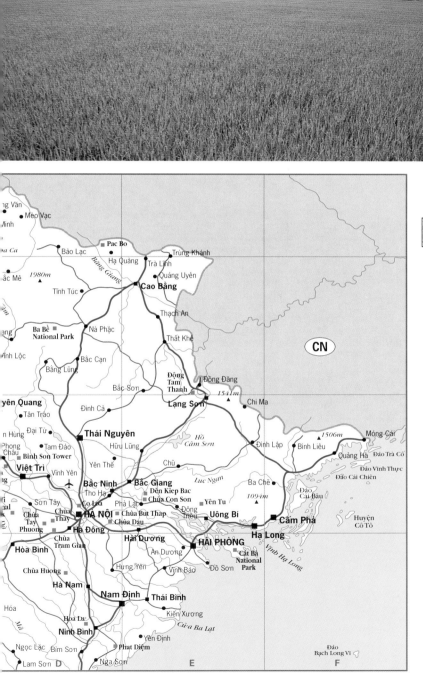

ng Văn
• Mèo Vạc
Minh

a Ca   • Bảo Lạc   ■ Pac Bo   Trùng Khánh
                          • Hạ Quảng   • Trà Lĩnh
ắc Mê   ▲1980m   Quảng Uyên
                 • Tĩnh Túc   ■ Cao Bằng

ạng   Ba Bể ■   Thạch An   CN
       National Park   • Nà Phặc
                                         Thất Khê
ỉnh Lộc   • Bắc Cạn

       • Bằng Lũng   Động
                      • Bắc Sơn   Tam   • Đồng Đăng
yên Quang   Thanh   ▲1541m
       • Tân Trào   • Đình Cả   Lạng Sơn   • Chi Ma

n Hùng • Đại Từ   ■ Thái Nguyên   ▲1506m   • Móng Cái
hong   • Tam Đảo   Hồ   • Đình Lập • Bình Liêu
Châu   Bình Sơn Tower • Hữu Lũng Cẩm Sơn   Quảng Hà • Đảo Trà Cổ
■ Việt Trì • Vĩnh Yên   • Yên Thế   Chũ   • Đảo Vĩnh Thực
al   Ba Chẽ   Đảo Cái Chiên
nal   • Sơn Tây ■ Bắc Ninh ■ Bắc Giang Lục Ngạn   Đảo
      Chùa   Đền Kiep Bac   ▲109+m   Cái Bầu
l   Tây   • Thọ Hà ■ Chùa Con Sơn   Huyện
      Phương ■ Cổ Loa • Phả Lại • Yên Tu   Cô Tô
                ■ HÀ NỘI ■ Chùa But Thap Đông
      Chùa Thầy   Chùa Dâu Triều ■ Uông Bí   ■ Cẩm Phả
      ■ Hà Đông   ■ Hạ Long
Hòa Bình Chùa   ■ Hải Dương   Vịnh Hạ Long
         Tram Gian   ■ HẢI PHÒNG
   • Chùa Hương   • An Dương   Cát Bà
                                 National
   ■ Hà Nam   • Hưng Yên   Park
                    • Vĩnh Bảo • Đồ Sơn
Hóa   ■ Nam Định ■ Thái Bình
         • Kiên Xương
   ■ Ninh Bình   Cửa Ba Lạt
• Hoa Lư
Ngọc Lặc • Bỉm Sơn   • Yên Định
• Lam Sơn D • Nga Sơn • Phát Diệm E   Đảo   F
                                      Bạch Long Vĩ

Above: nothing goes to waste. Here weed is being collected from flooded fields for use as pig fodder
Below: terraced fields and the homes of a highland minority near Cao Bang

small industries keep the pot boiling. Abundant rich clay furnishes the local brick kilns in villages such as Bat Trang and Tho Ha, which have been churning out pottery for over four centuries. Here, too, are centres of silk-making and folk painting (the latter at the village of Dong Ho – see panel opposite), while this same delta area gave birth to the art of water-puppetry a thousand years ago. To the south lies Chua Huong (Perfume Pagoda), North Vietnam's greatest pilgrimage site, while elsewhere, hidden in the trees, are countless ancient pagodas that shelter superb statues and intricate woodcarvings.

However, times change and bombs fall: much of this region is now a characterless sprawl of half-built villages connected by potholed roads and inhabited by unsmiling, drab-looking people. Three decades of war overlapping with two decades of catastrophic socio-political changes have, not surprisingly, left their mark here.

The only viable way to visit this area is to take day-trips from Hanoi, as acceptable accommodation is non-existent in the region and in any case few sights lie over 50km from the capital (see also pages 67–9).

Minority trail Move west into the mountains, and it is

an altogether different story. This magnificent, isolated region is home to the greatest concentration of Vietnam's ethnic minorities, whose villages lie scattered over the slopes and valleys that rise towards Laos and China. Their history of autonomy and support for the Northerners during the Vietnam War has left them with relatively decent conditions as well as political representation. In many cases lifestyles have not changed for centuries, and this is, of course, an added attraction for visitors. In the case of Sa Pa, tourism is already having an effect on local traditions, but elsewhere the trail remains little trodden, mainly due to bad communications.

The far-from-comfortable Highway 6 that loops up to Lai Chau in the north-western corner of the region necessitates a rented jeep or robust Russian motor bike – buses are only for masochists. Budget travellers should either join tours from Hanoi or take the train to Lao Cai and Lang Son, both border crossings into China. A faster alternative is to fly in or out of Dien Bien Phu, the decisive battleground in the war for independence from the French.

Unadulterated Nature-lovers are in their element in the mountainous areas. Unlike Vietnam's defoliated wastelands further south, the northern mountains escaped bombing entirely due to their proximity to China: the US government judiciously avoided tempting the devil. However, this same proximity spelled disaster in 1979 when the Chinese army destroyed the border towns between Lang Son and Lao Cai. Another legacy of this period is the presence of mines, which continue to cause fatal accidents.

Outside the few urban areas, nature is free and abundant. Forests, though eaten into by cultivated plots, clad the mountains right up to the peaks and are home to rare tigers and leopards, as well as hundreds of bird and reptile species. Closest to Hanoi is Tam Dao, a mountain resort offering good nature trails, while further afield lies the beautiful Ba Be National Park, rivalling Sa Pa in the nature stakes. Ha Long Bay also has its national park, on Cat Ba Island, with the added bonus of beaches where you can recover from the arduous northern trail.

Dong Ho folk paintings
A Northern art form that is passed down through the generations is that of hand-painted woodcuts, produced above all in the village of Dong Ho, near Thuan Thanh (about 25km east of Hanoi). These satirical, naïve drawings illustrate legends and moral tales, often with animals as their chief protagonists. The paintings can now be bought in many art galleries in Hanoi.

79

THE NORTH

Tourist services
● Cao Bang Provincial
Trade & Tourism, Cao
Bang (tel: 026 852245/
852404).
● There is no tourist office
in Cat Ba, but all hotels are
good sources of informa-
tion. Huu Dung restaurant
(up the unnamed street
facing the jetty; no phone)
offers motorbike and boat
rentals, treks and general
information, as well as
serving food from a wide-
ranging menu. The outdoor
beer-stall by the jetty is
where boatmen gather; ask
for Du and Cuong, whose
boat (called *Hai Long*) is
the most comfortable.

*Cat Ba Island's main
harbour, a village
in itself*

► Ba Be National Park 77D3

High in the province of Cao Bang, about 250km from Hanoi, lie three interconnected lakes (Ba Be means 'Three Seas') rimmed by forested peaks. This magnificent area has recently been declared a national park to protect the forest and the large colonies of waterbirds that live on the two islands, Po Ga Mai and An Ma. Boat-trips penetrate the shadowy 300m-long **Puong Grotto►**, which soars to heights of 30m and drips with stalactites and stalagmites, or take you on an hour-long journey to the **Dau Dang Waterfall**, a tiered 100m cascade. Access to this remote area takes a full day from Hanoi, making three-day all-in tours the best option.

►► Bac Ha 76C3

Bac Ha looks set to join Sa Pa (see pages 92–3) as an ethnic-minority tour destination. This extended mountain village lies about 55km east of Lao Cai and has only just been 'discovered' by tours from Hanoi. At the weekend market, Giays, Tays and Daos pour in from surrounding villages, making for a colourfully diverse crowd. Local specialities include plums and corn wine, the latter more of an acquired taste. Accommodation, though very basic, is gradually expanding and there are plenty of hikes in the region. Motor bikes or jeep taxis can be hired from Lao Cai station, or Bac Ha can be combined with Sa Pa on all-in tours from Hanoi.

► Cao Bang 77E3

Few visitors attempt the long and potholed ride to Cao Bang, barely 30km from the Chinese frontier but with no official crossing point. If they do, it is to visit another Uncle Ho memorial, **Pac Bo►**, 60km to the north-west. These caves are where Ho Chi Minh organised Viet Minh resistance in 1941 against the Japanese occupation, ironically helped by American advisers (see page 43). Virtually invisible from the air, and with a tunnel link to China, Pac Bo became Uncle Ho's think-tank; he even found time to carve a stalagmite into a resemblance of Lenin when not penning poetry or naming a local peak after Karl Marx. Cao Bang market pulls in local Dao, Tho and H'Mong ethnic minorities, accompanied by their cattle and goats.

►►► Cat Ba Island 77E1

This unspoilt island makes a viable alternative to staying in touristy Ha Long City as it lies

Entrance to the
Cat Ba ferry dock in
Hai Phong

on the southern perimeter of Ha Long Bay (see pages
86–7) and is reached by ferry from Hai Phong in under
our hours. First stop is Cat Hai, a small fishing village on
he north coast, but Cat Ba's main harbour and ferry dock
s at the southern end of the island, curling around an
extensive floating village where karaoke cafés are visited
by sampans and basket boats from the nearby houseboats. On land, Cat Ba town straggles between a government hotel in the east and the market in the west, with
several small hotels in between. The local boatmen
organise tours of Ha Long Bay over one or more days,
generally for better rates than can be found at Ha Long
City (count on US$5 per hour for a boat accommodating
up to ten people). From the eastern end of the town a
path climbs over a headland to two exquisite coves,
where soft white sand gently slopes into the emerald
sea; the first has beach-huts and a café, while the second
s more deserted and dramatic.

The island's inhabitants are friendly and the present
infrastructure achieves a good balance of being limited yet
at the same time perfectly adequate. Cat Ba Island is the
biggest (354sq km) of an archipelago of 366 islands, and
its untouched interior of primary tropical forest, coastal
mangroves and offshore coral reefs are now protected as
a national park▶▶ (Admission charge cheap; guides
available and recommended). Some 745 plant species
have so far been identified in the park, including the rare
kim giao tree, while other species counts record 20
mammals, 69 birds and 30 reptiles. White-headed
monkeys bound along the limestone escarpments, and
mountain goats, deer, wild boar, kingfishers, hornbills and
hawks are all relatively common. The park lies 15km from
Cat Ba town and is easily reached by motor bike or bus.
Local cafés organise day-treks through the park to the
east coast, from where a boat ferries the group back to
the main harbour.

Life after Pac Bo
In August 1942, just inside
the Chinese border, Chiang
Kai-shek's police arrested
Ho Chi Minh. Ho had been
on his way from Pac Bo to
contact the Chinese leader
in an attempt to gain
support for the resistance
movement against the
Japanese, despite the
fact that his communist
sympathies did not find
favour with the nationalist
Kuomintang. For 15 months
Ho Chi Minh was dragged
from prison to prison (30 in
total), sometimes forced to
walk 50km a day. He was
held in chains together
with common bandits and
assassins, locked in
stinking, infected cells,
fed a meagre diet and,
inevitably, became
extremely sick. This was
when Ho Chi Minh's force
of will was most apparent
as, despite the execrable
conditions, he managed to
write over 100 poems (in
Chinese, so as not to raise
any suspicions).

The princess's sacrifice
Chua Tuyet, the highest of a string of seven cave-temples at the Perfume Pagoda, was the legendary abode of a princess who, against her father's will, chose to retreat to this cave to dedicate herself to Buddhism. Some time later her father contracted leprosy, leading to blindness and atrophied hands. After consulting the experts, the emperor was told that he would only regain his health if one of his subjects made the voluntary sacrifice of his own hands and eyes. Word reached the princess, who self-sacrificially carried out the deed. On learning of this tragedy, the emperor himself became a Buddhist and started to transform the caves into temples.

▶▶   **Chua Huong (Perfume Pagoda)**   77D1

This extensive network of pagodas and cave-temples, dedicated to Quan Am (the Goddess of Mercy) and built into a wooded mountainside beside the Yen Vi River, lies 60km south-west of Hanoi (*Admission charge* expensive). At Ben Duc wharf, flotillas of wooden rowing-boats wait to transport the hordes of pilgrims who descend on the site come rain or shine, peaking during the festival season (mid-January to mid-March), as this is the mecca of North Vietnamese Buddhists. A one-hour glide through peaceful rural scenery passes several minor pagodas before arriving at a jetty serving the main pagoda, **Thien Tru**, founded in the late 15th century and gradually extended to encompass numerous smaller temples. Unfortunately the complex suffered extensive fire damage during the war against the French, so much of it is very recent restoration. Ponds, tombs, a lovely bell-tower, gardens and monks' quarters all cluster around the mountain at the top of a staircase which, in the rain, becomes a natural waterfall.

From here, a steep 3km path leads up past four cave-temples to the soaring **Huong Tich (Rice-barn Grotto)**, while another 3km branch ends at the Chua Hinh Bong pagoda. Two other jetties closer to Ben Duc serve countless other shrines and pagodas, including the popular Chua Tuyet (see panel). All are well served by food-stalls and vendors, so you will not go hungry or thirsty on the climb.

Come rain or shine, hundreds of boats make their way to the pilgrimage sites of the Perfume Pagoda

▶   **Dien Bien Phu**   77D1

In the extreme north-west of Vietnam, knocking on Laos's door, lies the site of France's momentous defeat in Vietnam – Dien Bien Phu. Today, the former battlefield displays the reconstructed bunker of Général de Castries alongside various artillery pieces, a vast Viet Minh cemetery and a memorial erected on the 30th anniversary of the battle to the dead of both sides. A small, very didactic **Army Museum** (*Open* 8–11, 1–4. *Admission charge* cheap) relates the battle through models, photos and weapons. Some 20km away, in the forest of Muong Phang, is the newly rebuilt bunker of General Giap. The small, prospering town itself offers reasonable accommodation and an airstrip, and there is plenty of ethnic and nature interest in the surrounding hills.

A French war relic at Dien Bien Phu

▶ Hai Phong 77E1

Industrialised Hai Phong, Vietnam's third-largest city, is a fairly rough and dusty destination. Life revolves around the port, whose containers, cranes and tankers sprawl along the mouth of the Cam River. Investment here is high, and the city is currently enjoying growth of over 12 per cent.

Much of the city was bombed first by the French and then the Americans, but a central grid of tree-lined streets conserves the colonial style, including the colonnaded **Grand Theatre** (1904), the **History Museum▶** (66 Dien Bien Phu. *Open* Tue–Sun 8–11, 2–6.30. *Admission charge cheap*) and the main hotels and restaurants. A couple of blocks north is Ben Bach Dang, the dock for ferries to Ha Long City and Cat Ba Island, while the railway station lies about 1km south. Near here is the **Hang Kenh Communal House▶** (1856), renowned for its exceptional dragon wood-carvings and dedicated to Ngo Quyen (see page 35). Further south lies **Du Hang Pagoda▶**, Hai Phong's oldest pagoda (10th century, but rebuilt in 1672) which houses some impressive statuary and antique furniture.

Less convenient is Hai Phong's new Kien An Airport, about 15km west of town along a potholed road, which has now virtually replaced the older Cat Bi Airport (if travelling by plane, check which airport your flight leaves from). Relief is, however, offered by **Do Son Beach▶**, 22km south-east of Hai Phong and occupying a forested promontory that was first developed by the French, some of whose venerable edifices can still be seen.

Le dernier débâcle
Dien Bien Phu was where General Vo Nguyen Giap led the historic assault on 16,000 French troops (mostly Foreign Legionnaires, Moroccans and Algerians), who had been entrenched for several months in a misguided attempt to lure the Viet Minh into the valley. The French plan backfired, and between March and May 1954 Giap, using unbelievable logistics to bring in his equipment, systematically assaulted base after base before finally planting the Vietnamese flag on a hill named Claudine, the last stronghold. Some 3,000 French soldiers died, another 3,000 were seriously injured and 10,000 prisoners were led away to camps. The Viet Minh toll was even higher, with an estimated 8,000 dead.

Do Son Beach, 22km south-east of Hai Phong

Mountain minorities

■ **Usually seen trekking up steep slopes or crowding into local markets, Vietnam's northern minorities maintain a colourfully high profile. Countless subgroups have each developed their own dialects and costumes over the centuries, and altogether this peripatetic population is a fascinating showpiece of the country's still flourishing ethnic cultures.** ■

H'Mong death rites

H'Mong deaths are occasions for animist rituals orchestrated by the shaman (*nong rua*). It is he who washes and dresses the corpse in its best clothes before it is placed on a stretcher near what the H'Mong regard as the sacred pole – the main column holding the roof of the house, which also assumes the more esoteric role of a bridge between the earth and the world of the spirits. From here the body is transferred to a room where it holds court: relatives and friends pay their respects over several days. Buffaloes and pigs are slaughtered and the dead person is 'fed' by the widow or eldest son. The final funeral ceremony is accompanied by prayers and music before the body is buried in a marked grave.

Muong One of the largest groups (numbering nearly a million) is the Muong, mainly concentrated south and west of Hanoi in the provinces of Hoa Binh, Yen Bai and Thanh Hoa. This Austroasiatic group is thought to share its origins with the Viets, but subsequently avoided all Chinese influence and maintained feudal rulers. Soberly dressed in dark clothes that are highlighted by embroidered panels and silver jewellery, the Muong are known for their literary imagination.

Thai Not to be confused with the inhabitants of Thailand, the Thai (or Tai) of Vietnam are subdivided into Black, White and Red groups. Altogether they number about a million, and live in stilt-houses in scattered villages through the valleys of the Red (Hong) and Black (Da) rivers, in the North-central interior and over the border into Laos and Thailand. They have developed efficient rice-farming techniques that put them in direct competition with the neighbouring Viets. Red Thai women wear superb bright costumes with tasselled turbans, their bodices embroidered with fish, birds or monkeys and edged with tinkling silver beads.

Tay Of the same Tai-Kadai family as the Thai are the 1.3 million Tay (Vietnam's largest minority), who live to the north and north-east of the Red River Delta. They are thought to have arrived with the Viets from southern China in the first centuries BC, but their unique script indicates that they might then have split off from the delta population. Related to them are the **Giay**, more visible in the north-west and also more recent arrivals from southern China, probably reaching the region in the 18th century. In contrast to the generally sober, indigo clothes of the Tay, Giay women wear riotously coloured costumes with multiple bands of embroidery, checked headscarves and embroidered puttees. The Giay honour the Goddess of Childbirth and believe in the transmigration of the soul, while the more integrated Tay share Viet religious beliefs.

H'Mong Waves of nomadic H'Mong (or Meo) started crossing from China into northern Vietnam and Laos about three centuries ago and now number about 750,000. Their preference for high altitudes has made them one of the most isolated groups. They maintain strong religious beliefs that are governed by a shaman who presides over funerals involving animal sacrifices, or arranged marriages that are preceded by mock kidnappings. Bride prices are paid in money, pigs and alcohol.

Both men and women wear indigo clothes made from hemp: the women sport long 'aprons' and embroidered waistcoats over baggy shorts and puttees, their hair rolled into a turban; the men wear skullcaps, loose trousers, shirts and a long waistcoat with an embroidered mandarin collar.

Dao Of unclear origins but probably contemporary arrivals of the H'Mong, the Dao (or Zao) inhabit the highest areas of the northern provinces and number about 800,000. Their aristocratic-looking women shave and wax their hair and eyebrows, leaving a high brow crowned with a large red, bejewelled turban, and wear densely embroidered indigo 'aprons'. Men's clothes are similar to those of the H'Mong, with the addition of an embroidered turban. The Dao still worship a canine ancestor whose five colours are used in their exceptionally fine needlework. In addition to usual burials and cremations is the practice of air burials: the corpse is placed in an elevated bamboo cage until only the bones remain, these eventually buried in an urn.

Minority traditions are gradually disappearing in more accessible areas

Independent nature
It is only since the early 1990s that foreign visitors have been able to penetrate the remote mountains of North Vietnam. Even the French had only a cursory relationship with the minorities of Tonkin, who actively opposed colonialism by joining guerrilla forces. Barely touched by outside influences, most survive on rice cultivation, slash-and-burn farming and, occasionally, commercial crops. The creation in the mid-1960s of two autonomous regions responded to the independent character of the minorities, but these were abolished post-1975. Today, the various ethnic groups have proportional representation at the National Assembly.

85

Opposite: Black Thai woman and child near Hoa Binh
Below: longhouses with woven bamboo walls in a Thai village near Son La

Ha Long Bay's myriad islets float in the mists of the horizon

►►► Ha Long Bay (Vinh Ha Long) 77F1

The magic of this vast, mysterious bay, covering an area of 1,500sq km up to the Chinese border, stems from the 3,000-plus jagged limestone islands that rise out of the South China Sea here. Eroded over time by the wind and sea, these dramatic pinnacles have become national emblems and are virtually an obligatory tourist destination.

The name Ha Long ('Descent of the Dragon') derives from the legend of an enormous creature of the deep which one day awoke from its sleep to thrash its way to heaven, in the process creating myriad rocky islets. Geologists say otherwise: the island-studded bay emerged at the end of the Primary era when the crumbly limestone was worn away by the waters of the numerous outlets of the Red River.

History, too, was made here, as it was after Capitaine Rivière failed to capture the coal mines of Hon Gai in 1882 that France launched a full-scale expedition against the entire country. More recently, Ha Long Bay was the departure point for hundreds of boat-people fleeing the economic miseries of the late 1980s and steering their little boats towards Hong Kong.

Access options Hon Gai, a working port, and the adjoining resort of Bai Chay have recently been given new, united status under the name Ha Long City. The 160km road from Hanoi is the usual bus or car route for visitors, and luckily plans are afoot to improve this overloaded and far-from-adequate road. Longer but more interesting alternatives are to take the two-hour train journey from Hanoi to Hai Phong, then catch a bus (two hours) or ferry (three to four hours) to Bai Chay or to Cat Ba Island (see pages 80–1). Those with extra suitcases of dong can also arrive directly by heli-jet from Hanoi. The easiest budget option is to take a two- or three-day tour from Hanoi, which may include sleeping on a boat: this sounds ideal, but much depends on the company and the weather. Tours that include hotels are generally not the best. Another alternative is to use tranquil Cat Ba Island as a base.

Coastal bases The greatest concentration of tourist facilities is at **Bai Chay (Ha Long City West)►**, a typical Vietnamese beach resort with lovely views and mercilesss vendors of coral, shells and chunks of stalactites. Plans are afoot for a US$10 million resort (due to open in 1998) that would shape the atmosphere definitively. Some 5km east lies **Hong Gai (Ha Long City East)►**, the provincial capital, which lives off coal mining and fishing. As Hon Gai is not overloaded with tourists, it offers a less artificial environment and reasonably priced hotels.

From both harbours boats can be hired to tour the bay, usually making a quick circuit of a couple of grottoes and including a swimming stop. As a result, the section of the bay nearest these towns has become polluted with tourist garbage. A far better plan is to arrange an extended trip that includes one night on board, as this offers a chance to penetrate the clear emerald waters to the east, where coral reefs lie beneath the surface.

Cavernous highlights Several spectacular island caves make obvious stopovers on the aquatic tour. The most astounding, **Hang Dau Go►►** (*Admission charge* moderate), 8km south of Bai Chay, harbours three chambers that are rife with glistening stalagmites and stalactites. Ninety steep steps climb to the first gaping cavern, inhabited by a silent crowd of dripping columns that fire the imagination. **Bo Nau (Pigeon Cave)►** is a shorter cave but has beautiful views over the bay, an aspect once appreciated by flocks of seabirds. **Bo Han Island** is the perfect spot for meditating on the sunset, while the 2km-long cave of **Hang Hanh►** (*Admission charge* moderate) offers another rock-formation extravaganza. Other islands harbour troops of monkeys and everywhere there are exquisite, idyllically secluded beaches.

87

Tourist boats from Bai Chay home in on the cavernous wonders

Tourist offices
● Hoa Binh Tourism,
54 Phuong Huu Nghi, Hoa
Binh (tel: 018 854374;
fax: 018 854372).
● Lai Chau Trade and
Tourism, Lai Chau (tel: 023
852112).
● Lang Son Tourism Export
& Import, Le Loi, Vinh Trai
Lang Son (tel: 025
871507/6).

► **Hoa Binh** 77D1

In the foothills of the Hoang Lien Son mountains 70km south-west of Hanoi is Hoa Binh, whose prehistoric finds prove that this was where man first started cultivating crops in Vietnam, about 10,000 years ago. Progress moves on, however, and the construction of Vietnam's largest hydroelectric plant on the Da River has transformed the nature of the area. There are numerous ethnic villages in the hills and the town centre is virtually monopolised by the sale of their wares, though this is very much geared to day-trippers from Hanoi.

►► **Lai Chau** 76B3

It is hard to get more remote than this town, lost in the magnificent mountains of north-western Vietnam. Highway 6, which snakes over 500km from Hanoi to reach Lai Chau, first traverses the **Pha Din Pass►** at about 1,000m; the name means 'Heaven and Earth', an appropriate description for this wild region of plunging gorges and soaring peaks. Some 23 ethnic minorities live in the province, notably the Thai and the H'Mong, and their hamlets pepper the cultivated slopes (these include opium plots) between huge tracts of forest. Highway 6 is a euphemism at this point as atrocious road surfaces, switchbacks and steep climbs make it an arduous stretch to say the least – a four-wheel drive or robust Russian motor bike are the only feasible vehicles. Flooding is a perennial problem in the valley where the town is located, and a project is being mooted to create a vast reservoir that would seal Lai Chau's fate for eternity.

Some 23 ethnic groups inhabit the province of Lai Chau, bordering on Laos and China

88

▶ **Lang Son**   77E2

Along with Lao Cai (see below), Lang Son is the main border-crossing town into China. China's calamitous attempted invasion of Vietnam in 1979 (see panel) left its toll on Lang Son and the actual border post of Dong Dang, 14km to the north, but since the border reopened trade (both legal and illegal) has boomed. The abundant fruit crops of the area add to the interest of Ky Lua Market, also visited by minority people. Just outside the town are the three **Tam Thanh Grottoes**, replete with rock formations and shrines, although more sociologically interesting is the market at **Dong Dang**, where Tay and Thai porters squat among buffaloes, cows, Russian Minsk motor bikes and a garish array of cheap Chinese goods. Night trains from Hanoi arrive at an unsociably early hour, but the only alternative is Highway 1, which ends in a memorably inglorious state at Lang Son to make the six-hour bus trip another northern endurance test.

'Friendship Gate', the border crossing to China at Lang Son, is still a strategically sensitive area

▶ **Lao Cai**   76B3

Anyone heading for Sa Pa or Bac Ha, or crossing into Yunnan in China comes through Lao Cai, the terminus for the train from Hanoi (a ten-hour journey, best undertaken at night). The hot, dusty town (rebuilt after the 1979 Chinese onslaught) sprawls along both banks of the Red River opposite the gleaming Chinese high-rises of Hekouvaoju the other side of a steel bridge. About 150m east of the bridge is the hilltop pagoda of **Chua Den Thuong▶**, beside which is a gigantic banyan where Chinese tourists come to burn joss-sticks. Two prayer-halls and several outdoor shrines offer views over the border. Lao Cai's main market is on the west bank of the river just behind the bus station, and there are several reasonable hotels and restaurants.

▶▶ **Mai Chau**   76C1

This lovely valley is a classic stopover on the north-west tour as well as a target for overnight tours from Hanoi, 130km away. Between Hoa Binh and Mai Chau the road climbs over the **Doc Koon Pass**, with superb views over the cluster of thatched stilt-houses that is Mai Chau and beyond to its mountainous backdrop. There is only one hotel, but tour groups or those travelling with a guide usually stay in minority houses where song and dance is laid on and *ruou can,* the local rice wine, liberally consumed.

Surprise attack
In February 1979, when Chinese tanks appeared on the border, the Vietnamese were completely taken by surprise. The attack was launched in response to Vietnam's anti-ethnic Chinese campaign and its invasion of Cambodia, but the Chinese still had not realised the long and resourceful Vietnamese defensive tradition. After three weeks of fighting, with tens of thousands dead (the true figures were concealed by both governments) and several towns ruined, the Chinese withdrew, deeming their attempted invasion a 'great success'. Sporadic skirmishes carried on for a few more years and both sides still remain suspicious of one another.

■ **Despite government attempts at suppression, opium-smoking and cultivation is still entrenched among certain northern minorities. Yet less than a century ago, its processing and trade were monopolised by the French colonial government, many of whose officials frequented opium dens to dream of things other than red tape.** ■

Getting high

'Any time anybody went to the rear they had to bring back liquor for the officers and hot beer, but for the rest of us they brought back smoke…we used to get Party Packs which was ten rolled joints to a pack. We paid $5 to the pack… Then they came up with another one they used to call 100s, which was longer than a cigarette. But they cost you a dollar for a joint. Those were soaked in opium… A half of one of those joints – and those guys were smoking two or three joints by themselves and just getting mellow – half a joint got six guys high…you couldn't function on that smoke.'
From *Nam* by Mark Baker (1987).

19th-century opium-smokers approaching terminal inertia

Opium farming was banned in Vietnam in 1954, although cultivation for personal use was permitted, and since 1986 all cultivation and possession has become illegal. Although attempts have been made to encourage farmers to grow the substitute cash crop of Panax Pseudo-Ginseng, which is sold to the Chinese for traditional medicines, it is impossible to control poppy cultivation in the remote north, and nor is it easy to eradicate what, in many cases, is an addiction. An estimated 30 per cent of H'Mong in Laos and Vietnam are regular users, and it is not unusual for tourists to be offered a sticky ball of opium at local markets or while trekking through the mountains.

The poppy seeds are sown after the rains in September, then harvested in February–March. When the petals drop off the poppy the remaining capsule is incised to allow sap to ooze out and oxidise. After 24 hours it has become a brown gum, which is then scraped off and rolled into easily transportable balls.

Origins Opium originated in Turkey and Persia, from where it spread west to Ancient Greece and east to India, before being introduced to China by Arab traders in the 13th century. Initially used for its pain-killing properties, opium was first taken for pleasure in the 17th century. In 1729, a Chinese emperor made a first, unsuccessful attempt to prohibit opium-smoking. During the same period, the H'Mong started their drift

south into Vietnam, bringing opium cultivation with them. In the 1860s the Chinese community was given the opium monopoly to finance the huge Vietnamese war indemnity owed to the French. Meanwhile, in the West, opium-smoking came to be regarded as a mellow and legal alternative to alcoholic intoxication, the French poet Baudelaire being one of its more lyrical apologists.

French monopoly By the time the French took over, opium dens proliferated among Vietnam's Chinese communities, the raw substance being brought from the mountains along a network of paths that later developed into the Ho Chi Minh Trail. Like the British in India and China, the French saw the economic potential of this trade and added opium to their monopolies of alcohol, salt and tobacco, the four altogether furnishing nearly 60 per cent of Indochina's tax revenues by 1914. French authorities justified this monopoly by stating that price regulation was necessary to avoid colonists being cheated by Chinese middlemen. At the *manufacture d'opium* (opium-processing factory), the raw substance, delivered in large balls wrapped in poppy leaves, was refined and then packed into boxes of between 5g and 100g, ready for sale and consumption. It was only in 1909 that a concerted inter-governmental attempt was made to restrict the sale of the drug as its extensive use was by then generally recognised as harmful.

A rebound in usage occurred during World War II under the Japanese occupation, the new overlords eager to keep the populations of 'Great East Asia' happy – and inactive. The horrors of the Vietnam War also invited extensive use of opium, as well as of its derivative, heroin, still a major urban problem in Vietnam today.

Ritual Embossed silver opium pipes are sold in 'antique' shops from Hanoi to Ho Chi Minh City, but these are not quite the metre-long pipes that were once so common. Opium dens grew in popularity as they took the hard work out of smoking – pipes took up to ten minutes to prepare, and in any case smokers were hardly *compos mentis* after they had inhaled a few. Smokers stretched out on mats or beds, their heads on a hard pillow, while a small ball attached to a needle was toasted and twisted over a spirit-lamp until it acquired the perfect treacly consistency; at this point the pipe bowl was heated and the soft pellet of opium inserted. Holding the pipe bowl over the flame, the smoker then inhaled, still using the needle to centralise the pellet. And then he dreamed...

A nation, a religion
'The first pipe paralyses and crushes me. I lie on my back, incapable of batting an eyelid. And that lasts one, two, three minutes. The boy, very patiently, offers me the second pipe. But I continue to revel in the minute signs of my intoxication, greedily savouring the mad turbulence in my brain, still incapable of dealing with the first attack of the divine poison. Only when the voluptuous vertigo starts to dissipate do I slowly raise my head and offer my lips to the second pipe... Opium is really a nation, a religion, a strong and jealous bond that holds men together. And I feel more brotherly towards the Asians who are smoking in Fou-Tcheou Road than to those inferior Frenchmen who vegetate in my native Paris.'
From *Fumée d'Opium* by Claude Farrère (1900s).

91

Intricately carved opium pipes on sale in Ho Chi Minh City

*Right: Dao women profit from Sa Pa's fast-developing tourist trade
Below: Sa Pa's glorious landscapes lose some of their appeal during the rainy season*

▶▶▶ Sa Pa   76B3

Of all the northern minority towns, Sa Pa justifiably draws the greatest number of visitors despite its isolation. Once a French hill-station and for centuries before that a market-place for ethnic highlanders, it is now smoothing its rural edges to accommodate a flow of tour groups from Hanoi. These all arrive for the weekend market, so during the week Sa Pa is relatively empty. Crowds of diminutive H'Mong in their indigo outfits and the more regal Dao, crowned by their bejewelled red turbans, flock to town, marketing or touting their beautifully embroidered clothes. *'Joli, joli! OK? Non!'* (French for 'Pretty, pretty! OK? No!') is the minority password here, which reaches a shrill soprano among the friendly though persistent H'Mong. Sa Pa also offers superb walks, while Vietnam's tallest mountain, Phan Si Pang (3,143m), looms in the background.

Paradise Sa Pa lies 40km from Lao Cai at the end of a tortuous mountain road that winds around valleys and passes minority villages and rice-fields before climbing to the pine-tree environs of the village. The settlement radiates from the church, football field and market-place, the latter soon set to move to a new purpose-built structure down the hill. Hotels, guest-houses, restaurants, a bank and a post office are dotted along the main road and the downhill street, this becoming a dirt-road that runs south through the valley.

Motorbike taxis or jeeps can be rented to explore further, the latter at exorbitant cost, but Sa Pa's delights lie in the countless mountain trails that lead from the town in all directions (note that these all include steep slopes). The entire valley south of Sa Pa was designated a nature reserve in 1986: despite extensive cultivation and local hunting habits, 56 mammal species have been identified here, including 17 that are rare or endangered, as well as 150 species of birds.

Walks A path behind the church leads up steps to wind around a dramatic boulder-strewn landscape over several peaks that offer breathtaking **valley views▶▶**. Bulbuls, flycatchers, niltavas and countless butterflies wing their way through the skies. West of the village, a track twists down past the picturesque ruins of a French villa to Catcat Waterfall, then, a few kilometres further on, reaches the

H'Mong village of **Sin Chai**►►. After following and then crossing the river, a trail finally rejoins the main valley road to loop back to Sa Pa: allow about four hours. A longer alternative is to follow the road south beyond the Giay village of Lao Chai to Ta Van (about 12km); between here and the Dao village of Chai Man are a series of prehistoric **rock-carvings**► that have so far eluded identification. Any walk along this valley road, however short, will take you past groups of H'Mong and Dao villagers whose stamina puts Westerners to shame. At the same time, fabulous views to Phan Si Pang accompany you all the way.

Weekend fever Sa Pa awakes on Saturday morning to troops of Dao heading for the market, their back-baskets laden with goods that they have carried from up to 15km away. Sadly, the Saturday night wooing tradition by which young girls chose their mate for the night has all but disappeared – overtly at least. Sunday morning sees more Giay and groups of good-humoured H'Mong, most clasping umbrellas and threading hemp, although some young men carry ghetto-blasters playing recordings of their own music – a sign of the changing times.

►► Son La

76B2

This classic stopover on the long north-western haul offers some basic accommodation and the chance to see fascinating minority villages of the Black and White Thai, H'Mong and Muong. **Ban Hin**►, a typical Thai hamlet about 3km from Son La, lays on rice wine and dances. Pine forests, caves (**Tham Ke** and **Tham Ta Toong**) and hot springs (**Suoi Nuoc Nong**, to the south, and **Ban Mong**, to the north-west) add to the attractions. A restored French prison in the town centre is a grim reminder of hill-tribe repression. Before the French era, the Son La region was ruled by the Black Thai, and from 1959 to 1980 it was an autonomous region.

A suspended bridge in the high plateau of Son La

Tourist services
● Sa Pa has no tourist office as yet, but some shops sell an excellent little publication in English (*Sa Pa*, The Gioi Publishers) covering walks, bird and mammal check-lists, and even ethnic-minority vocabulary. Train tickets can be ordered through a sub-post office on the main street south, and the Auberge Hotel organises jeeps and tours, albeit at steep rates. Tourist buses operate twice daily to connect with Hanoi trains at Lao Cai; alternatively, motorbike taxis should cost little more than US$5.
● Son La Tourism, Quyet Thang, Son La (tel: 022 852702).

The ornate entrance to Chua Den Va at Son Tay

Triple peaks

Tam Dao literally means 'Three Isolated Islands', a reference to the three highest peaks of the range that rise in dramatic style above the hill-station. The middle peak, Thach Ban ('Stone Table'), is named after a large stone slab that lies on its summit, said to be a meeting point for male fairies who, in free moments, come down from heaven to play chess – although no one seems to know what they use for pieces. To the left is Thien Thi ('Celestial Market'), less ethereally home to a telecommunications tower but also with a cascading waterfall, while the highest peak, rising 1,400m, is named Phu Nghia ('Bearer of Good Things').

Defend the country!

'The Hung Kings have the merits of building the country. You and I should be the ones to defend the country.' Uncle Ho in a speech to his Viet Minh forces, September 1954.

▶ **Son Tay** 77D2

Today, only fragments of the citadel walls that once rimmed Son Tay remain. The walls incorporated four gates, were surrounded by a moat, and enclosed the ruler's Kinh Thien Pavilion and a barracks for the military protectors of the Trinh Dynasty (1673–1788), whose capital was at Thang Long (Hanoi). Of more interest is **Chua Den Va▶▶**, dating from the 10th century and located in the nearby village of Duong Lam. This intricately carved pagoda incorporates a courtyard designed for giant chess games: the pieces are brought out during the temple festival on the last day of the twelfth lunar month, just before Tet. More impressive still is **Chua Mia▶▶▶**, founded in 1632. Its 287 statues are made from a variety of materials that range from wood to ground sugar cane, the latter lacquered and gilded (*mia* means 'sugar cane'). For Ba Vi National Park, located to the south-west, see page 67.

▶ **Tam Dao** 77D2

This relaxing hill-station, developed by the French in 1902, lies high in the Tam Dao mountains about 85km north of Hanoi and is reached by a circuitous route. The small town is at an altitude of 880m, making its average temperature 10°C lower than that of Hanoi and its climate uncomfortably cold and damp in winter. Some colonial villas are now being restored, but the main interest here lies in walks and bird-watching. Xa Huong Lake, a waterfall and several pagodas are also close at hand.

Tam Dao is also a good base for exploring two major sights to the west. **Binh Son Tower▶▶**, near Lap Thanh, is an incredible 14th-century architectural feat (extensively restored post-1975) rising on 11 levels to a tapering point, its bricks finely etched with floral designs. The **Hung Kings Temple▶▶**, a few kilometres further on towards Phong Chau, is a complex of temples and shrines rife with legends of Vietnam's first dynasty 4,000 years ago. The five structures rise up Nghia Linh Hill and date from the 15th century, while numerous prehistoric artefacts have been excavated at the base of the hill.

► **Tho Ha** 77D2

Some 30km north-east of Hanoi, Highway 1 passes through Bac Ninh. For an amusing break stop at its outskirts at the village of Tho Ha, which spans the Cau River. The village has been renowned for its pottery since the 15th century; remnants of the trade can still be seen, pieces being made from a local clay and fired at high temperatures to produce a natural brown glaze. Here, too, is a beautiful pagoda and community-hall complex, **Dinh Tho Ha►►**, built in large enclosed grounds in the late 17th century. The interior is richly carved and is decorated with a major highlight, the Throne of the Golden Turtle (spirit of the temple), guarded by life-sized sentries.

Pine therapy
The pines on Yen Tu include three varieties: the white, the green and the red. Taxol, a substance found in the bark and needles of the Himalayan red pine, is helpful in curing breast, ovarian and lung cancers, but as it is also the slowest-growing tree in the world, supplies for pharmaceutical research are in very short supply.

►► **Yen Tu** 77E2

This is yet another scenic pilgrimage destination, reached via a strenuous 15km hike from Uong Bi, 40km west of Ha Long City. Once called White Cloud Mountain, not without reason, Yen Tu is unclimbable in the rainy season (May–September).

The mountain achieved notoriety in the 13th century when successive Tran Dynasty emperors came here to practise Buddhist meditation. In 1299 Tran Nhan Tong founded the Tru Lam sect here, which aimed to integrate religion into life through meditation. He built numerous pagodas, towers and shrines along the trail to the summit, planting the main stretch with 274 pine trees that have now reached immense proportions. These pines are said to contain mysterious energies that magnetise men (see panel on page 126). Several Tran Dynasty emperors were buried on Yen Tu, and Minh Mang later erected stelae by their tombs.

*Above: Yen Tu's pagodas fade into the ever-present clouds
Below: Dinh Tho Ha is reached by ferry*

■ From the Trung sisters to the contemporary writer Duong Thu Huong, Vietnam has a long history of women protagonists who have not hesitated to shoot on sight or denounce repression. Furthermore, the social upheavals of the Vietnam War have released women's domestic roles from the stranglehold of the Confucian cult of male authority. ■

Mother of Vietnam
According to legend, around 2800 BC King Lac Long Quan married the immortal Au Co, who bore him no fewer than 100 children. Fifty of the children followed their mother back to her mountain domain while the others accompanied their father to the Nam Hai Sea, where they founded the first kingdom of Vietnam.

Early to market

Centuries-old images of the Vietnamese peasant woman trotting along rural roads, heavy yoke over shoulders, bent double planting rice in the paddy-fields or squatting in her coolie hat at the market still hold true. Other, more sophisticated images project the urban woman in immaculate *ao dai*, gently but purposefully talking a man into her pocket in the age-old concubine tradition. This, too, is true. But beyond these stereotypes are countless heroines, named and unnamed, who have taken up arms, built roads or committed suicide in moral despair.

Pioneer sisters Vietnam's original Joans of Arc were the Trung sisters, Trung Trac and Trung Nhi, who in AD 40 rose up against their Chinese rulers and for three years headed an independent state. Both sisters are said to have fought while pregnant, their bodies encased in gold-plated armour, and eventually, along with 12 women generals, capturing some 65 citadels in the Red River Delta. At their home town of Me Linh they built their own citadel, from where they initiated reforms and reduced the oppressive taxes imposed by the Chinese Han Dynasty.

This utopia was to be short-lived, however, as in AD 43 the Chinese returned with reinforcements and soon defeated the Trung sisters' forces. True to historic interpretation, there are two versions of their fate: one says that they were executed and beheaded by the Chinese, the other that they committed suicide by throwing themselves in the Day River to avoid capture. Whatever the truth, the sisters continue to be worshipped at Hanoi's Hai Ba Trung Temple, where their annual festival is celebrated on the 6th day of the second lunar month (see page 56).

Self-sacrifice Similar in spirit was Trieu Au, a young girl from the province of Thanh Hoa who in AD 248 decided to take over from her dead brother in an uprising against the Chinese. Seated in a gold palanquin atop a fighting elephant, this Vietnamese Boudicca courageously led her compatriots into battle, but again defeat was imminent, inevitably followed by her suicide. Her grave stands by the memorial pagoda of Den Ba Trieu in Phu Dien village near Thanh Hoa. Self-sacrifice is an ongoing theme in Vietnamese history and legends, the latter usually involving lovers sent to war, betrayal or, in some cases, spiritual concerns, as in the case of the cave princess of the Perfume Pagoda (see panel on page 82).

War changes It was during the 20th century that the greatest changes in the

Northern woman's role took place, these evolving parallel to the tragedies and errors of war and the absurdities of the 1950s land reforms. From the 1930s onwards, women were recruited into the Communist Party, led demonstrations against the French and fought in Viet Minh guerrilla battles, often armed only with scimitars and poles. As the independence war merged into the war against the South and its American allies, Northern women became highly trained, well-armed soldiers fighting side by side with men.

Meanwhile, those that manned the home fort had to take over tasks that had previously been the male domain. Many also worked as guides, leading army platoons through impenetrable jungle, while tens of thousands helped build and maintain the Ho Chi Minh Trail.

Heroines or victims? One recorded occasion of the prowess of the Northern women took place in Hue during the Tet Offensive, when 11 teenage girls defeated an entire US battalion. Another famous photo shows a tiny woman, rifle in hand, capturing a lanky GI almost twice her height, his head bowed. However, it was not heroics all the way: only three women survived from the writer Duong Thu Huong's volunteer group of 40, and in the post-1975 political upheavals thousands of women ended up working in factories in the Soviet Union as their only chance of survival.

Women unloading coal from a Red River barge

Quan Am
Quan Am, the Goddess of Mercy and of Mother and Child, is a uniquely Vietnamese deity. Legend has it that after an argument with her husband she was turned out of the house and took refuge in a monastery disguised as a monk. Her good looks attracted the amorous attentions of a young girl, who later came to the monastery with a baby and accused Quan Am of fathering it. Refusing to denounce the girl, Quan Am was turned out yet again and spent her life begging with the baby until, on her death, her feminine identity was revealed. The Chinese emperor subsequently made her the guardian spirit of mother and child.

THE NORTH-CENTRE

REGION HIGHLIGHTS ◄◄◄◄◄

Dragons raise their heads to survey the ruins of Hue's Imperial City

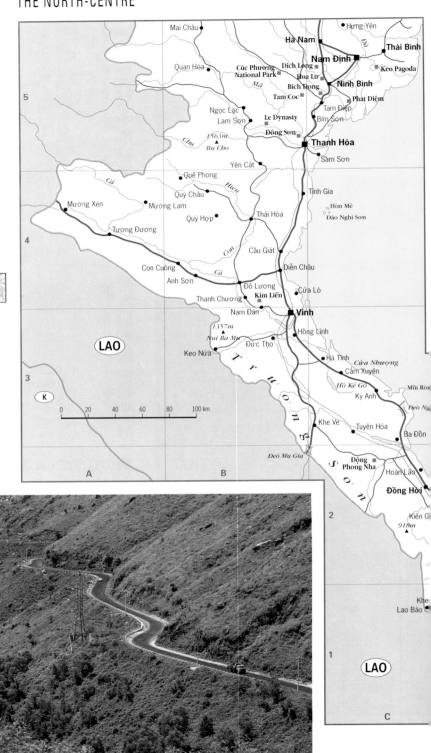

Mai Châu
Hưng Yên
Hà Nam
Thái Bình
Quan Hóa
Cúc Phương
National Park
Dịch Long
Nam Định
Keo Pagoda
Hoa Lư
Ninh Bình
Mã
Bích Động
Phát Diệm
Tam Cốc
Tam Điệp
Ngọc Lặc
Le Dynasty
Bìm Sơn
Lam Sơn
Chu
Đông Sơn
1563m
Bù Chơ
Thanh Hóa
Yên Cát
Sầm Sơn
Quế Phong
Cả
Tĩnh Gia
Hiếu
Hòn Mê
Quỳ Châu
Đào Nghi Sơn
Mường Xén
Mường Lam
Quỳ Hợp
Thái Hòa
Tương Đương
Con
Cầu Giát
Con Cuông
Cả
Diễn Châu
Anh Sơn
Đô Lương
Cửa Lò
Thanh Chương
Kim Liên
Nam Đàn
Vinh
1357m
Hồng Lĩnh
Núi Ba Mụ
Đức Thọ
Keo Nửa
Hà Tĩnh
Cửa Nhượng
Cẩm Xuyên
Hồ Kẻ Gỗ
Mũi Ròn
Kỳ Anh
Đèo Ng
Khe Ve
Tuyên Hóa
Ba Đồn
Đèo Mu Gia
Động
Phong Nha
Hoàn Lão
Đồng Hới
Kiến G
918m
Khe
Lao Bảo

LAO
K
LAO

0 20 40 60 80 100 km

Trường Sơn

100

The North-centre From Nam Dinh to the Hai Van Pass, the extreme northern and southern points of this region, Highway 1 (once the Mandarin Road) skirts the coastline for 650km, leaving the parallel railway occasionally to swing inland. At its narrowest, the coastal plain is only 40km from the Laotian border, which curls along the endless Truong Son mountain range to the west.

Most foreign visitors head straight for Hue, the queen of central Vietnam, completely skipping the entire northern stretch from Hanoi. This is a pity because the towns of Nam Dinh, Ninh Binh and Thanh Hoa were all major sites during the formative days of independent Vietnam from the 10th to 15th centuries, and harbour some fascinating, albeit scattered relics. Earlier still, during the Chinese dominion over the North, the region south of Thanh Hoa was a battleground between their culture and that of Indianised Champa. And a millennium earlier still, it was near Thanh Hoa that the sophisticated Dong Son civilisation emerged. Not least, here are Ho Chi Minh's origins, both his native village near Vinh and Hue, where he spent part of his childhood.

Hoa Lu tortoise

Hardship and wars The north-central stretch is also one of Vietnam's poorest regions, where farmers and fishermen have to deal with harsh climatic extremes, be they flash floods, typhoons or bitterly cold winter winds

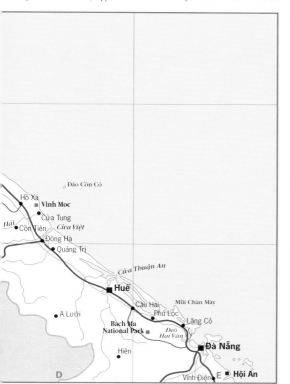

Obsessive reminder
'At Con Thien or along the My Chanh river which marked the front in Spring 1972, mud-diggers are still at work like in Khe Sanh. Even in Hue, every morning we watched from the Huong Giang Hotel terrace as children in masks dived from sampans, again and again, into the Perfume River. The fragments of shells or bombs that they brought to the surface were never very big. A tiny profit but an obsessive reminder. In front of the Hue citadel, a young girl was selling tourists old Kalashnikov or M-16 bullets that had been mounted on pendants.'
From *La Colline des Anges* by Eric Guillebaud and Raymond Depardon (1993).

Opposite: trucks crawling up the Hai Van Pass

Hue's schools and colleges are the best in the country

Rowing songs
One of Hue's many wide-ranging creations is a repertoire of rowing songs that were developed by boatswomen according to the task in hand. The *ho mai day* is sung when the sampan is heavily loaded or is rowed against fast currents: its fast and insistent rhythm encourages the rower to push harder. The *ho mai nhi* has a slower rhythm and accompanies easier trips. All songs express a melancholic love of river and water, as in the following: 'Evening, before the King's pavilion:/ people are sitting, fishing, sad and grieving,/ loving, in love, remembering, waiting, watching,/ Whose boat plies the river mists?/ – offering so many rowing songs/ that move these mountains and rivers,/ our Nation.'

carrying a high salt content picked up from the sea. If travelling from the South, the standard of living drops noticeably north of Hue, deteriorating further as far as Thanh Hoa province: bare feet, child beggars prostrating themselves in front of cars, drab houses and clothes (forget the pristine white *ao dai* of the South), few private cars or even motor bikes, and the return of the ox-cart are just some of the indicators.

Add to this the repeated and still visible devastation caused by the wars against the French and the Americans, and the North-centre region acquires some depressing aspects. This was where some of the bloodiest confrontations took place in 1967–72, whether hand-to-hand fighting, artillery sieges or carpet bombing. Towns that were flattened by bombs have since been rebuilt in uninspiring concrete and huge tracts of no man's land are still pitted with craters and/or completely defoliated, although Hue's bombed Forbidden Purple City is perhaps the most evocative reminder of the period. The DMZ (Demilitarised Zone) is where war buffs should head to gain insight into the terrible battles that took place along the defensive McNamara Line, and which ultimately broke the morale of the Americans while leaving tens of thousands of Vietnamese dead.

Cheering up On a brighter side, this coastline harbours some magnificent unspoilt beaches (Lang Co, Cua Tung and Hon La, among others) and two spectacular passes, the Hai Van Pass and the equally stunning Ngang Pass, about 70km north of Dong Hoi. Both were used as borders between ancient kingdoms and, centuries ago, the Ngang Pass even incorporated a wall running from the mountains to the sea, built by the Northerners to keep the Annamites at bay.

North from Thanh Hoa province, the landscape is characterised by dramatic limestone pinnacles rising beside paddy-fields and above canals that once attracted royal attention. Here there is a wealth of ancient pagodas, these now picturesque stops on canal-boat tours. Wildlife and primary forest are also present, at both Bach Ma and in the vast wilds of Cuc Phuong National Park. And everywhere the infrastructure is improving: ferries are being replaced by bridges and industry creeps in to provide essential employment.

Grande finale Above all, it is Hue that draws the crowds. Its inhabitants, aristocratic and highly educated, set themselves apart from the rest of the country, if only by their accent. The city's facilities are improving by leaps and bounds, and Hue's unique cuisine necessitates several days of indulgence. Whether drifting down the Perfume River, exploring the Imperial Tombs, cycling through the leafy lanes of the citadel or investing in the city's still lively crafts tradition, all visitors consider Hue to be one of the highlights of Vietnam.

Orchids add a splash of colour to Bach Ma's forests

104

► ▮ Bach Ma National Park   101E1

Directly inland from the Hai Van Pass at an altitude of 1,200m, and lying some 50km south-west of Hue, is this small national park, which surrounds a former French hill-station. Access is from the village of Cau Hai on Highway 1 along an atrocious road that leads to the park headquarters, and from here it is a steep 15km climb to the ruins of Bach Ma itself, yet another victim of the Vietnam War. Trails inside the park are good and offer panoramic views to Da Nang and the coast. Few mammals survive, but there are plenty of birds in the tracts of primary rainforest, as well as countless orchid species. There is no entrance charge, but a guide is obligatory, partly due to human danger in the guise of armed poachers.

► ► Cuc Phuong National Park   100B5

Cuc Phuong, about 40km due west of Ninh Binh (*Admission charge* moderate), covers an area of 25,000 hectares that is punctuated by the cave-ridden limestone outcrops typical of this region. In between, vast tracts of primary tropical forest harbour an astonishing 2,000 plant species, including magnificent rare hardwoods, some of them 1,000 years old and rising 50–70m, as well as reptiles, insects and over 130 species of birds. Mammals theoretically include elephants, tigers, deer and flying squirrels, but they are harder to spot. There is also a breeding centre for the spotted deer that once roamed freely here and is now being reintroduced.

This isolated primeval forest was only discovered in 1959, and the park, Vietnam's first, was inaugurated by Ho Chi Minh three years later. Long treks lasting several days can be organised through agencies in Hanoi, otherwise a local guide is advisable – even for day-treks. Bungalows, a restaurant and a campsite are located near the park entrance.

▮ Dong Ha   101D2

Little can be said about this nondescript estuary town, which stands on the edge of the desolate DMZ (Demilitarised Zone) 60km north of Hue in one of Vietnam's poorest provinces, Quang Tri. Entirely reconstructed post-1975, Dong Ha serves only as a base for information, guides, accommodation and uninspiring restaurants for visitors exploring the DMZ in depth. Alternatively, you can cover the ground on a day-trip tour from Hue. The town is also prospering thanks to the goods (legal and not so) that arrive from the Laotian border, barely 100km to the west, and to its fast-developing port.

The only historic sight is **Quang Tri Citadel►**, 20km to the south, built in 1824 by Emperor Minh Mang but now a pile of rubble interspersed with craters. In 1972, after capturing the citadel from the ARVN, the North Vietnamese Army occupied it for 36 days, suffering the heaviest and longest artillery and bombing attacks (equivalent to eight times the force of the Hiroshima atomic bomb) ever launched by the Southern forces.

Left: surprising comfort at a Cuc Phuong tourist chalet
Below: a common sight (in Bach Ma and Cuc Phuong), the male pheasant
Bottom: a crater near Dong Ha, completely destroyed by American bombs

► **Dong Hoi** *100C2*

Like Dong Ha (see opposite), by 1972 Dong Hoi had been virtually razed to the ground, so today most of the town is a reconstructed breeze-block showpiece on the banks of the Nhat Le River. However, the odd sight does remain and anyone wishing to visit Phong Nha Cave (50km north-west – see pages 124–5) will need to spend the night here. Elements of the old town ramparts, which ran from the foot of Dau Mau Mountain to the mouth of Nhat Le River, still stand and have even been restored. The main entrance, **Quang Binh Gate►**, is a good example of the Nguyen Dynasty architectural style, and was built in 1630 as part of a defensive system to protect Hue, the imperial capital, from the rival Trinh lords to the north.

Along the coast here are several sandy beaches: **Hon La►**, 30km north, has a wonderful expanse of sand-dunes and casuarinas; while closer to town are **Nhat Le** and **Da Nhay (Ly Hoa) beaches►**, with calm, protected waters. Bird-lovers can organise a four-hour boat-trip to **Dao Chim (Bird Island)**, a gathering point for countless species of seabirds.

Tourist offices
● Quang Tri Tourism, Highway 1A, 15 Le Duan, Dong Ha (tel: 053 852213/852725; fax: 053 852292).
● Quang Binh Tourist, 50 Quang Trung, Dong Hoi (tel: 052 822669; fax: 052 822404).

The DMZ

Symbolic bridge

Crossing the Ben Hai River on Highway 1 is the Hien Luong Bridge, a steel-girder construction built by the French in 1950 which later became the border post between North and South Vietnam – thereby escaping bombing, unlike most other bridges. War was not without its petty human rivalries: half the bridge was painted red (the North) and half yellow, while in their attempt to outdo the Southerners, the Northerners finally produced a giant flag measuring 120sq m that fluttered at their end of the bridge. Today, their flag-post has become yet another social-realist monument to victory.

When France signed away its supremacy at the Geneva Conference in July 1954, the treaty stipulated that a demilitarised zone be created between Ho Chi Minh's North and President Diem's regime in the South, theoretically a temporary measure pending elections. The zone covered 5km on either side of the Ben Hai River at the 17th Parallel, extending about 90km from the river mouth inland to the Laotian border. However, the elections were never to be, and by 1972 the DMZ had received 45,000 tonnes of napalm and chemicals, and seen tens of thousands killed.

Natural camouflage For the Northerners, the DMZ was an ideal battleground: forested ridges, peaks and ravines combined with coastal sand-dunes and swamps to create perfect concealment for their battalions; reinforcement and supply lines were short, and emergency sanctuary was never far away. Add to these the steady drizzle that fell from October to May, and this confrontation point inevitably spelled disaster for the American forces and their allies.

In October 1966, General Westmoreland set up a series of strongholds along an electric fence (named the

McNamara Line), backed up a few kilometres south by a string of bases that included Camp Carroll, the strategic observation post known as the 'Rockpile', Ca Lu and the notorious Khe Sanh. Little did the Americans realise that the North Vietnamese had been preparing the terrain for months, digging foxholes and building artillery-proof bunkers that were protected by 2m-thick walls of bamboo, grass and packed earth. Mortars, rockets and bombs from both sides devastated the area during the first confrontation of 1967, and from then on some 25 per cent of all American forces' deaths took place along the DMZ.

From coffee to scrap Khe Sanh, 55km west of Dong Ha, had originally been an area of coffee plantations developed by the French in the fertile volcanic soil. The sophisticated base built by the Americans, which included a metal-plate runway, was where 6,000 US soldiers and 2,000 South Vietnamese aimed to control the Ho Chi Minh Trail as it skirted into Laos. When the NVA attacked Khe Sanh in early 1968 as a diversion from the Tet

*Above: Hien Luong Bridge
Bottom left and right: the
Truong Son memorial and
its war graves*

Offensive, they used tanks
for the first time, and this,
combined with artillery shelling
from over the Laotian border,
contributed to their final
victory, albeit with thousands
of casualties.

After the 75-day siege, US
forces evacuated the base,
burying untold tonnes of
ammunition, weapons and even vehicles which they
subsequently bombed with B52s. This heritage spelled
the riches and the doom of hordes of Vietnamese who,
from 1976 onwards, moved in to dig for their scrap-metal
fortune. Some became dong-millionaires, others lost
their arms or legs, and in the entire Quang Tri province an
estimated 7,000 lost their lives.

Ho Chi Minh Trail The Duong Truong Son (Ho Chi Minh
Trail) was another of North Vietnam's ingenious strate-
gies, and was developed to supply the Viet Cong in the
South with equipment, supplies and men. In 1959 it was
a mountain track only traversable on foot, horseback or by
bicycle. By 1964 trucks were using it, but only at night,
crawling behind a runner dressed in white to avoid using
headlights. In 1973, the CIA's map of the trail showed
thousands of kilometres (some say 16,000km) of all-
weather road looping into Laos, and with multiple
branches in case of attack on one line (described by one
US pilot as 'a plate of spaghetti'). Despite this, nearly
20,000 North Vietnamese were killed along the trail, and
another 2,000 died of malaria. A section can be seen near
the Cuban-built Dakrong Bridge, just east of Khe Sanh,
but it holds only symbolic interest.

National Cemetery
The Truong Son National
Cemetery lies south of the
Ben Hai River near Con
Tien (meaning 'Hill of
Angels') and the village of
Camlo. Some 11,000
cement headstones,
grouped according to the
soldiers' North
Vietnamese home
provinces, cloak the hills,
while at the centre is a
group of gigantic statues
and a large stela inscribed
with a tribute to the men
and women who kept the
Ho Chi Minh Trail function-
ing. In 1973, a year after
the NVA had occupied
nearby Dong Ha, President
Fidel Castro of Cuba came
to pay his tributes here.
The cemetery will soon be
more accessible via a
direct road link to
Highway 1.

■ **After surviving the inferno of the Vietnam War, the English photographer Tim Page continues to return regularly to the region, whether on assignment for magazines, preparing one of his six published books, lobbying the Hanoi authorities to build a memorial for the media victims of the conflict, or quite simply monitoring the changes.** ■

With a Vietnamese experience that spans over 30 years, few Westerners have gained such a close insight into the nation's soul as Tim Page, and nor have they been so intimately linked with the vagaries of its recent history. Perhaps this is because, as Page himself says, 'You learn more about yourself than about Vietnam'. When he landed in Vietnam in 1965 he was only 20, a 'long-haired young snapper' who soon managed to establish himself as one of the most fearless and talented photographers both on the ground and in the air. Within 2½ years this kamikaze approach had led to three serious injuries which he only just survived. Several subsequent months spent in the US covering anti-war demonstrations gave Page a clearer insight into the context of the war as well as editorial needs. Back in the war zone in time to witness the 1968 May offensive, Page continued to bombard the world press with his often harrowing pictures, spelling out the truth of a conflict that was at its destructive zenith.

Playing with fire 'The images had to come from our side,' he states, 'It was hard to be anti-war or anti-American when you were hanging out with GIs and getting rides in their helicopters. But the truth about the struggle dawned very quickly as one was treated to the best commentaries of journalists such as David Halberstam and Neil Sheehan.' In the heat, dirt, smell and

horror of battle, a handful of photographers echoed such analyses by capturing a visual truth that gradually shifted world opinion. 'It was the most vain war ever fought,' says Page. 'Though counting the days till their return, GIs would happily pose for photos. Meanwhile we [the press] established our grapevine of madness to get information. But things changed in the early 1970s when the war was winding down and there was greater drug consumption, lower morale and less discipline.'

In 1969, while on an assignment for *Life* magazine, Tim Page stepped out of a helicopter onto an exploding mine. Declared dead on arrival at hospital, he was eventually evacuated to the US, where he underwent major surgery.

Mentally and physically scarred for the next decade, it was finally his return to Vietnam in 1980 that acted as a catharsis.

In memoriam Witnessing today's changes leaves Page in a privileged position that he is not content merely to exploit for the ends of the Western media. Over the last few years he has repeatedly lobbied the Hanoi government for permission to erect a memorial to the 300 or so members of the press who died during the war, an action that is finally bearing fruit. A large tract of land near Dong Ha in the former DMZ has now been designated as a People's Park in which a nine-storey *thap* (Buddhist tower) will arise. Around its base will be inscribed the names of all the press killed in Vietnam from 1945 to 1975, including those from the Saigon side. Meanwhile, Page has worked in Bangkok with the IMMF (Indochinese Media Memorial Foundation) to set up a school for journalists from the region, an essential step in encouraging a modicum of free press which ultimately may help to expose the endemic corruption that riddles the Vietnamese system.

Like a lotus Whatever the purpose of each visit, Page admits the strong hold Vietnam has over him. 'It's a privilege to understand a society that's not in terrible shape – what is their role model after all? But finally it's the most magnetic part of the planet. Understanding it is like peeling back the petals of a lotus-flower.'

Those eyes
'Anticipation, fear, relief, the joy all poured out at once; you really had to focus on the people in choppers: it was like being inside a giant blender, but the light was machine-lit, subtle, with those oil-painting tones that make masterpieces… Those eyes could have kept me there forever; it never seemed as if I had enough to make a tome. Occasionally a few would see the light of print, but mainly they sat in box files being shuffled into slide shows, trying to erase why they'd been shot, why I'd been there.'
From *Tim Page's Nam* by Tim Page (1983).

The perils of death
'A photographer in wartime knows that his job might entail the sacrifice of his life. He knows the perils of death just as closely as a soldier; and in Vietnam, without question, a photographer faced danger far more than the average US soldier. The majority of the half-a-million GIs serving in Vietnam at the peak of the American presence were supply soldiers or clerks (at the Rear-Echelon)…'
From *River of Time* by Jon Swain (1996).

Dante's Inferno revisited at the Tam Coc caves

Dynastic beginnnings
Hoa Lu, once extending over 200 hectares and the capital of Vietnam from AD 968 to 1010, was built in rustic style according to the laws of geomancy and included an eye for a strategic position: mountains afforded lookout posts against the Chinese and the Hong River provided easy access. The first rulers of independent Vietnam were the Ngo Dynasty (939–65), but in the 960s they were conquered by Emperor Dinh Bo Linh, who ruled for 11 years. Then came the turn of the Early Le Dynasty, led by General Le Hoan, who intelligently married Dinh Bo Linh's widow and greatly expanded Hoa Lu. In 1009 power moved to the Late Ly Dynasty, whose leaders moved the capital to Thang Long (Hanoi) and abandoned Hoa Lu's palaces.

▶▶▶ **Hai Van Pass (Deo Hai Van)**   *101E1*

This 496m pass is Vietnam's geographic and climatic frontier, and once formed the north–south divide between Annam and Champa. The serpentine road that twists up to the pass is a severe testing ground for local buses: breakdowns are frequent, as is rain (Hai Van means 'Pass of Ocean Clouds'). If there is a gap in the shifting mists, breathtaking views sweep over the indented coastline south to Da Nang and the Marble Mountains, and north to the lagoons just south of Hue. Behind looms Ai Van Son (1,172m), while the zigzagging railway track keeps to a safer altitude below. A ruined French fort, a post office, a 'café in the clouds', a short path to a lookout point and hordes of vendors in woolly scarves and hats are the local fixtures.

▶▶▶ **Hoa Lu**   *100C5*

The idyllic and dramatic landscapes of the ancient capital of Hoa Lu, where waterways meander between rice-fields and monumental limestone outcrops, also encompass ancient pagodas and cave-temples, making it a major destination for domestic tourism (*Admission charge* moderate). The entire region was once a gulf which subsequently dried up to leave this remarkable landscape, often known as the 'dry Ha Long Bay'. Hoa Lu itself contains over 30 caves and was the capital of the Viets from the 10th to 11th centuries, although little remains of this today. It is easy to spend an entire day here, dividing your time between boat-trips, climbs to mountain shrines, walks, exploring pagodas and fending off the numerous vendors.

Regal shrines The entrance to the royal capital lies 14km north of Ninh Binh in a site chosen for its river and encircling mountains. On the site of the audience hall which once fronted the palace stand two outstanding pagodas. The first, **Den Le Hoan**▶▶, was rebuilt in 1696 in memory of General Le Hoan and contains several shrines, one devoted to his wife, a former empress, and another to his three sons, incarnated in superb wooden statues. Exuding its six centuries of seniority is the second pagoda, **Den Dinh Tien Hoang**►►►, standing a few metres further on in a walled garden with a gilded sedan chair outside its main doors. Inside, intricate wood-carvings, chests and Emperor Dinh Bo Linh seated in his gilded throne emerge from the thick incense smoke. The emperor's grave lies on **Ma Yen Hill**►, which looms up in front of these pagodas: 300 steps zigzag up the slopes to a rocky summit with fabulous views to the south. A path around the base of this hill leads to a canal where boats offer leisurely three-hour tours.

About 5km further on lies **Ban Long Pagoda**►, founded 600 years ago and located in a superbly remote and rural site hacked into the rock-face. Four Buddhist nuns live here, watching over the cave shrine which, in 1947, sheltered Viet Minh guerrillas.

Grottoes Some 8km south of Ninh Binh lies a watery extension of Hoa Lu. This is served by a large jetty with souvenir stalls, restaurants and boats that are geared to day-trippers from Hanoi. At the beginning of the route to **Tam Coc (Three Caves)**►►► (*Admission charge* moderate) stands the lovely **Den Thai Vi Pagoda**►►, fronted by a two-storey community hall. Two- to three-hour boat-trips lead along a river past high rocky outcrops edged by rice-fields and through three dark and dripping grottoes. Accompanying sounds are the creaking oars, birdsong and the bleating of goats, the only animals capable of scaling the sheer rock-faces. Each cave is a Dante-esque underworld, the devil's role enacted by floating vendors lurking in the shadows.

Bich Dong Pagoda►► (*Admission charge* moderate) lies 3km west of the jetty. The three sanctuaries date from 1228 but were enlarged and altered in the 16th and 18th centuries. From the garden pagoda of Chua Ha below, steps wind up through caves to Chua Trung, where Buddha statues are picked out in the gloom by children with torches. Finally, you reach the summit pagoda, Chua Thuong, where spectacular views encompass the essence of this magnificent area. Another boat-trip can be taken from Bich Dong to the Dong Tien Grotto.

Bich Dong Pagoda

Tourist services

● Hue City Tourism (for city information), 1 Truong Dinh, Hue (tel: 054 823577/823406; fax: 054 825814).
● Hue Tourist Office, 15 Le Loi, Hue (tel: 054 822369; fax: 054 824806).
● Thua Thien-Hue Tourism Company (for the province), 9 Ngo Quyen, Hue (tel: 054 823288/822990; fax: 054 823502).
● Apart from the official organisations listed above, several private agencies organise DMZ tours, Perfume River boat-trips (which never cover the promised itinerary), and train, air and tourist-bus tickets. The ubiquitous Sinh Café has an office by the Hung Vuong Hotel, 2 Hung Vuong (tel: 054 822121; fax: 054 825910), while DMZ/Huetour at 26 Le Loi (tel: 054 825242; fax: 054 824806) offers an equivalent service.

A gateway leading into the heart of Hue's walled city

From 1802 to 1945, Vietnam's Imperial City saw 13 successive Nguyen emperors who bequeathed a vast citadel and their rural tombs to the nation. After extensive wartime damage, phoenix-like Hue is now rising from its ashes, showing a dynamism that has partly been stimulated by Unesco's attention to its monuments since 1983. The city's 300,000 inhabitants include a large number of students who maintain Hue's reputation as a centre of learning, while thousands more are now employed in tourism. New hotels, souvenir and antique shops and cafés open regularly, while every morning the Perfume River (Song Huong) throbs with the engines of tourist dragon-boats. Tradition is nevertheless alive, seen in the sampans punted by women, in the houseboats with their tiny rooftop shrines, in the superb Hue porcelain and in the delicacies of imperial cuisine. Again, this is a town with great bicycle potential (easily rented) and, even if you are not pedalling around the tombs, the verdant backstreets of the citadel offer plenty of interest.

Layout Most hotels are located on the south side of the Perfume River, with a luxury concentration at the confluence of the rivers, and good middle-range establishments on and off Hung Vuong, a main artery that links the Trang Tien Bridge with the airport and Highway 1. The elegant tree-lined backstreets in this former French quarter have plenty of old colonial architecture, as well as necessities such as banks, post offices and tour agencies. Across the river lies the ancient citadel, which radiates from the Imperial City, while immediately east of Dong Ba Canal is the old Chinese quarter of Phu Cat, home to numerous pagodas.

Old Hue Eleven stone gates surround this walled citadel of over 500 hectares, laid out in a square that is crisscrossed by canals and encloses vegetable gardens, lakes, residential backlanes and, at its heart, the Imperial City. Bicycle or take a cyclo around the entire area as it is full of surprises, including **Lake Tinh Tam** with its 'floating' pavilion. Here, too, is the hyperactive **Dong Ba Market►►**, located right by the dock where Dong Ba Canal joins the sedate Perfume River. Immediately north lies Phan Dang Luu, an intriguing street with a juxtaposition of herbal medicines, festival costumes and motorbike spares.

Closer to the Forbidden Purple City are two museums worth investigating. The **History Museum►►** (23 Thang 8. *Open* 7–11, 1.30–5. *Admission charge* moderate) covers Sa Huynh, Dong Son and ethnographic exhibits in an impressive timber building; a neglected upstairs altar-room is inhabited by bats. An annexe across the lawn houses the **War Museum**,

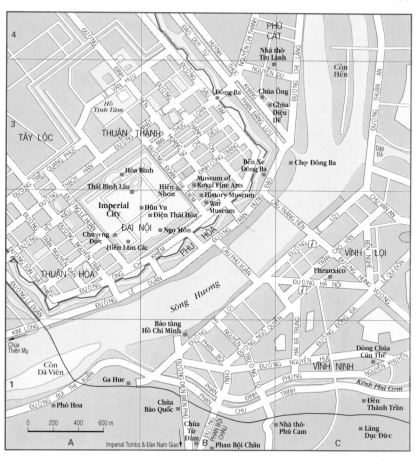

covering the period 1954–75 with reconstructions, photos, weapons, and guerrilla accessories such as rice cards, tyre sandals, cleavers and catapults. The English captions are, not surprisingly, one-sided, but altogether this section gives a clear picture of some of the suffering that Hue underwent. Behind this is the **Museum of Royal Fine Arts►►** (3 Le Truc. *Open* 6–6. *Admission charge* moderate). This lovely, colonnaded wooden palace (1845) houses a fine display of regal paraphernalia, from Emperor Khai

Dinh's inlaid dragon-bed to brocade robes, embroidered boots, Hue porcelain, ivory, silverware and inlaid *objets d'art*. In front stand bronze cannon, statues of mandarins and huge bronze incense-burners.

Dragon-boats ferry tourists to Thien Mu Pagoda and the Imperial Tombs

Bitter-sweet revenge
During the Tet Offensive, Hue witnessed some of the bloodiest fighting and underwent some of the cruellest retribution of any town during the Vietnam War. After the North Vietnamese Army had painlessly taken over the city, they set about revenging themselves on the population – or rather removing all 'uncooperative' elements. For 25 days, the army rooted out their chosen victims, these numbering about 3,000 civilians and including Buddhist monks, priests, intellectuals and anyone considered remotely sympathetic to the Southern regime. Their fate was either execution by firing squad, decapitation or being buried alive. There is, of course, nothing about this in Hue's War Museum.

Imperial exhibits at the Thai Hoa Palace

The Imperial City▶▶▶
Open: daily 7–5.30. Admission charge: expensive.
Building on the Great Enclosure (containing the Imperial City and the Forbidden Purple City) lasted from 1802 to 1833, during which time a gracious landscape of gardens, terraces, palaces and pavilions was created, rimmed by a walled moat and entered through four gates. Each precinct had a specific function, whether ceremonial, residential or spiritual, and all were laid out according to geomantic principles. However, of the original 300 edifices only 80 remain, and many of these are sadly decrepit. Devastation started in 1947 with a fire, but above all it was the 1968 Tet Offensive that put the final touches on its destruction. After taking Hue, the North Vietnamese forces held out for 25 days, their standard fluttering defiantly from the flag-tower. Retaliation from the South came hard and strong, and for two weeks much of the citadel area was bombed and shot out, leaving the Forbidden Purple City flattened and thousands of civilians dead. Today, although restoration continues, the Imperial City is a forlorn place where fast-encroaching vegetation accentuates the climatic and human destruction.

Heart of the empire The labyrinthine architectural complex is entered from the south through the majestic, U-shaped **Ngo Mon Gate (Noon Gate)**. Its central yellow doors, opening into a tunnel, were once reserved exclusively for the emperor while court officials were relegated to the side entrances. With restoration complete, the upper floor now houses an information room containing a model of the entire site and offering good views. The colourfully tiled roof pavilion was where the emperor would make public appearances and where Bao Dai officially abdicated in 1945.

From here, walkways and terraces lead past lotus-ponds to the **Thai Hoa Palace (Palace of Supreme Harmony)**, a colonnaded ironwood construction surmounted by dragons, its interior resplendent in red and gold. This houses the Throne Pavilion, where the emperor would receive delegations and preside over major ceremonies from his ornate throne. At the back is a courtyard flanked by two pavilions where the mandarins prepared for ceremonies: imperial costumes can be hired at the mock throne room in the restored **Huu Vu Pavilion** for photo calls. Two large 17th-century bronze cauldrons with decorative flora and fauna reliefs dominate the courtyard.

The ruined walls north of here once enclosed the **Forbidden Purple City**, the residential palaces of the emperor and empress where, apart from the imperial family, only eunuchs and concubines dared to tread.

Today it is a bombed-out no man's land of scrub, cacti, and rubble, with only sections of walls still standing. However, on the east side of these ruins stands the beautifully restored royal reading room, the **Thai Binh Lau**, displaying intricate mosaic work on its roof and enclosing a pretty pond and rock garden. From here, paths lead round the northern perimeter, passing Hoa Binh Gate and the partially intact, atmospheric pavilions of the **Queen Mother's Residence** near the west gate. A walk south from this precinct leads through well-tended vegetable plots to the last major cluster of surviving pavilions, located in the southwestern corner.

Dynastic honors Here, two pavilions erected to honor the Nguyen monarchs flank a courtyard displaying the **Cuu Dinh (Nine Dynastic Urns)**, each one dedicated to an emperor. These bronze urns were cast in Hue in 1835–1837, weigh 3,500–5,700 pounds each, and are laced in delicate classic motifs (sun, moon, meteors, clouds, mountains, and so on). Their craftsmanship is remarkable, making the symbolism (power, stability, and continuity) even stronger. The largest, central urn, also the most ornate, is dedicated to the first Nguyen emperor, Gia Long. Inside the **The To Temple** (1821) is a wonderful array of miniature thrones, candlesticks, silk parasols, and carved chests (façades only), each one an altar honoring one of the ten Nguyen emperors (dethroned or emigrant kings were not so honored). Opposite, behind the urns, is the very beautiful restored **Hien Lam Cac Pavilion**, the only three-story edifice in the entire Imperial City.

The restored Ngo Mon Gate, the main entrance to the Imperial City

Imperial measurements
The perimeter of the citadel measures 6 miles, while the trapezoidal walls that delineate it rise 21 feet and are more than 6 feet thick—it is said that 20,000 men worked on their construction. Eight villages (subsequently relocated) occupied the 2.3 square-mile site of the Imperial City, this taking 27 years to build and with 1.5 miles of walls. Inside this, the Forbidden Purple City covered 22 acres and was surrounded by 3,900 feet of walls that rose 11 feet and were 3 feet thick.

Detail on royal reading-room wall, the Forbidden Purple City

■ **Many of Vietnam's older buildings – from the Imperial City and tombs of Hue to the traditional merchants' houses in Hoi An – were constructed according to the ancient laws of geomancy, a practice that originated in China as *feng shui* and that aims to balance *yin* and *yang*.** ■

Take to the hills
'On a rock hill you must take an earthy site; on an earth hill, a rocky site. Where it is confined, take an open place; where it is open, take a confined space. On a prominence, take the flat; where it is flat, take the prominent. Where strong comes, take weak; where weak comes, take strong. Where there are many hills, take water; where there is much water, take hills…'
Extract from a Chinese *feng shui* manual.

For over a millennium, the Chinese-influenced cultures of Southeast Asia have drawn on the popular yet esoteric set of geomantic practices designed to integrate man and nature. This concern has led to the age-old science being dubbed 'mystical ecology'. *Feng shui* literally means 'wind and water', and its basic principle is that the manner in which man affects his environment (or landscape) will subsequently influence and control his fortunes. It is not surprising then that even today towering office blocks in Singapore and Hong Kong are built in collaboration with geomancers. Nor is Vietnam an exception to this deeply rooted tradition.

In the balance The venerable geomancer, armed with a special compass and a pendulum, examines the proposed site to determine the direction of *chi* (cosmic energy) and the *yin-yang* balance. *Yin*, the female aspect representing darkness and passivity, often governs northerly sites considered optimal for burial. *Yang*, the brighter, more active male element, leads to south-facing dwellings considered ideal for habitats or even cities (as in Hue's Imperial City or at Hoa Lu). Modern geomancers will also take into account crossroads, traffic and telegraph poles, all thought to adversely affect the flow of *chi*.

Ideally, dwellings should back on to northerly mountains or hills and face water, either a river or the sea, to the south. This seemingly logical rule for houses in cooler climes was originally partly inspired by defensive considerations. The geomancer then takes into account the future inhabitant's birth sign, which through complex calculations allows him to determine the configuration of the house. Linked to this, too, are auspicious days to build, auspicious proportions and specific rites to enact during construction. Finally, geomancy does not end at the outer walls; even the layout of furniture should allow for an uninterrupted flow of *chi*, the breath of life.

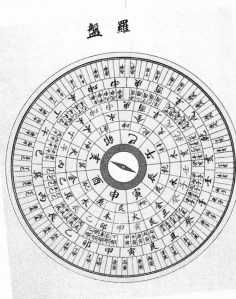

羅 盤

A Chinese geomancer's compass spells out feng shui

Excursions

Thien Mu Pagoda (Celestial Lady Pagoda)►► Some 4km west of the citadel on a hill overlooking the Perfume River stands Hue's postcard symbol, an octagonal seven-tiered tower. This was built in 1844 in front of the main pagoda, dating from 1621. Each tier is dedicated to a Buddha who appeared in human form (*manushi buddha*), incarnated here as statues, while the name 'celestial lady' supposedly originated from an ageing goddess who appeared to a Nguyen ancestor, telling him to build a pagoda on this hill. The tower (Phuoc Duyen) is flanked by two small pavilions, one sheltering a huge marble tortoise surmounted by a large stela (1715) relating the development of Buddhism in Hue, and the other a bronze bell (1710) over 2m in height which, when rung, can be heard 15km away.

Behind the tower, a gateway guarded by six dramatic statues leads to the main temple, a dark hall illuminated by a shiny brass laughing Buddha. Outside, on the left, stands the Austin car that in June 1963 was driven by Thich Quang Duc (a monk from this pagoda) to Saigon, where he took his pacifist stand of self-immolation (see panel on page 177). Behind are monastery buildings and gardens that lead to a wall overlooking a peaceful hillside cemetery. Thien Mu can be reached either by bicycle, straight along the waterfront road, or by boat.

Nam Giao Esplanade (Nam Giao Dan)► Located 3km south of the river, and hidden behind pine trees on the road to the tombs, is this imperial curiosity borrowed from China and built by Gia Long in 1806. This was where the emperor would pay ritualistic homage to heaven and earth in a secret ceremony involving the sacrifice of hundreds of specially raised animals. The top, circular level (Vien Dan) symbolises heaven, the square middle terrace (Phuong Dan) represents earth, and the lowest terrace represents man, all enclosed by a rectangular wall. The ceremonies were so costly that from the reign of Thanh Thai they only took place every three years.

The Thien Mu Pagoda obeys geomancy laws by facing the river and having its back to the mountain

Climatically led leisure
If the notoriously bad Hue climate follows its usual pattern of *crachin* (drizzle), cloud or more vehement downpours, temporary escape lies at the water-puppet theatre by Phu Xuan Bridge at 11 Le Loi (tel: 054 828020). Fifty-minute shows are held continuously from 4pm to 8pm by a small but enthusiastic troupe, not as ambitious in scale as the Hanoi version, but an entertaining interlude none the less. Taped commentaries are in French and English.

On the other hand, when the heat of the sun is too great for river trips or cycling, head for the riverside cafés along the north bank between the bridges. This breezy, shady spot offers a cacophony of rival café soundtracks and endlessly absorbing views of river traffic.

The ponds and gardens at Minh Mang's tomb are laid out in the shape of the Chinese ideogram for longevity

Tu Duc's eulogy
The stela eulogy relating an emperor's virtues and lifelong achievements was usually written by his son or successor. Tradition changed somewhat when childless Tu Duc found himself writing his own. This rather tragic figure, who would listen to music and write poetry in the Xung Khiem Pavilion by the lake, nevertheless had 104 wives and concubines and lived a life of true imperial luxury – including drinking tea made with dewdrops collected from lotus leaves. It is said that his remains do not actually lie in his tomb, but are buried together with priceless treasure in an unknown spot: all 200 servants who attended the burial were subsequently beheaded.

Imperial Tombs►► Of the 13 Nguyen emperors, only seven had tomb complexes built. Far from being mere mausoleums, these were miniature palaces set in gardens and overlooking lakes. Built according to the laws of geomancy under each emperor's supervision, all are located close to the river south-west of the citadel. They are best reached by road (car or bicycle), although Tu Duc, Dong Khanh and Minh Mang are within walking distance of the river. Below are descriptions of the most outstanding.

Gia Long►► (*Admission charge* expensive) lies 16km from Hue by road or 19km by river; this is the southernmost tomb and is difficult of access so it sees few visitors. If coming by car, a river crossing followed by a few kilometres on foot are necessary. It is also the oldest mausoleum as Emperor Gia Long was the first of the Nguyen Dynasty. Much of the complex is overgrown and some pavilions are now roofed in corrugated iron, but the peaceful, undulating lakeside setting of pine trees and seven mausoleums overcome this. The main tombs are **Thien To Huu**, opposite the Gia Thanh Palace, which contains the sepulchre of Gia Long's second wife; and **Thien Tho**, where Gia Long himself is buried beside his first wife. Flanking his mausoleum is the stela pavilion and the Minh Thanh Temple. Five other mausoleums situated closer to the river contain 17th-century ancestors.

Khai Dinh► (*Admission charge* expensive) was the last of the Nguyen Dynasty's great tombs, built in 1920–31. No expense was spared on its elaborate, semi-Europeanised style which borders on the kitsch. Less pastoral than the other tombs and inaugurating the era of concrete (now weathering badly), it stands in imposing isolation on a hilltop, reached up a flight of 109 steps. Half-way up is the Honour Courtyard, where an army of mandarins, horses and elephants surrounds the octagonal stela pavilion. At the top looms Thien Dinh, the main mausoleum, decorated with murals of fragmented porcelain and glass set in concrete. Inside, a bronze statue of an enthroned Khai Dinh stands above his body, buried several metres underground. Khai Dinh's tomb lies 10km from Hue in the village of Chau Chu.

Minh Mang▶▶▶ (*Admission charge* expensive) is the only tomb to lie west of the river, so anyone coming by road needs to take a ferry at the confluence of the river. A perfect example of geomancy, this harmonious tomb complex, surrounded by a lake, lies about 2km from the river. Although planned during Minh Mang's lifetime, the symmetrical design was built by his successor in 1840–3. The Dai Hong Gate leads into the Honour Courtyard, peopled by mandarins and elephants, and followed by the stela pavilion. From here, an esplanade leads to the mandarin temples, followed by the beautiful Sung An Palace, a symphony of vermilions and golds splashing across its pillars, beams, lanterns and antique objects. Beyond this, the straight axis continues across the lake to the open-sided Minh Lau Pavilion, before crossing the Crescent Moon Lake past a row of fragrant frangipanis to the circular precinct of Minh Mang's tomb, a simple mound covered with pine trees (usually locked).

The construction of **Tu Duc▶▶▶** (*Admission charge* expensive), a vast, undulating royal garden, started in 1864, took 20 years to complete and was not without strikes and rebellions against its exorbitance. Luu Khiem Lake, edged with pleasure pavilions, fronts the main buildings, including Hoa Kiem Temple, used by Tu Duc as an office during his lifetime. In the back courtyard of this walled group is Minh Khiem Duong (1866), the oldest-surviving classical theatre in Vietnam. To the north stands the pavilion housing the stela (Vietnam's largest), behind, in another walled compound, is Tu Duc's tomb, and at the tip of the lake is the tomb of the empress.

The last of the concubines
Although each dead emperor was guarded by his stone mandarins, he also had some livelier company, namely the concubines who survived him. When the writer Crosbie Garstin visited Minh Mang's tomb in the early 1920s, he encountered a ghostly crowd of them, obviously ensconced there since the emperor's death in 1840. 'One by one, a host of old witches appeared, materialising silently out of the surrounding gloom, issuing from behind the pillars, from black nooks and corners, rising up off the floor where they had been asleep. One rose from under a table even; I trod on her... Round I went..., the old hags creeping noiselessly behind me, blinking rheumy-eyed in the candle-light, half real, half shadow...a company of sad old ghosts.'

119

Honour Courtyard at Khai Dinh's tomb

■ **For over a thousand years Vietnam followed the precepts of Chinese traditional medicine, and today, after decades of Western medicine, it is now experiencing a strong resurgence. Back come the *yin* and *yang*, as well as antler velvet, ginger, fungus, bark and countless untranslatable remedies.** ■

120

Cupping
A common sight on the skin of Vietnamese people is a strange cluster of round red blotches that appear too symmetrical to have been caused naturally. In fact, they derive from cupping, a practice whereby the troubled area is treated by heating a small glass and placing it on the skin with the open end downwards. The high temperature causes a temporary vacuum that sucks the skin into the cup, causing small vessels to break and leaving a round, red bruise. Misguided individuals occasionally attempt self-treatment to remove the 'bad wind' by burning a painful spot with a cigarette.

The French medical biologists Pasteur, Calmette and Yersin may still be honoured by street-names and their institutes may continue valuable research, but the focus of contemporary Vietnamese medicine has made a volte-face. There now exist two major schools of traditional medicine, one in Hanoi and one in Ho Chi Minh City, as well as an acupuncture institute and 17 hospitals dedicated to traditional treatments. Western students also study at the institutes, a result of the growing worldwide interest in these 'natural' practices. Disciplines include acupuncture, therapeutic massage, respiratory exercises, and classical and popular herbal recipes. Although by law every village has a plot of land set aside to grow curative herbs, these have not replaced biochemical treatments; the aim of Vietnamese medicine is to combine the two successfully, and each province's public health service has parallel offices devoted to both systems.

Pioneers Traditional remedies were first analysed by the Buddhist monk Tue Tinh in a book of essays, probably in the 14th century, then exhaustively categorised by the 18th-century mandarin Lan Ong in a 66-volume encyclopaedia, the *Bon Thao*. This remains the bible of

Vietnam's traditional doctors and is consulted throughout the Far East. However, during the French colonial era a new attitude developed. The colonial authorities regarded traditional practitioners as quacks and closed down the Hue school of traditional medicine. As a result, the urban élite turned to Western medicine, although the rural sector continued to rely on trusted ancient remedies.

In the balance Central to the oriental concept of health is the *yin-yang* philosophy of the human body. Essentially, the body and its organs are subject to and generate their own positive and negative energies. Any imbalance of these brings disorder to that part or function of the body. 'Full' organs such as the heart, liver and lungs are *yin* (am in Vietnamese, and representing the female force); 'empty' ones such as the bladder, bowel and intestine are *yang* (duong, or the male force). In its turn, each organ has two sides. In the heart, for example, the blood and muscle are *yin* while the energy driving the muscle is *yang*.

Too much *yang* leads to fever, thirst, hot extremities, a rapid pulse or constipation, while an overdose of *yin* energies produces the opposite: cold, shivering, diarrhoea, swelling and a weak pulse. Diagnoses are made by looking at the eyes, the tongue, the unhealthy organ and, above all, by measuring 12 different pulses, the meridians of *chi*, the life force. The doctor then prescribes a cure based on precise recipes for herbal remedies, and these

Moxibustion
Moxibustion is particularly good for arthritis, and involves applying heat to acupuncture points by holding the glowing end of a burning paper tube containing moxa wool (made from common mugwort) near the skin, or attaching lit moxa cones to acupuncture needles inserted in the skin.

may be accompanied by therapeutic massage and acupuncture (practised for 23 specific disorders).

Natural fix *Dau con ho* or *dau con cop*, a mentholated ointment similar to Tiger Balm, is commonly used for aches and pains; it is widely sold by itinerant vendors alongside other less healthy items such as cigarettes and chewing-gum. Liquorice is prescribed for coughs and fever, wild cinnamon for stomach-ache, mint for headaches or colds, ginger for vomiting or flu, and chrysanthemum for skin disorders. More complex preparations of pills and potions are made up by the pharmacist in his fabulous emporium of little drawers, jars and

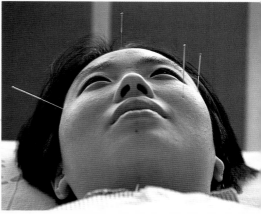

Top: the elixir of life?
Above: acupuncture in progress

sacks full of the vital ingredients, be they dried roots, leaves, bark, herbs, fungus, seeds, nuts or fruit. Some of the weirder ingredients commonly seen in China or Hong Kong that originate from endangered species such as bears, tigers and rhinoceroses are rarely seen in Vietnam, as such trade is officially illegal. However, belief often overrides principles and under-the-counter commerce does go on.

THE NORTH-CENTRE

Recycling

'The chief business up here is scrap recycling, though the pickings are thinning. There is probably no accurate total of how many pieces of ordnance, how many rounds were fired in these fields. What goes up has to come down. The earth is impregnated with chunks of extended firepower. Ten years after liberation, the road and railside were still littered with carcasses of armoured fighting vehicles, T-34 and -54 turrets plopped down in paddies and on dunes. These are the rich and easy pickings, high-grade recyclable metals, destined for smelting to ingots in the mills in Long Binh, to be shipped to Japan and Korea, only to return as Sapporo six-pack beer cans, Toyotas and Hondas.' From *Derailed in Uncle Ho's Victory Garden* by Tim Page (1995).

Khe Sanh   *100C1*

High in the devastated mountains of Quang Tri province near the Laotian border lies Khe Sanh, best known for having been the scene of the most humiliating American defeat of the Vietnam War, which cost 10,000 NVA their lives and later cost General Westmoreland his post (see pages 106–7). There is little to see at the battleground itself (3km from town), an inferno of red-ochre soil pockmarked with scrap-hunters' craters and rimmed by the hills where the NVA was entrenched.

The border post itself is at **Lao Bao**, notable for smuggling and karaoke cafés, about 10km to the west. Highway 9, which links the border with Dong Ha on the coast, is still a patchy ride, although plans are afoot to create a throughroad to Laos, Thailand and Myanmar (Burma). Defoliated hills have been replanted with eucalyptus, and coffee and pepper are becoming viable crops. Although Khe Sanh was entirely bombed, its 35,000 inhabitants are now surprisingly prosperous – partly as a result of the sometimes fatal scrap-metal business (see panel).

►► Lang Co   *101E1*

This idyllic little coastal fishing village, sandwiched between a lagoon and the ocean, lies immediately north of the Hai Van Pass. Water is on every side, as rivers flow into lagoons and these in turn spill into the sea. The white sandy beach offers good swimming in clear water and the village has seafood restaurants in abundance. Unfortunately, the only hotel profits from its monopoly, and is hardly recommendable.

▶ **Nam Dinh** *100C5*

The attractions of this large industrial town (90km south of Hanoi) lie resolutely in its environs, where relics of the Tran Dynasty include some exceptional pagodas. Under the French, as early as 1889, Nam Dinh developed into Tonkin's most important textile centre (producing above all silk), an industry that survives today together with a few elegant buildings from the colonial era.

The relics of the 'Golden City' of the Tran Dynasty (1225–1400) lie scattered over a wide expanse of paddy-fields, starting about 5km north of the centre. The **Thap Pho Minh Pagoda**▶▶ is defined by an astonishing 13-storey tower that rises 21m above the walls and trees surrounding the temple. Its richly decorated first level is of blue marble, the following ones are of brick and the summit is of stone. Founded in 1262 as a centre of Buddhism, it was extended in 1305 to include a lovely tiled, hexagonal building that was restored during the colonial era. Nestling in trees near by is the **Tran Mieu**▶, the 1239 memorial temple for the Tran Dynasty which adjoins the **Co Trach Temple**, dedicated to the princely general, Tran Hung Dao, who defeated the Chinese in the 13th century. His altar statue is flanked by those of his brothers, with his parents and sons aligned behind. Tran Mieu itself houses 14 altars, each one honouring a Tran ruler.

One of Vietnam's most important Buddhist landmarks, the 11th-century Co Le Pagoda

Some 20km south-east of Nam Dinh stands the striking **Co Le Pagoda**▶▶▶, founded by the Ly Dynasty (1009–1225), although later embellished by the Trans. In front of the temple is the Thap Cuu Pham, a beautiful stupa tower set on the back of a stone turtle. Inside is one of Vietnam's largest Buddhas, rising over 21m, which was erected to commemorate the bonze Minh Khong, who spread the Buddhist word in Vietnam. Behind is a glass case containing a remarkable sandalwood Buddha dating from the 12th century.

Completing the spiritual offerings near Nam Dinh is the **Keo Pagoda**▶▶▶, which lies about 17km east across the river in Thai Binh province. The road is rough and access complicated, but it is well worth making the effort. This vast, lakeside complex of 16 temple buildings was founded in the 11th century but has been rebuilt and extended since the early 17th century, when much was destroyed by floods. The main temple houses an impressive, crowded pantheon covering the 17th–19th centuries and dominated by the Emperor of the Heavens, with the gods of the stars holding the books of births and deaths. The complex is completed by a magnificent three-storey bell-tower, considered a masterpiece of carving, and by cloisters that house dragon-boats brought out during the festival on the 10th to 16th days of the ninth lunar month.

Left: Lang Co's white sands

Tourist office
● Nam Ha Tourism, Nguyen Due, Nam Dinh (tel: 035 849439).

Tourist offices
● Ninh Binh Tourism, Trang Hung Dao, Ninh Binh (tel: 030 871483/872037; fax: 030 872090).
● Thanh Hoa Tourism, 25a Quang Trung, Thanh Hoa (tel: 037 852517/852957).

Construction and destruction
Although Phat Diem was the sad recipient of eight US bombs in 1972, there is no sign of the damage. The blast tilted the cathedral by an angle of 20 degrees, blew away most of the roof and badly damaged doors and stone reliefs, as well as flattening St Joseph's Chapel and tilting St Peter's. Restoration started immediately and took two years to complete. However, this was nothing compared with the technical problems that were faced during construction a century earlier. Timber was brought from up to 200km away, marble from 60km away in Thanh Hoa, and stone from 40km away. These huge blocks and trunks were then transported along the river on bamboo rafts, before being hauled to the site by men and buffaloes. A labour of love indeed.

►   **Ninh Binh**   100C5

There is nothing of interest in Ninh Binh itself, yet another concrete town built in the wake of extensive B52 bombing, but it makes a perfect base for several major sights. Hoa Lu, Bich Dong and Tam Coc (see pages 110–11), Cuc Phuong National Park (see page 104), the cave-temples of Dich Long, and Phat Diem (see below) all lie within easy striking distance by motor bike or even bicycle. Ninh Binh's handful of budget and mid-range hotels also offer excellent value and have particularly helpful staff, making a welcome change from Hanoi.

►►►   **Phat Diem**   100C5

This extraordinary complex (Open 7.30–11.30, 2.30–5. Masses held Mon–Fri 5am and 5pm; Sat–Sun 5am, 10am and 4pm) is Vietnam's most important Catholic centre. The construction of the cathedral, its five chapels and the bell-tower (1875–99) was spearheaded by Father Sau, the local Jesuit priest, and by 1901 it had become the seat of the new diocese, the Vatican of Vietnam. Catholic persecution from 1954 to 1975 led to the imprisonment of priests and the closing of the seminary, but since 1985 doi moi (open-door policy) has eased the situation and the priests have returned.

The uniqueness of Phat Diem lies above all in the incredible blend of oriental structures and Catholic functions. A lake (with an island statue of Jesus Christ replacing the usual Quan Am) and artificial grottoes add to the wonderland aspects that create a major focal point for the 134,000 Catholics of Ninh Binh province, as well as for numerous pilgrims. At the front stands the superb bell-tower►►, built in the style of the communal houses of Vietnamese villages and the last edifice to be completed. Steps from a side entrance wind up to a platform which offers good views of the entire region as well as of the cathedral façade. The **cathedral**► is built of brick and stone, with an 80m-long interior dominated by 48 hefty ironwood pillars, all intricately chiselled, lacquered and gilded. The lateral naves house 15 stone reliefs depicting the life of Jesus. Of the five chapels, that dedicated to **St Peter**►► is perhaps the most striking: its jackwood interior displays magnificent carvings on the pillars and tympanum.

To gain access to the locked chapels, contact one of the Jesuit priests at the entrance: these highly educated and often polyglot individuals are also happy to act as guides, but make sure you buy one of their publications and/or make a donation. The village of Phat Diem lies along a pleasant rural road about 20km from Highway 1 and offers several interesting churches (there are 200 in the province), including **Phuc Nac**►, a beautiful twin-towered 19th-century edifice whose brightly renovated interior includes a richly carved altar and a blue ceiling decorated with gold stars. The entrance to the church is through gardens at the rear.

►   **Phong Nha Cave (Dong Phong Nha)**   100C2

The 14 grottoes of Phong Nha (Open 7.30–6. Admission charge expensive), 50km north-west of Dong Hoi and accessible by boat from Son Trach, are best visited on an organised tour from Dong Hoi. The caves were used back in the 10th century as sanctuaries by the Chams, who left some shrines and inscriptions, but today the main interest is geological: a waterborne itinerary winds past 1,500m of stalactites and stalagmites that have acquired endless imaginative identities.

Sanctuary

'Immediately below us stood, sat and lay the whole population of Phat Diem. Catholics, Buddhists, pagans, they had all packed their most valued possessions – a cooking-stove, a lamp, mirror, wardrobe, some mats, a holy picture – and moved into the Cathedral precincts. Here in the north it would be bitterly cold when darkness came, and already the Cathedral was full: there was no more shelter; even on the stairs to the bell tower every step was occupied; and all the time more people crowded through the gates, carrying their babies and household goods. They believed, whatever their religion, that here they would be safe.'

From *The Quiet American* by Graham Greene (1955), relating a battle between the Viet Minh and the French.

Phat Diem's popularity leads to overflows at Sunday mass

Thanh Hoa   100B5

Few visitors stop along this monotonous stretch, but Thanh Hoa offers some historical connections. The town itself was built as a citadel under the Ho Dynasty in 1397, and four granite gates and foundations remain. Not least, it is near the site of Vietnam's influential Bronze Age excavations, named **Dong Son** after the village 8km to the west. There is nothing to see here, but about 30km further on, near Lam Son, lie the **Le Dynasty graves▶**. This large walled lakeside complex, sadly dilapidated, dates from the 15th to 17th centuries and includes a 1433 stela commemorating the Le Dynasty's victory over the Chinese Ming (see page 36). Light relief is available at **Sam Son Beach▶**, 16km east of Thanh Hoa, which conserves some French villas dating from the turn of the century.

■ **A bonsai buzzes past on a motor bike, a bus passenger clutches a seedling as if his life depends upon it, topiary bushes outnumber deities at a pagoda, nursery gardens are at every street corner...Vietnam has an obsessive and touching preoccupation with the world of plants, cajoling them into the most extraordinary forms.** ■

Tree worship

Vietnamese reverence for plants also extends to receiving the 'vital fluid' of trees. This strange curative habit, known as *thai thu khi*, was apparently used for centuries by Buddhist monks but was only put to the test in 1944 by a Professor Bui Long Thanh, who led a pilgrimage up Yen Tu Mountain (see page 95). The 700-year-old pine trees on this sacred mountain were reputed to emanate a life force that Bui Long Thanh demonstrated by remaining glued to the tree for half an hour. Others who underwent the same magnetic arboreal force apparently experienced extremes of hysteria, from laughter to tears or even deep sleep.

Shoots and cut flowers look for a new home

The age-old national hobby of cultivating ornamental plants is as diversified and time-consuming as the grower's imagination and sense of aesthetics will allow. Yet it is not a mere horticultural pastime, as behind the shapes and arrangements lies a philosophy of form inextricably linked with the seasons and passage of time. Plants become status symbols, and certain potted creations are passed on as family heirlooms. At one extreme is the nocturnal scene of a family, all seated around their prize *Phyllocactus* plant as they await the magical moment when one creamy bud breaks into flower. At the other extreme are the elaborate miniature rock gardens found in pagoda forecourts or private homes. And in between are armies of bonsais and zoos of animal topiaries, their creepers trained around wire frames.

Controlling nature It may take several years to prune and manicure a plant into the desired shape. Each posture represents an ideology: a plant growing straight with an exposed lower trunk is called a *truc* ('vertical posture'), while a plant with horizontal shoots or branches is a *hoanh* ('horizontal posture'). A plant pruned to have only two branches, one large and one small, becomes a *phu tu* ('father and son plant'). Imagination runs riot in miniature rock gardens, a tradition that started under Emperor Le Dai Hanh in 986. These worlds in miniature are peopled by tiny ceramic figures, and even the surrounding ponds have miniature lotuses and goldfish.

Vinh 100B3

The provincial capital of Nghe An, yet another impoverished North Vietnam province, is a mere staging post on
Highway 1. For the Vietnamese, its importance lies 10km
west at **Kim Lien (or Sen)**▶, where Ho Chi Minh spent his
childhood in a typical wattle and daub dwelling. This,
together with a museum, lies in wait. The entire province
has a long history of resistance and, as a result, Vinh
suffered during the independence war, was rebuilt but
was destroyed again by US bombing (it received 6,000
tonnes of bombs in one month alone). Post-1975, East
Germany poured in reconstruction aid, highly visible in the
dingy, rat-ridden apartment blocks on the outskirts. In
1989 US Veterans built a clinic here. Some 18km east lies
Cua Lo▶, a long beach with beautiful white sands but
rather tacky facilities.

Tourist offices
● Nghe An Tourist
Company, 8 Quang Trung,
Vinh (tel: 038 844692/
844825).
● Tourism Guides Office,
Kim Lien Hotel, Vinh
(tel: 038 844751).

►► Vinh Moc 101D2

Although the tunnels of Vinh Moc are not nearly as extensive as those at Cu Chi (see page 203), their remote location has prevented them from being turned into a circus.
They lie on the coast some 25km north of Dong Ha facing
Con Co Island, which was an NVA supplies base. After
seeing their village flattened in 1966, Vinh Moc's inhabitants spent 600 days secretly removing earth with
baskets and barrows to create a 2km network with 13
entrances and four wells. The walls were hard-packed
enough to withstand typhoons, and bomb shelters were
dug 24m below ground. Family rooms, a meeting room
for 50 people and even a clinic (where 17 babies are said
to have been born) made up the underground habitat,
which altogether accommodated 250 people in 1968–72.
Villagers were well armed to carry out commando
actions, and also ferried supplies to and from Con Co –
frustrating for the South Vietnamese and the Americans,
who knew this base existed but never located it. At the
entrance, a small but interesting museum gives a descrip-
tive display with English and Vietnamese captions, and
includes domestic and military relics. The main exit from
the tunnels opens on to magnificent **Cua Tung Beach**▶.

*Essential ventilation
for the Vinh Moc
tunnels came partly
from an opening on to
the beach*

127

THE SOUTH-CENTRE

REGION HIGHLIGHTS ◄◄◄◄◄◄

*Hoi An's backstreets
reveal quintessential
images of old
Vietnam and an
idealised life-style*

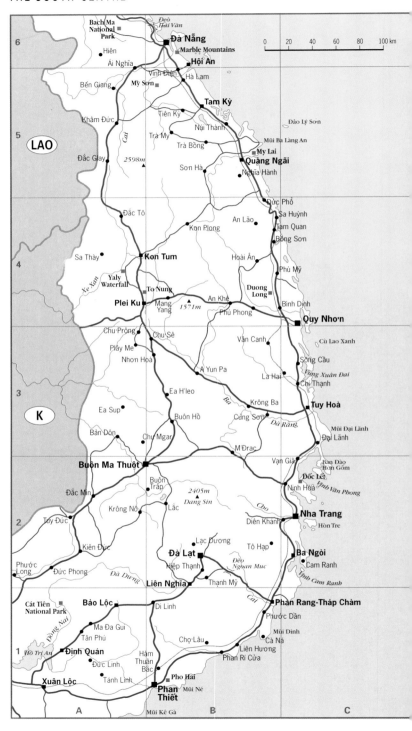

The South-centre

The **South-centre** The sublime landscapes of south-central Vietnam represent the country's greatest diversity. As the flat deltaland of the south rises into the Truong Son mountain range, swathes of red-ochre soil alternate with pine forests and waterfalls, and, further north, with patchy primary forest where tigers once roamed. To the east, the slopes descend sharply into a narrow, cultivated coastal belt edged with the country's most beautiful beaches which in turn overlook the mesmerising palette of emeralds, jades and turquoises that is the South China Sea. Millennium-old Cham towers rise from hilltops, a bountiful marine harvest is heaved ashore from colourful wooden boats, and luminously green paddy-fields worked by coolie-hatted farmers abut the foothills. Paradise? Not quite. This same area saw some of the Vietnam War's heaviest fighting, accompanied by extensive defoliation, bombing and death. Da Nang, Nha Trang, Quy Nhon, Cam Ranh Bay and Plei Ku were all major bases for American forces, while the province of Quang Ngai was an important Viet Cong stronghold.

Reminders Over two decades later, the war has mostly been forgotten. But then suddenly the traveller is confronted with a reminder, whether at Nha Trang's fairground where children whirl around in recycled tank turrets, or, more seriously, among the depressingly desolate hills of the highlands where dioxin has eternally poisoned the soil, or, most moving of all, at the My Lai memorial ground.

View from the Marble Mountains outside Da Nang

Linguistic excess
'What's your name? Where you from? How old are you? Madame! Madame!' Coca-cola, cigarettes, chewing-gum and postcards are lobbed at every tourist from all directions, along with the inevitable conversational gambits. This part of Vietnam is where people have the time and, above all, the motivation to learn and practise English, as well as some well-chosen French phrases for good measure. Every urban waiter makes an unbelievable effort, and every menu is methodically translated into English – of sorts.

*Above: elephant rides
are the big attraction
at Ban Don near Buon
Ma Thuot
Below: coffee-beans
have created a boom
in Buon Ma Thuot*

A more positive spin-off is that English is widely spoken as a large number of civilians were employed by the American army. And, going further back in time, it was the French who built the magnificent stretch of railway that dips and swings precipitously along the coastline.

Highland specials Da Lat, a honeymooners' destination, is the most popular town in the Central Highlands and presents a refreshingly prosperous, friendly face to the world. Lakes, waterfalls and old French villas are the main attractions, as is the climate: here, the steamy nights of the tropics fade to a bad dream.

Vietnam's other former colonial hill station and coffee producer, Buon Ma Thuot, is a definite step down in ambience. An added aggravation is the appalling state of the access road from the coast (average speed 40kph) although this may improve. Buon Ma Thuot and its environs, Plei Ku (in contrast served by an excellent new road) and Kon Tum are all best visited with tours as their infrastructures are still underdeveloped and sights often lie far from town. Many of the minority villages in this region, home to the various Montagnard peoples (see pages

42–3), are particularly deprived, with little compensation or the loss of their agricultural land to logging and defolia- on. Tour groups may home in on less 'authentic' villages ith song and dance laid on, but at least the hosts are illing accomplices.

oastal temptations Back on the coast, there is a tanta- sing choice of cultural and sybaritic pursuits, all backed o by a good hotel network. Fun-seeking Nha Trang is an bvious stop as it offers a relaxed combination of both. he tiled Chinese roofs of Hoi An shelter a wealth of storical and cultural interest, and the town is on a pleas- ntly walkable scale and has endless commercial distrac- ons: inveterate shoppers will be in their element here. Da ang, the largest port and town along this coast, is less nticing, partly due to its immense size, industrial base nd rougher urban society. Nevertheless, the museum ere is a must for Cham enthusiasts.

Anyone unacquainted with the Cham civilisation will oon be longing to learn more after visiting this stretch, which at one time formed the kingdom of Champa. Cham owers abound, covering a period of over eight centuries nd offering some wonderful panoramas, intricate carv- igs and extraordinary building techniques. Despite enturies of looting and more recent bombing, their capi- als survive at My Son and at Tra Ban near Quy Nhon. And this isn't enough, the ocean offers round-the-clock visual istractions in the form of coral reefs, rocking and rolling asket boats and the flickering lights of night fishermen.

Rubber future
Since the 1920s, rubber has been a major money-spinner in the Central Highlands, above all in the province of Dac Lac. However, these monotonous plantations of surprisingly spindly *Hevea* trees (whose seeds were originally smuggled out of the Amazon by an unprincipled Englishman about a century ago) seem set to clad nearly 400,000 hectares of the region by the year 2005. This represents a hundred-fold increase on the area exploited by the French, and could well be a government pipedream. Alternatively, it could be the solution to the barren hillsides and lack of employment.

133

A train trundles up the Hai Van Pass

An Ede minority farmer at Tur near Buon Ma Thuot

Tourist office
● Dac Lac Tourist, 3 Phan Chu Trinh, Buon Ma Thuot (tel: 050 852108/852324; fax: 050 852865).
● The only way to visit the Dac Lac region is by rented car as local buses are basically motorised carts. The tourist office can help, but compare rates with a small private agency, Banme Tourist (tel: 050 852820).

Through dark glasses
'The whole district of the Dak Lake is seen as if through dark glasses. There is not a great deal of colour. It is a study in smoky blues, greens and white. The light has a cool Nordic quality and the lake itself is an Icelandic *vatyn* with the mountain reflections blurred in the dim sparkle of the frosted surface.'
From *A Dragon Apparent* by Norman Lewis (1951).

► ► ► **Bao Loc** 130A

For those journeying from the south, Bao Loc marks the beginning of the Central Highlands. This is a land of tea, coffee, strawberry and mulberry plantations, a local speciality being delicious crystallised fruits. Some 18km north-west of town is the thundering 90m **Dam Waterfall**►►, the highest in the area. After following a rough turn-off from the highway, access to the cataract involves a steep climb, but the pay-off is the spectacular views. **Bay Tung Waterfall**► lies about 10km south-west of town and has swimmable pools. Bao Loc itself is a modestly scaled, unspectacular town with a handful of hotels set around a small lake.

► ► ► **Buon Ma Thuot** 130A

High in the Central Highlands stands the capital of the huge province of Dac Lac, whose name adorns countless buses heading from north to south. It is hardly the most scenic of Vietnam's offerings, lying as it does beyond a wasteland of defoliated valleys where minority villagers eke out a living, yet newfound coffee-bean prosperity is having positive repercussions. New hotels mushroom and the environs offer ethnographic and nature interest, but local tours are, for the moment, extremely limited.

In amongst the corrugated iron, Buon Ma Thuot (pronounced 'Ba Me Toot') has some interesting old timber architecture, although ambitious town-planning schemes are advancing destructively. Outstanding are the **Archbishop's Palace**► (on Phan Chu Trinh), a gabled tiled construction, and **Bao Dai's Villa**► (4 Nguyen Du), on the corner of tree-lined Doc Lap boulevard. The latter stands in a huge, neglected garden; over the last decades the villa served as a 'people's guest-house', but the main building is now being renovated. Nearer the central roundabout, whose former tank monument has been replaced by a symbol of peace, stands the **Ethnographic Museum**►►, showing a nteresting display of Montagnard artefacts, instruments, ools, weaving and baskets. Minority women, easily identi- ed by their backpack baskets, congregate around the narket area four blocks south of the central monument.

Out of town The abysmal road to **Lac Lake▶**, 56km south f town, is luckily under repair, but again the landscape is poilt by scarred hillsides. Minority longhouses, a bombed hurch and paddy-fields soon announce the village of Lac. What is often called a villa belonging to Bao Dai is in fact is ruined 1950s hunting lodge, perched on a hilltop over- ooking the lake and now a target for graffiti. Just beyond he market a track leads through the M'nong village of **Jun** o the lake, where sweeping views reveal long dugout anoes, islands and distant hills. The longhouses of Jun ive a close-up on impoverished minority life, and the illagers still use elephants – although in the daytime they re out in the forest hauling logs.

There are numerous minority villages in the province, articularly Ede and M'nong settlements, but visiting most f them amounts to cultural voyeurism which, considering heir present difficulties, they could do without. **Tur▶** is an de Protestant village 14km south-west of Buon Ma Thuot with a French-speaking village leader and is used to receiv- ng visitors. It is a good example f self-sufficiency, as manioc, offee, corn, rice and fruit are ultivated, and chickens, ducks, igs and cattle roam near by.

Elephants Dac Lac abounds in nountain waterfalls, most otable being **Draysap▶** (mean- ng 'Fall of Mist' in the Ede anguage), about 30km to the outh-west. A 5km jungle trek rom here takes you to another vaterfall, **Gia Long▶**, where lephant rides can be arranged. These same creatures come into heir own at **Ban Don▶**, 50km orth of Buon Ma Thuot and a avourite with guided tours. Here, dozens of amiable lephants trundle along under heir high-priced tourist loads vhen not out helping to hunt wild lephants or haul logs. Some laborate chiefs' tombs point to Ban Don's illustrious past as a najor trading crossroads with a nulti-cultural character (M'nong, Ede, Giarai and Laotian), while ver 30km to the north stands a nonumental relic of the Chams, he **Yang Prong Tower**.

Popular tourist-pulls and essential agricultural companions: Ban Don's elephants

Elephant trapping
Wild elephant trapping and training is the hallmark of Ban Don, and prowess is still something to boast about among the men, most of whom belong to Montagnard minorities. Over 15 of them claim to have captured over 30 elephants each, while a 75-year-old veteran remembers the day he caught a rare white elephant. The local hero is a certain Kru, who has broken all records by successfully trapping 300 elephants. However, this livelihood is on the wane as the elephants are disappearing along with the forests.

Silk

■ Around 40,000 hectares of mulberry trees cloak the mountain slopes of Vietnam, nurturing the production of 3 million metres of silk a year – an output that the government aims to triple by the year 2000. Woven silk has become a burgeoning industry and few tourists leave the country without taking home a souvenir made from this luxurious fabric. ■

Dress codes
In Vietnam's imperial days there was a strict code governing dress: the cut and colour reflected the owner's social class and the occasion for which the garment was worn.
Working men were limited to black, brown and white, while yellow was reserved for the emperor, purple and red for mandarins, and blue for lesser court officials. Women had more liberty in terms of colour, but it was the *ao dai* ('long dress') that ruled. This holds true today, above all in the South among the middle classes, but more often than not this flowing tunic and matching trousers is made of rayon rather than the more traditional cotton or silk.

Up in the Central Highlands the production of silk fibre is thriving. The technique originated in China, where for 3,000 years it remained secret. It was then developed in North Vietnam during Chinese rule, and was brought to Da Lat by immigrants after reunification in 1975.

Gargantua Silkworm eggs (the best come from China) are left to incubate before the caterpillar breaks out in ravenous form, only interested in consuming large quantities of mulberry leaves (it sleeps only four days in 28). After a month or so the silkworms have grown to their mature size of 7cm and start rejecting their food; this means that they are ready to build their cocoons. At this point, a bamboo frame is laid over them so that they complete their construction vertically under the eagle eyes of the silk-producers, who are alert to any imperfections.

Cocooning For three days, the silkworms disgorge a sticky secretion that binds together a single 800m-long fibre into the cocoon shape. Occasionally, two lovestruck silkworms decide to build a cocoon in tandem, creating a tangled, less viable product. The next stage involves plunging the completed cocoons (some are rejected for flaws) into vats of boiling water to soften, loosen and then extract the thread. This is wound, twisted and spun mechanically to combine the fibre from ten cocoons into one weavable silk yarn. First- and second-grade silks are sorted at this stage, and the caterpillars are then fried and consumed as a delicacy.

Silk, from worm to cocoon to thread

►► Ca Na 130B1

A blissful white beach lapped by calm turquoise waters and home to a modest cluster of restaurants and beach-huts makes a relaxing stopover 30km south of Phan Rang. There is a prolific coral reef immediately offshore, so bring your snorkel and mask. The fishing village itself is a couple of kilometres to the north and can be reached on foot via the beach, although access includes negotiating a precari-ous ride in a basket boat across a lagoon. Villagers are particularly impoverished so the rare tourist tends to become a target for mild aggression, mainly from children.

► Cam Ranh Bay (Vinh Cam Ranh) 130C2

This vast and very beautiful deep-water harbour, just north of Phan Rang, has switched military hands several times over the last century. Japanese, Americans and Russians have used it consecutively as a naval base, but since the collapse of the Soviet Union in 1991 only a handful of Russian ships remain. Today, shrimp farms and salt-flats have been resuscitated, while old Soviet radars rust under the palm trees. Much of the bay is out of bounds, but at its southern end is a string of excellent seafood restaurants.

► Cat Tien National Park 130A1

The 3,500 hectares of this forested nature reserve lie about 40km along a rough turn-off from the main highway in the southern foothills of the Central Highlands. If arriv-ing from the south, watch for the 142km or 145km mark-ers with signs to Cat Tien. Guides can be hired at the forest station, although you are unlikely to spot the elephants, bison and rhinoceroses said to roam here. More immediately visible is the rich diversity of tropical hardwoods, including redwood and *bang lang*, which once cloaked most of Central Vietnam.

►► Dai Lanh 130C3

Another of the region's exquisite beaches languishes patiently at Dai Lanh awaiting infrastructure. Mountains descend steeply into the sea here, creating an idyllic half-moon bay lined with casuarinas. For the moment there is no accommodation, although small restaurants abound.

The striking sculptural coastline of Ca Na at sunset

Inland exploration
If the joys and beauties of the coast pall, try heading inland in search of the tomb of the colonial hero Alexandre Yersin (see panel on page 156). A short rural track at the northern end of Cam Ranh Bay, about 20km south of Nha Trang and near the village of Suoi Giao, leads inland to his grave. Steps dug into the earth climb to a mound that is crowned by a small obelisk inscribed with his name and an epitaph in French: '*Bienfaiteur et humaniste. Vénéré du peuple vietnamien*' ('Benefactor and humanist. Venerated by the Vietnamese people'). Recently burned joss-sticks indicate that veneration is still the case, over 50 years after his death. This site was chosen for its proximity to Yersin's farm in Suoi Giao, where he lived for a good part of 40 years.

▶▶ **Da Lat**   130B2

The last emperor
Bao Dai was the last emperor of the Nguyen Dynasty. Born in 1913, Bao Dai reigned 1926–45 before abdicating in favour of Ho Chi Minh and leaving for France in 1946. Three years later he returned from self-imposed exile in Hong Kong to resume his status as emperor under French and American sponsorship. By then he was terminally debauched and corrupt, and still not fluent in Vietnamese due to his French education, but for the French and Americans he represented the 'true nationalist spirit' (as opposed to Ho Chi Minh's Viet Minh terrorists). Bao Dai remained in power another four years, before being deposed by Diem in 1954 and fleeing to France. He died in Paris in July 1997.

Tourist services
● Lam Dong Tourist Company, 4 Tran Quoc Toan, Da Lat (tel: 063 822125/821351/822047; fax: 063 828330/822661).
● The tourist office organises accommodation in some spacious old colonial villas, as well as guided tours of the region.

An eternal spring reigns in this 1,500m hill-resort, developed by the French in the 1920s for its fresh climate. Art nouveau and art deco villas, lakes, pine forests, waterfalls, rose gardens, a golf course, minority villages, coffee plantations and silkworm factories make up today's attractions. For the Vietnamese, this is a classic honeymoon destination, and many of the facilities reflect this – swan-shaped pedalboats on Xuan Huong Lake in the town centre, kitsch souvenirs and surreal fancy-dress photo opportunities in strategic beauty spots. A darker side to Da Lat is its role in sex-tourism, an industry that is being led here by the Taiwanese.

Centre Although once called the 'little Paris' of Vietnam, Da Lat has since acquired the usual motley array of grey concrete structures, notable among these being the Soviet-style **market▶▶** building. This is the focal point of town and the envy of the country, where mountains of artichokes, avocados, guavas and strawberries vie with fragrant arum lilies, roses, gladioli and roses, and neatly arranged bags of delicious Da Lat coffee. Ruddy cheeked, soft-faced women in woolly caps and jackets knit, chat and sell; many of them are Montagnards whose easy, friendly nature is partly due to the fact that Da Lat completely escaped the war.

Above the market is a string of little cafés that includes Café Tung, once a hang-out for Saigon intellectuals. Café Stop and Go, a Da Lat institution popular with bereted artists and poets who look like they might have stepped out of 1920s Montmartre, is now on Ly Tu Trong, reached via Phan Boi Chau.

Da Lat's self-styled artist-poet at the Café Stop and Go

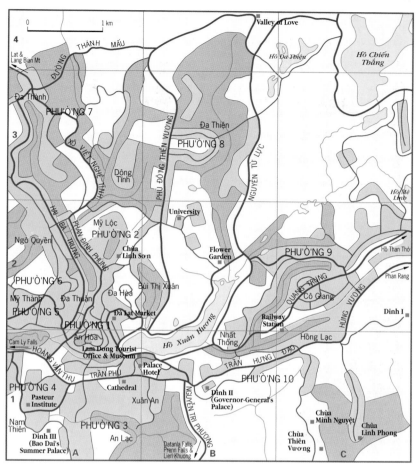

Palatial sights Stretching through the centre of town is the mirrored expanse of Xuan Huong Lake, with an 18-hole golf course on its northern slopes. This adjoins Da Lat's **Flower Garden**, where rare orchids, roses and lilies are cultivated. On the southern side a road climbs past the ritzily revamped Palace Hotel to the former **Governor-General's Palace►**, now Palace Hotel II, which stands on a forested knoll with lovely views to the south. This art deco jewel was built by the French architect Jean Doucoux in the mid-1930s.

Bao Dai's Summer Palace►► (*Open* daily 7–11, 1.30–4. *Admission charge* moderate) is located in its own hilltop pine grove beyond the Governor-General's Palace further up Tran Hung Dao and Tran Phu. This relic of the Nguyen Dynasty, dating from 1933, offers insights into the life of Bao Dai, who spent his last Vietnamese years here in the company of a concubine before final exile to France in 1954. The palace is rich in art deco furniture and design features, although it could do with a repaint. A 'Distraction Room' and 'Moon-watching and Breeze-getting Terrace' join endless memorabilia, a well-tended garden, pony rides

Private guide
An excellent local guide with impressive general knowledge and a wry sense of humour provides tours to silk factories and coffee plantations as well as the usual sights, so giving a rounded vision of Da Lat. He operates with a network of other equally competent private guides: Mr Hoang Van Quan, 9/19C Hem San Banh, Da Lat (tel: 063 825614). Contact him in the evening as he is likely to be out on the road during the day.

Crazy lady

Of Da Lat's many arty eccentrics, Dr Dang Viet Nga is perhaps the one with the highest profile. This Soviet-trained architect and erstwhile hippy came to Da Lat from Hanoi in 1983, and has since left an indelible architectural mark, most extraordinary being her 'Cobweb Mansion' (south-west of Xuan Huong Lake). This brightly painted concrete 'crazy house' (as the locals call it) winds itself around trees, mimicking their organic shapes. Once you get beyond the fairground creations of toadstools, giraffes and kangaroos it is actually an impressive feat, making Dang Viet Nga Vietnam's down-market version of a Gaudi or a Niki de Saint-Phalle. It functions as a guest-house and visitors can explore for a moderate entrance fee.

Gaudi eat your heart out, this is Da Lat!

and Santa Claus photo-calls to produce a well-rounded vision of past and present Vietnam.

Other sights within Da Lat include countless colonial villas, some of which now function as government-owned hotels and are concentrated along Tran Hung Dao near the palaces, while others are grouped north of the cinema. The attractive old *crémaillère* (cog railway) station▶ once saw trains arriving from Saigon, but these stopped running in 1976; a tourist train now functions for 7km. The **Lam Dong Province Museum**, near the tourist office, displays archaeological and ethnological artefacts from the area. Unspectacular churches and pagodas are plentiful, a minor exception being the 1930s cathedral on Tran Phu Street, just south of the lake. About half the inhabitants of the Da Lat region are Christian, many being Northerners who fled south in 1954.

Excursions Da Lat's environs are what most foreign visitors come to enjoy. Tea, coffee and mulberry plantations flank the hills, spaced between rotating crops (cabbages, potatoes and onions) and what little remains of the forest. Logging was made illegal in 1995, but as there is no alternative for domestic fuel (essential for heating during December and January, when night temperatures hover just above 0°C) the practice still goes on. Hiking, bicycling or motorbiking are the best ways to get around, although a local guide is necessary as the beauty spots are not easy to find. Permits were once required but this is no longer the case, although certain areas still remain out of bounds.

Watery landscapes Lakes (usually reservoirs) and waterfalls are plentiful in this mountainous environment, and include the **Valley of Love** and **Ho Than Tho (Lake of Sighs)**, a favourite for lovelorn suicides in both legend and fact, and nestling in rolling pineclad hills about 6km to the north. Ponies offer leisurely rambles around the hills, the ubiquitous paddle-boats and noisier motor boats allow lake tours, and stalls sell a mind-boggling array of souvenirs. You will not be alone: this is Da Lat's number-one tourist trap, dubbed by locals the 'Valley of Shoppers'.

Less visited for the moment is **Tuyen Lam Lake (Quang Trung Reservoir)** and Datanla Waterfall, about 5km south of town. A 1993 Buddhist meditation centre overlooks the reservoir, where there is also a waterfront orchidarium and replica indigenous village. Furry bears and Da Lat cowboys (photo-call specialists) lurk in the shadows, and cruising motor boats indicate a prosperous future. The turn-off to the **Datanla Waterfall**▶ (*Admission charge* cheap) lies a little way further south down the highway, and access involves walking along a pleasant forest trail that harbours plenty of birds and butterflies. Water tumbles 20m into a stream lined with flat marble, reputed to be a bathing ground for local fairies.

The most popular waterfall is **Prenn Falls**▶ (*Open 7.30–5. Admission charge* cheap), 10km south of town beside the main highway. This thundering curtain of water almost fades into insignificance beside the tourist structure that surrounds it: restaurants, kiosks, concrete paths and an artificial lake. Some 20km further on is the far more scenic and untouched **Lien Khuong**▶▶, a beautiful watery landscape where a river cascades over volcanic rocks to create pools and great clambering potential. Those bitten with the waterfall bug can continue a further 10km or so to see the highest cataract of the region, **Pongua Waterfall▶**, where torrents tumble over 40m into a lake.

Mountain villages Striking out to the north, a hike up **Lang Bian Mountain▶▶** (2,163m) will bring you in closer touch with local flora and fauna, although sadly the lower slopes are denuded. Five volcanic peaks crown the summit, which offers spectacular panoramic views. The trail to the top, easy to follow and taking three to four hours, leaves from the village of **Lat**. This settlement lies 12km north of Da Lat and is an obvious destination for anyone wishing to catch a glimpse of local minority life as it encompasses four different ethnic groups. Villagers live in basic wooden, thatched huts raised on piles, and scratch a living between cultivating crops and producing charcoal. Protestant and Catholic churches point to American and French influences.

Outside Da Lat on the Nha Trang highway is a K'ho settlement dubbed **Chicken Village**, a reference to its overscaled statue of a rooster. Various unlikely stories surround this recent apparition, but what is more striking is the extreme poverty of the place and the fact that the school only dates from 1995. Numerous stalls selling K'ho and Cham weavings await tourists, but as vendors are not local, profits do not go to the village.

Tigers?
'Da Lat is the playground of Indo-China and has a fair share of the dreariness so often associated with places thus advertised... It looked like a drab little resort in Haute Savoie, developed by someone who had spent a few years as vice-consul in Shanghai. Of Da Lat, though, one thing must be admitted; that life there, even in peacetime, is not entirely divorced from adventure, since there is a chance, one in a thousand perhaps, of knocking into a tiger if one strolls in the streets after dark.'
From *A Dragon Apparent* by Norman Lewis (1951).

141

Curtains of water mirror the fast-changing face of Da Lat, increasingly geared to the needs of southern Vietnam's new bourgeoisie and Asian tourists out for cheap thrills

■ **Nearly a million minority people inhabit the Central Highlands, most of them living in a state of limbo between their ancient customs and encroaching Vietnamisation. Just 30 years ago they resolutely obeyed traditions and animist beliefs, but today they are being forced into the role of Vietnam's underclass.** ■

142

Jars

When you see a row of jars lined up by a longhouse, it is never quite clear whether they contain water or wine. However, for the Montagnards these represent wealth, whatever their contents. Gongs, drums and jars were once prized possessions, some being of ancient Chinese or Cham origin and therefore highly valuable. Apart from being used to store rice wine, jars were accumulated as residences for spirits. When a spirit moved in, the owner was informed in a dream, a fact subsequently verified by independent assessors. As such, the jar acquired additional value and could be exchanged for a large number of buffalo.

A Jaraï spirit sculpture ponders its climatic fate

Four provinces of the Truong Son mountains are home to five major ethnic groups and numerous smaller ones. The Mnong, K'ho, Ede, Jaraï and Ba Na minorities are the Montagnards ('mountain-dwellers') of Central Vietnam, an all-encompassing name bestowed upon them by the French which is still widely used today. The unflattering old Vietnamese term, *Moi* ('savages'), originated in pre-colonial days when members of Vietnam's educated classes never even ventured into the interior. Court mandarins related stories of wild men with long tails to early French adventurers, but the French era of census-taking, rice taxes, forced labour and virtual slavery on rubber plantations put an end to this ignorance. Then, too, came missionaries, the first step in the 'civilising' of the hill people. French Catholics and, later, American Protestants vied for their souls, but it was the independence war and Vietnam War, when Montagnards were widely recruited and much of their land destroyed, that dealt the final blow to their autonomous existence.

Common traits Over the centuries when there were no borders between Laos or Cambodia, these minorities came to the Central Highlands in waves, although some were already present in the 5th century BC, a fact related in Chinese annals. The Jaraï (or Garaï), the K'ho (also Koho or Coho), and the Ede (or Rhade) all belong to the Austronesian racial group with Malayo-Polynesian linguistic traits, while the Mnong and the Ba Na (or Bahnar) belong to the Austroasiatic group and speak Mon-Khmer languages. Despite strong cultural differences, these minorities share many traits, notably in agriculture, house construction and domestic utensils.

Rituals The largest group, the Jaraï, probably numbers about 260,000, and is concentrated in the region of Plei Ku. Once great hunters and extremely ritualistic, staging buffalo sacrifices for any momentous occasion, many Jaraï have now adopted urban lives. However, those that remain in their stilt-villages to practise slash-and-burn agriculture reveal that animism continues in their local grave-yards. In a copse of trees they arrange model houses beside carved wooden statues. These primitive squatting figures, chin in hands, are carved by the deceased's family, who regularly take it food to appease the spirits. Sadly, the region's climatic extremes take their toll on the statues, as do collectors and antique dealers; together with the decline of this rare tradition, this means that the statues are increasingly hard to find.

Montagnards

Matriarchal In the Dac Lac province around Buon Ma Thuot, 27 per cent of the population is Ede, accounting for some 200,000 people. This is one of the most culturally acclimatised groups, and was considered the most advanced of the Montagnards by the French and the missionaries who made early contact with them. Traditionally, the Ede are matrilineal, each extended family living in a longhouse and with a woman elder responsible for community affairs. Christian villages usually include a small chapel, often doubling as a school, but are currently suffering from the government ban on large congregations among the minorities. Husbands are 'bought' by mothers for their daughters, previously with gongs and jars but today with more tangible dowries.

Little has changed over the centuries in the culinary techniques of the Muong and other Montagnards

Similarly matriarchal are the Mnong, who inhabit Dac Lac and the Da Lat area further south. This rebellious group only submitted to the French in 1939 and, even then, over the next two decades assassinated eight of their administrators. Today, their bare breasts, tasselled loincloths and tooth-necklaces have gone, but their immaculate longhouses with woven bamboo walls and thatched roofs remain, and they still indulge to the full in the Montagnard tipple of rice wine.

Montagnard villagers cope with the elements

Autonomy

The Montagnards have long considered autonomy a necessity to their well-being, and their present dire straits are proof that this still holds true. In 1964, despite extensive CIA manoeuvring and groundwork, the Central Highlands came under Viet Cong control because President Diem had refused to grant the minorities local autonomy as enjoyed by those in the North. By the 1970s–80s, a Montagnard resistance movement (FULRO – Front Unifié de Lutte des Races Opprimés) had based itself in the jungles over the Cambodian border and continually staged raids against Vietnamese army units. In late 1992, when barely 10 per cent of the original group survived, they surrendered to a UN peacekeeping force and were shipped out *en masse* to the USA.

A rare quiet corner in the commercial Marble Mountains

Tourist offices
● Da Nang Tourism, 92A Phan Chu Trinh, Da Nang (tel: 051 821423/ 822112; fax: 051 821560). For general information.
● Quang Nam–Da Nang Tourism & Service Company, 95 Hung Vuong, Da Nang (tel: 051 823993; fax: 051 824023). For organised tours and guides, including a special 'battlefields tour' aimed at veterans.

▶   **Da Nang**   *130B6*

Half a million people inhabit this major port, now Central Vietnam's main industrial base and its fourth-largest city. Sprawling around a deep-water harbour, with a mountainous promontory to the north, beaches to the south, an outstanding museum and a good hotel infrastructure, it has great tourist potential. However, there is a seedy and even aggressive air about the place, and this, combined with the highly visible relics of the city's major role in the Vietnam War, often leaves visitors with little desire to stay long.

Past and present Tourane, as it was called by the French, still harbours some impressive old villas, mainly located along the waterfront boulevard of **Bach Dang▶** (see No 42 in particular). This tree-lined stretch, with cafés edging the Han River and views across to Monkey Mountain, is Da Nang's most scenic area, where underemployed cyclo-drivers and *Honda oms* (motorbike taxis) hail from every street corner.

Walk a few blocks inland to the main street, Phan Chau Trinh, and you enter a Westernised world of computer and camera shops, rock-music cafés, mini-skirts and jeans. American army relics are still in daily use, from the tin spoons in cafés to the army trucks and jeeps that thunder along the city's main axes. Da Nang was where the first US marines landed in March 1965, and subsequently became home to a huge air force base as well as the notorious R & R resort of China Beach (see opposite). Ten years later, the city became the scene of total panic and chaos when half a million South Vietnamese found themselves abandoned in the face of fast-advancing Northern troops. Pillaging and rape preceded further frenzied scenes when planes and ships were mobbed. Today, dozens of derelict hangars stand as silent witnesses to the period.

Da Nang's main sight is the **Cham Museum▶▶▶** (*Open daily 7–6. Admission charge* moderate), a beautiful yellow colonnaded building at the southern end of Bach Dang. This breezy semi-open-air museum, surrounded by frangipani trees, was built by the École Française de l'Extrême Orient in 1915 to exhibit Cham sculptures and architectural fragments. Some 235 artefacts are displayed in chronological order, starting with 8th-century pieces from My Son in the east wing and ending with 12th–14th-century sculptures from Thap Mam. Highlights include a rare 7th-century fragment of a bas-relief depicting polo players, a very relaxed-looking Brahma on his birthday (from My Son), a magnificent Dong Duong altar flanked by two superb *dvara-pala* (guardians) in the back room, and some graceful 10th-century *apsara*

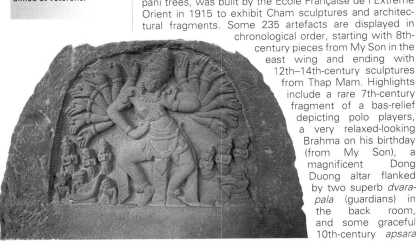

A Da Nang fisherwoman at work on the beach

(dancers), exhibited in a corner of the central Tra Kieu Room. A fabulously sculpted snake-eating *garuda* (mythical eagle) is one of several later masterpieces in the Thap Mam Room.

South of town Da Nang's biggest tourist pull, the **Marble Mountains►** (*Open* daily 7–5.30. *Admission charge* moderate), lies 12km to the south. Although marble now has to be imported from the north to make the thousands of statues and souvenirs, the mountains remain a major pilgrimage site. Commercialisation is everywhere and accompanies anyone who climbs the steep 157 steps to explore the cave-shrines and pagodas. Children show you into the darker reaches with torches, beggars beg, and incense and drinks vendors persist. Despite this, there are some lovely views and a few quiet corners: try finding **Tang Chon Dong►►**, a network of cave-shrines located behind the Quan Am statue by Linh Ung Pagoda. More popular is the striking **Huyen Khong Cave►►**, whose walls soar to a natural skylight. Shrines, statues and inscriptions lie in the cool gloom, as do a few bullet holes. In the early 1970s, Viet Cong used the mountain as a military base, successfully destroying US aircraft in the airbase below.

About 500m east of the Marble Mountains lies the old American R & R resort of **China Beach►**, a windy stretch of dunes and casuarinas edged by rough surf. The Non Nuoc Resort is the only structure here – at least for the moment. Plans for a massive US$243 million American joint venture resort collapsed in 1996, but this, or something similar, may well be resuscitated.

Like a sponge
'The Marble Mountains rise up out of the sandwaves like five great tusks. There is no other mountain, hill or even rock for miles, just these grey monoliths standing lonely and sand-blown on a desolate shore. Each is dedicated to a separate element. That to which my escort steered me was "Water" and the largest. Up innumerable steps of grey, white and rosy marble we climbed, to a terrace whereon was a small Buddhist temple containing the usual collection of gilt images, gongs and drums. The mountain was perforated like a sponge. A bonze appeared and led me up and down gloomy tunnels and galleries – the throb of the breakers echoing after us – through and through the rock from grotto to terrace, from view to view.'
From *The Dragon and the Lotus* by Crosbie Garstin (1928).

Cloth shops
Every central street in Hoi An is home to several 'cloth shops', where bolts of silk, rayon and polyester are piled up and vendors hover with tape-measures. Tailoring prices are low, but however enticing the fabrics, play safe. Order direct copies of your own clothes or of one of the shop's existing styles. Choose heavier fabrics (such as raw silk) and keep things simple. A tried and tested cloth shop is Tin Tin at 88 Le Loi.

Hoi An's early prosperity stemmed from the presence of intersecting rivers right by the coast

▶▶▶ **Hoi An** 130B6

This is one of Vietnam's most delightful places, a small, atmospheric harbour town little changed for 200 years and with a friendly population that is gunning hard for late 20th-century tourism. A few days spent here compensate for many of the country's more difficult destinations, and no one will leave without a made-to-measure outfit tucked into his or her bag. Apart from its extensive cultural offerings, Hoi An has enthusiastically seized upon the commercial potential of cheap fabrics and seamstresses: tailors almost outnumber antique and souvenir shops, which is saying something. However, the town's popularity has outstripped accommodation, so if you plan coming here in the high season make sure you have a room booked and/or arrive early. Commercialism has also invaded the historic family houses, and nowhere is without its obligatory souvenir stand; a bonus is that English and French are widely spoken, giving a welcome boost to communication.

Active past Hoi An's lengthy history is suitably eclectic, its name alone changing over the centuries – Haifo, Haiso, Cotam and Faifo are just some of the variations. It was under the Champa Kingdom that it developed as a port on the Thu Bon River, reflected in the discovery of numerous Cham wells and artefacts as well as Islamic and Chinese porcelain. By the 15th century Viet hamlets were growing up around their activities of trade, pottery, fishing and birds'-nest collecting. The following two centuries saw a massive influx of Chinese and Japanese settlers, who set about controlling trade in the South China Sea and establishing their own autonomous districts within the town. Portuguese, Dutch, English and French merchant ships soon started docking at cosmopolitan Faifo (as Hoi An was then known), and trade in silk, porcelain, pepper, tea, mother-of-pearl and lacquer boomed.

Catastrophe struck with the Tay Son Rebellion in the late 18th century (see page 38), when much of the town was destroyed, and continued with the gradual silting-up of the Thu Bon River. By the time the French appeared in Vietnam, Da Nang had taken over as the country's main port. With a few notable

Centuries of maritime trade have left Hoi An with a multi-cultural legacy

xceptions, most structures in Hoi An date from the 9th century, and this alone creates an outstanding rchitectural harmony.

ayout The centre of Hoi An covers a small grid of streets dging the river. Bach Dang, the waterfront road lined vith excellent open-air restaurants, links the Japanese ridge at the western end of town and the market and rench quarter at the eastern end. Running parallel are nree streets along which the town's main historic build- ngs are located, above all Tran Phu, the former Japanese uarter. To the north, Tran Hung Dao acts as a perimeter, onnecting the bus station with Cua Dai Beach, 4km to the ast. This easy scale encourages walking or cycling (rental ikes are readily available) around the sights, further elped by the ban on cars in the centre.

A visit to the small **museum►** (7 Nguyen Hue. *Open* –5), housed in a former pagoda, makes a good starting oint before you strike out into the numerous old houses, agodas and Chinese congregation halls (*hoi quan*) that epper the centre. Exhibits include ancient pottery, jars nd stone earrings, 10th-century Cham sculptures, a ovely wooden statue of the Japanese Emperor Tran Vo emoved from the bridge), old documents, 1930s photos nd temple artefacts. A courtyard with goldfish pond leads o the **Quan Cong Pagoda►►**, this in turn opening on to ran Phu (it is at No 24). Founded in 1653, the pagoda ocuses on an impressive statue of General Quan Cong, anked by his mandarin lieutenants and white horse. laques sealed into the wall list the names of Chinese lonors, while the ceiling is decorated with symbolic carp.

A few doors further east at 10 Tran Phu stands the Iainan Assembly Hall►, built in 1883 in memory of over hundred Hainan seamen who were killed after they were nistaken for pirates. Exceptional here is the superbly arved and gilded altar screen depicting Chinese court life.

House design

Of Hoi An's estimated 600 historical houses, these fanning out along the three main streets, two-thirds maintain their traditional design, with brick exteriors, wood-panelled interiors and tiled roofs (alternating *yin* concave tiles with *yang* convex ones). This mixture of materials keeps the house cool in summer and warm in winter. Their design, similar to southern Chinese homes, is based on three modules built on a narrow plot at least 35m in depth. From the front of the house an altar area leads to the main living space, this in turn opening on to a central courtyard. Here, sloping eave overhangs keep the lower rooms cool and free of rain, and the area is overlooked by upper-floor balconies. The courtyard is multifunctional: it provides light, air and space for plants, and also allows rainwater to be collected. Beyond this is the kitchen area. Beds may be in the living area or upstairs.

The Japanese Bridge

Following Tran Phu west to No 46, you cannot miss the **Phuc Kien Assembly Hall**► (*Open* daily 7.30–12, 2–5.30), touted by the tourist office as Hoi An's best hall but now fronted by a garish 1975 gateway and paved garden. Founded in 1786, this Fujian temple is partly dedicated to Thien Hao, the Goddess of the Sea, whose statue stands in the second hall. The front hall contains a mural depicting the six founding Fukien (Fujian) families escaping persecution under the Chinese Qing Dynasty in 1644.

Further west is the **Museum of Trading Ceramics**►► (80 Tran Phu. *Open* 8–5), a fabulous ironwood house built at the turn of the century and immaculately restored by a Japanese association in 1993. This is worth seeing for the structure alone, but also houses a small collection of ancient ceramics, architectural fragments and drawings.

Next stop, at No 77, is the 300-year-old **Quan Thang House**►►► (*Open* 8–6. *Admission* donation), with an impressive example of ornately carved doors and screens, Japanese beams, slatted windows and a carved stone pillar from China. The walls beneath the skywell display exquisite reliefs representing mythological beasts and scenes from daily life. Eight generations of this Fujian family are worshipped at the ancestor shrine.

To the bridge At the western end of Tran Phu, at No 176, is the **Cantonese (Quangdong) Assembly Hall**► (*Open* 6–7.30am, 1–5.30pm). It was dedicated in 1786 to Quan Cong, and displays a writhing ceramic dragon in its courtyard fountain and an elaborate illuminated altar fronted by huge pivotal doors. Beyond this lies Hoi An's major claim to fame, the **Japanese Bridge**►►►, which curves gracefully over a tributary of the Thu Bon River. The first roofed bridge was built in 1593 to link the Japanese and Chinese communities, but the present construction dates from 1719. This date is inscribed above its small temple, Chua Cau, although the bridge has since undergone several alterations. At the western end stand two statues of dogs and at the eastern end two monkeys, said to symbolise

he years in which construction of the bridge was started and completed. Once a gathering point for beggars, vendors and fortune-tellers, the bridge is now guarded by a policeman on the lookout for motor bikes, which are banned from crossing it.

Over the bridge at 4 Nguyen Thi Minh Khai, in the 17th-century Chinese quarter, is the **Phung Hung House**►►► (*Open* 8–6. *Admission* donation), a 200-year-old family house that combines many of the architectural details for which Hoi An is renowned: a Japanese crabshell-shaped ceiling; Chinese balustrades and pivotal doors with vertically sliding shutters; and Vietnamese inlaid furniture and

Chinese congregations
Congregations still play an important social, professional, commercial and sometimes political role among Hoi An's Chinese population. Community assembly halls (*hoi quan*) enable each regional group to preserve its traditions and dialect, to venerate its founding fathers and Taoist gods, and, not least, act as a business meeting point. Hoi An's Chinese population originated in the regions of Fujian (formerly Fukien; the majority), Guangzhou (formerly Canton), Chao'an (formerly Chaozhou) and Hainan, and each group continues to respect its own traditions.

149

antiques. During the 1964 flood, 160 neighbours took refuge upstairs, probably watching the surging waters below through the trapdoor. The suspended family shrine is dedicated to Thien Hao, who watched the family's ancestors as they sailed from China.

Back in the centre, walk a few steps from the Japanese Bridge towards the river to reach Nguyen Thai Hoc, a street that once opened directly on to the river. At No 101 stands the **Tan Ky House**►►► (*Open* 8–12, 2–4.30), a well-preserved 200-year-old dwelling that has been home to seven generations of a Chinese merchant family, their warehouse conveniently located on the upper floor. The same narrow but deep layout, crabshell ceiling, suspended Japanese beams and central courtyard define the Hoi An style, while inlaid mother-of-pearl panels idolise nature through Chinese poems. There is also some stunning antique ebony furniture beside newer reproductions. A few doors further on at No 80 is the **Diep Dong Nguyen House**►, interesting above all for its collection of antiques.

A final pilgrimage should be made to the **Tran Family Chapel**►► (21 Le Loi. *Open* 8–5), entered through a shady, luxuriant courtyard. Built in 1802 by the Chinese mandarin Tran, it displays some remarkable items, including fine ivory carvings, scrolls and embroidered panels. On the family altar stand boxes, each containing the names and death dates of family members, with lotus symbols denoting women and circular gold plaques for men. At the back of the chapel is a pretty garden containing some bonsai trees.

Chinese craftsmanship at Tan Ky House (above left) and blackwood furniture at Diep Dong Nguyen House (above)

The Phuc Kien Assembly Hall was completely renovated in 1990 by the Fujian community

Recovery Hoi An's central market is a wonderful place to return to the present after this historical immersion. Numerous stalls sell herbal remedies, a Hoi An speciality, and market life is at its liveliest early in the morning when fresh produce is unloaded at the wharf. A boat-trip on the river at this time is also recommended. East of the market is the **Cam Nam Bridge**, leading to a small island (pleasant for a bike ride), and beyond this on Phan Boi Chau is the French quarter, dating from the 1880s onwards. **Tran Duong House▶** at No 25 Phan Boi Chau (*Admission* donation) bears no comparison to the sumptuous houses of the centre, but the stuccoed, colonnaded façade and art deco furniture are interesting none the less.

Excursions An obvious destination is **Cua Dai Beach▶▶**, reached by a pleasant rural cycle ride past paddy-fields and hamlets. Follow Tran Hung Dao 4km east from the Hoi An Hotel to reach this wide expanse of dunes and casuarinas, where deck-chairs, restaurants and persistent child vendors lie in wait.

North-west of Hoi An are two pagodas, one of which is thought to be the oldest building hereabouts. To get there, go straight up Le Loi until you reach Le Hong Phong; turn left here and then right at a large nursery garden. The sandy road leads to **Chuc Thanh Pagoda▶▶**, set in large, unkempt grounds that are dotted with old and new tombs. It was founded in 1454 by a Fujian Buddhist monk and was most recently restored in 1955; bullet holes in the walls testify to wartime suffering. Today, only five monks live at the pagoda, worshipping A Di Da, the laughing Buddha, whose statue is centrally placed in the beautiful old sanctuary alongside 18 *arhat* (saints) and some exceptional ritual objects.

From here, head about 500m west along a sandy path past gardens and over a canal to reach the more imposing **Phuoc Lam Pagoda▶▶**, a mid-17th-century building set in a peaceful garden, again with numerous tombs, some encrusted with ceramic fragments. The monks here remain discreet, so it is not always possible to enter the pagoda.

■ **A highly visible Chinese cultural import to Hoi An is the belief in animals and plants as symbols of good fortune. Buddhist temples, assembly halls and private homes all display variations on the zoomorphic theme, carved into wood, cast in bronze, painted on ceramics or moulded in clay.** ■

Eyes Anyone visiting a traditional Hoi An house will notice an 'eye' over the door. This wooden object, nailed into the lintel, is usually shaped as a chrysanthemum and incorporates an octagonal figure or the *yin-yang* sign, representing the sun, the cosmos and the evolution of the world. Occasionally a bat may appear to symbolise happiness, or the eye may simply be depicted as the Chinese ideogram for longevity. Door eyes on temples are more ornate and may be shaped like a tiger or, as in the Phuc Kien Assembly Hall (see page 148), a *yin-yang* sign surrounded by two pairs of dragons, one worshipping the sun and the other the moon.

Fishing for fortune One of the most popular images is the carp, symbol of motivation and abundance, and regarded by Hoi An's seafaring people as a good omen. According to myth, the fish must struggle against the currents to reach the Dragon Gate, where it is metamorphosed into a dragon – thus it perfectly embodies quest, success and, a logical conclusion, prosperity. Equally prized are the *giao long*, serpentine young dragons that writhe around pillars. These are thought to have been used extensively in place of 'real' dragons as the latter were reserved exclusively for royalty under the Nguyen Dynasty. Cranes or storks are signs of longevity, closely followed by tortoises, deer and peaches.

Fertility Apart from long life and prosperity, Chinese homes also incorporate symbols of domestic harmony. Marital bliss is depicted as a pair of swimming fish, the orchid and the lotus both represent conjugal happiness, while sexual union is symbolised by a lotus stem and pod. Being an essential part of the family business, children (preferably male) are encouraged by the fertility symbols of pomegranates, watermelons or lotus pods, all fruits that bear abundant seeds.

Out they come
According to Chinese belief, on the 5th day of the fifth lunar month, *yin* (negative forces) are believed to emerge. These elements include ghosts responsible for disease, accidental death and financial disaster. Five so-called poisonous creatures – the snake, the centipede, the scorpion, the gecko and the toad or spider – are said to proliferate at this time. Precautions taken against these ghosts include hanging up pungent stalks that are said to repel evil.

Still bright-eyed on its rooftop perch...

An astonishing Ba Na village house watches over imported customs

Cham finds
At the village of Tra Kieu, once the Cham administrative capital of Simhapura and located 6km from the main highway, 20km from My Son, there is a fascinating little collection of Cham artefacts in the Catholic church (Dia So Tra Kieu). These have been brought to the local priest over the years by local farmers who continue to unearth relics deep in the soil. Sadly, nothing is left of Simhapura itself except the ramparts, while all major sculptures are preserved at the Cham Museum in Da Nang (see page 144).

► **Kon Tum** 130A4

This provincial capital lies on the banks of the Dakbla River in a high valley in the Central Highlands. French colonialists arrived in the 19th century, following earlier missionaries who started proselytising among the minority people back in 1651. A grim reminder of this period (and now open to visitors) is the large prison built by the French to intern dissidents, later used by the South Vietnamese for captured Viet Cong. Heavy fighting went on in the area in 1972 and mines still lie around Dak To, 42km north of town.

Minority groups abound, above all the Ba Na, the first Montagnard group to write in their own language and famed as skilled hunters. Their stilt-house villages encircling the town can be visited, preferably with a guide; as elsewhere in the Central Highlands, use your discretion and sensitivity. As Kon Tum means 'Village of Many Lakes' in the Ba Na language, it is not surprising that the impressive **Yaly Waterfall**, cascading 60m over terraced rocks into the Po Co River, lies near by – about 30km south-west of town.

►► **My Son** 130B5

These sadly scarred relics of the powerful kingdom of Champa stand in verdant isolation in a valley 60km south of Da Nang (*Open* daily 8–4. *Admission charge* expensive). Access is along a severely rutted and complicated 30km dirt-road that leaves the main highway just outside Hoi An, so a reliable vehicle and driver is a prerequisite. From the entrance-ticket office, visitors are taken by jeep across a bamboo bridge (this recently replaced the need to boat across the river, although it sometimes collapses) then on a few more kilometres to the site. A trail meanders around the hilly terrain, crossing streams and cutting through the thick undergrowth; do not venture off it as the area was once heavily mined.

Isolation From the 4th to 13th centuries, a uniquely long period among Southeast Asia's civilisations, My Son was the religious centre of the Indianised Chams, who kept their administrative settlement separate at Tra Kieu, 20km away. This remote setting between mountain and sea preserved an estimated 68 brick temples, erected by successive rulers and incorporating divinities carved in their image alongside Siva, the founding god of Champa. Wooden buildings reserved for the religious communities surrounded the graceful temples, but subsequently these rotted away in the tropical climate.

Six centuries of abandon, invasion by nature and repeated looting ended in the late 19th century, when Henri Parmentier and the École Française de l'Extrême Orient started excavations. Numbers were given to each building and the most outstanding sculptures were carted away to the Cham Museum at Da Nang (see page 144). Then came war and, in 1969, American B52 bombers tracking Viet Cong guerrillas: the site masterpiece, labelled A1, was destroyed and five other temples were badly damaged. Since then, some questionable restoration work

has been undertaken by Polish archaeologists.

Layout The first groups encountered – B, C and D – are also the best preserved. B-group, dating mainly from the 10th century, includes the boat-shaped roof of B5 which once sheltered sacred texts and ritual objects for ceremonial use in B1, the central tower of this group, while B4 displays some superb exterior carving. In the corner of the group is B3, a beautiful example of a pyramidal Cham tower. Many of the façades contain statues (some cumbersomely restored in concrete) and elaborate decorative carving. There is less to see of C-group, with its 8th-century shrine to Siva.

From the two D edifices, the trail leads east across a stream to the devastated A-group, once the jewel of the site but now a pile of rubble, although some finely carved fragments include part of a grimacing *kala* (Javanese monster). The trail continues north up a small hill to G-group and, beyond a bomb crater, to 7th-century E- and F-groups, where a linga (the phallus symbol of Siva), a statue of Nandin (the bull god), stelae inscribed in Sanskrit and decapitated statues lie forlornly in the ruins.

Arizona
The ancient Cham tracks stretching from My Son to the sea at Hoi An became important Viet Cong infiltration routes in the late 1960s. My Son was an ideal strategic refuge for the VC, lying at the heart of a wild region that was called 'Arizona' by the US marines based at Da Nang. When the B52s started unleashing their formidable bombs, followed up by helicopter fire, brick towers that had survived over a millennium were shattered and their delicate *apsara* (dancer) carvings pockmarked with shrapnel, if not totally destroyed. Incensed by this cultural aggression, Philippe Stern, curator of Paris's Musée Guimet and an expert on Champa, begged the Americans to spare 'humanity's heritage'. The Americans did take heed, but in some cases it was too late.

153

B-group, the best preserved at My Son

■ **Accomplished builders, sculptors, farmers, traders, seamen and even pirates, the Chams formed one of Southeast Asia's longest-surviving early cultures. For more than ten centuries they reigned over Central Vietnam, until they were absorbed by the Khmer and annexed by the Viets – although even this was not quite the end of their hybrid culture as 100,000 Chams survive today.** ■

Chams today
Thought to number about 100,000, today's surviving Chams are scattered between Vietnam, Cambodia, Thailand and Malaysia. Of the 60,000 Chams in Vietnam, about a third have converted to Islam to form the country's only sizeable Muslim community. Their villages are concentrated in Phan Rang and along the coast north to Nha Trang, where they grow rice, raise cattle or cultivate grapes, but are never fishermen. Like many ethnic minorities, they have not been well integrated into the mainstream economy. Weaving is traditionally highly valued in courtship and family life, and in some villages 80 per cent of the households still practise this craft.

Champa, caught between the flourishing Khmers of the south and the onward-marching Viets of the north, and isolated on its narrow coastal strip, was finally swallowed up in 1471. Until then, it had miraculously survived by playing a cat and mouse game with the Chinese, the Javanese in the 8th century, the Viets in the 10th century, Kublai Khan's Mongols in the 13th century and, during much of the period, the powerful Khmers of Angkor.

Siva rules The Chams were of Malayo-Polynesian descent, described by a 4th-century Chinese traveller as 'possessing a large, straight nose, dark, curly hair, and practising a funeral rite that uses incineration to the sound of a drum'. Chinese texts indicate AD 192 as the year a local ruler rejected the Chinese authority that held sway over the region and founded his own independent kingdom by uniting several neighbouring principalities.

It was when Champa extended its control to the Funan Kingdom in the Mekong Delta during the 4th century that it encountered Hinduism, a religion with sophisticated socio-political structures that was already marked by Buddhism. Cham rulers then moved into another dimension, and set about creating their own Sivaite monuments and icons. Indian and Khmer art had strong influences, but the Chams developed their own specific techniques for erecting the magnificent tower shrines (*khan*), many of which still stand in the central coastal belt.

Cham style The reign of Indravarman I (875–*c*. 895), who built the remarkable Buddhist monastery of Dong Duong (50km south-east of My Son), marked the apogee of Champa. Just before this period, the Po Nagar towers of Nha Trang rose up (see page 157), only to be sacked in the 10th century by the Khmers. Javanese influences appeared in the form of ferocious *kala* (monsters) and *makara* (sea monsters), while Siva, Vishnu, Ganesh, Laksmi and *dvarapala* (guardians) all contributed to the Hindu pantheon. Although they never modelled their surroundings or created grandiose constructions to the extent of the Khmer, the Chams nevertheless had a clear concept of their religious architecture, which was aimed at deifying their ruler. They were also extremely gifted in producing three-dimensional sculptures destined for altars inside the tower shrines, as opposed to the bas-reliefs common to Indian culture.

Sinister past
An Italian Dominican monk, Gabriel de San Antonio, who visited the conquered Chams in the 16th century, gave an interesting insight into their earlier culture in his account. For him, Champa was brilliant but unbalanced, like the civilisation of the Aztecs. Technically advanced, able to devise new agricultural methods (including developing a fast-growing variety of rice) and undertake vast irrigation projects, sensitive to arts and science, Champa nevertheless possessed another, more sinister face. On certain auspicious days, massive human sacrifices were made, sometimes numbering up to 6,000 victims, all in the name of the ruling god-king.

Questioning the merits of the Po Klong Garai towers, one of the last major Cham sites before their definitive defeat by the Viets in 1471

Thanks to the École Française de l'Extrême Orient, a wealth of Cham sculptures has been conserved at Da Nang's museum

The ochre-brick towers followed a familiar pattern: a tall, central, rectangular cell with a west-facing entrance and ornately carved 'blind' porticoes was crowned by a soaring pyramidal roof composed of a series of diminishing pavilions. Pilasters and mouldings with vegetal reliefs decorated the façades, sculptures of deities stood in niches and worm-like ornamentation was used liberally. All this disappeared gradually as My Son and Dong Duong came to an end when the Viets captured the region in 980, forcing the Chams to move their capital south to Tra Ban, near Binh Dinh and just north of Quy Nhon.

Final creations Although the Chams made a brief return to My Son in the 11th century, most of their artistic effort from then on was concentrated on several groups of towers in Binh Dinh, these named after precious materials (ivory, gold, silver and copper – see pages 164–5). Built in a far more sober style and with minimal ornamentation, these towers emphasised the beauty of their proportions and sites (all were located on hilltops). This decline in decorative prowess was probably partly due to the spread of Buddhism, a less hierarchical religion in which god-kings had no place, and partly an expression of a reduced dynamism. The Po Klong Garai group outside Phan Rang (see page 160) probably represents one of the last major Cham sites, dating from the late 13th century, before Champa was definitively defeated by the Viets in 1471.

156

Monsieur Yersin

Alexandre Yersin was an exceptionally multi-talented man. Doctor, explorer, botanist, photographer, agriculturalist, meteorologist and amateur astrophysicist, he was in his element in the pioneering days of French Indochina. After working with Pasteur in Paris, he became a ship's doctor on the Indochinese route, a ploy that allowed him to explore Vietnam's interior: it was thanks to Yersin that the hill-station of Da Lat was developed. In 1894, while in Hong Kong, he made the momentous discovery of the bacillus responsible for bubonic plague. After founding his Nha Trang laboratory, he concentrated on crop experimentation, and it was he again who brought *Hevea*, the rubber tree, to Vietnam. He died in Nha Trang in 1943, a revered though solitary figure. Even in today's post-1975 climate, many roads continue to bear Yersin's name (see also panel on page 137).

A slow start on Nha Trang's city beach

►►► Nha Trang   130C2

Nha Trang is Vietnam's all-time favourite seaside resort, a breezy, Riviera-style seafront edged by a wide, palm-lined boulevard that boasts open-air cafés and seafood restaurants. A 6km white-sand beach running the length of town, offshore islands, colonial architecture, a burgeoning range of hotels and exceptionally outgoing inhabitants all contribute to make Nha Trang one of Vietnam's most pleasurable and relaxing destinations – that is when you have managed to escape the thriving population of beach masseurs and vendors. Above all, the site is endowed with a natural beauty that survives despite the expanding town, now home to 200,000 people.

Precursors Today's Korean, Chinese, Western and domestic tourists are not the first to have discovered Nha Trang's joys. The earliest to leave their mark were the Chams, who erected the elaborate Po Nagar towers at the mouth of the Cai River. Several somnolent centuries later, in 1891, the remarkable Swiss explorer Dr Alexandre Yersin arrived, and was so enraptured by the idyllic fishing-village setting that he decided to settle and found Vietnam's second Institut Pasteur here (the first was in Saigon). It was his move that set the wheels of colonial building in motion. Emperor Bao Dai was similarly struck by Nha Trang's exceptional beauty, and in 1923 had a complex of villas built on the southern headland. Then, some 40 years later, an American naval base was established here and GIs came to live it up during their R & R breaks. After 1975, Nha Trang continued to ply its tourist trade to Russians working at the large naval base of Cam Ranh Bay, but today the resort has donned decidedly more cosmopolitan colours.

Layout The main action takes place along Tran Phu, a road that stretches 5km from near the river estuary south past the airport to the main harbour beyond Bao Dai's headland. Nocturnal motorbike and bicycle cruising is a favourite local pastime along the northern stretch, and any pedalling foreigner is likely to strike up a conversation

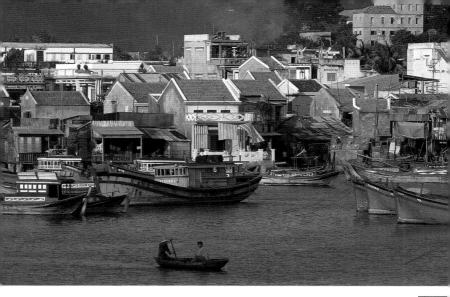

Fishing boats are a permanent feature in the Cai estuary

n route as every teenager seems to be learning nglish. A buzzing concentration of hotels and facilities is rouped around the junction with Le Thanh Ton, a major rtery that runs inland to the rail and bus stations and to ong Son Pagoda.

The older, leafy district north of Le Thanh Ton is the ommercial centre; the market is located here, as are umerous colonial villas that have been converted into otels. Modern mini-hotels are also appearing in the ewer streets to the south. Quang Trung, a major orth–south artery, leads over the Xom Bong Bridge to the Cham towers and to Hon Chong Beach. Getting around lha Trang is easy, as cyclos are plentiful and bicycles and motor bikes both widely available and cheap to rent.

owering beginnings Looming to the north of the estu-ry on a rocky hilltop is **Po Nagar (Thap Ba)**▶▶▶ (*Open* aily 8–5. *Admission charge* cheap), where four of the riginal eight Cham towers remain. They were built etween the 7th and 12th centuries, survived sporadic ttacks by marauding Malays, Khmers and Chinese, and till hold spiritual significance for Buddhists who come ere to burn incense at the altars. Unfortunately, any mystical ambience is instantly destroyed by the hordes of elentless child vendors and photographers.

Brick columns that once enclosed a meditation hall stand t the base of the hillock; from here, a staircase climbs to hap Chinh (AD 817), the 23m main tower which shelters a much-venerated statue of a ten-armed Bhagavatti, wife of Siva. Above the entrance is a restored statue of Siva, while Sanskrit inscriptions face the walls of the antechamber and the door-frame. Grouped around it are three smaller owers, less ornate and less well-preserved, although an mpressive linga is housed in the south tower.

A bicycle detour along the next turn-off west from the ighway takes you down to the river, where you will find boat-builders constructing the impressive fishing boats hat cluster in the estuary and subsequently cover distances as far as Ha Long Bay.

Tourist services
● Khan Hoa Tourism, 1 Tran Hung Dao, Nha Trang (tel: 058 822257; fax: 058 824206). This official tourist office is of little help bar selling a map of the town and booking tours. Far more helpful are the private tour agencies, branches of Ho Chi Minh City's backpackers' haunts:
● Linh Café, 4 Nguyen Thien Thuat, Nha Trang (tel: 058 825064; fax: 058 824991). Central Highlands tour, minibus network, island boat-trips, good café/restaurant, helpful staff and guides.
● Ha Phuong Tourist Company, c/o Hanh Café, 5a Tran Hung Dao (tel: 058 829015). Similar to above, plus own hotel, ticketing and visas.

Island hopping
Five islands lie a few kilometres out from the harbour. The largest, Hon Tre (Bamboo Island), offers a good, sheltered beach on its north coast. Hon Mun (Ebony Island), the furthest offshore of the main string, offers extensive coral reefs and is where swifts' nests are collected for the Chinese gourmet delicacy of bird's-nest soup (this is more common at distant Hon Yen, which requires a four-hour boat-ride). Hon Mot is just a rocky blip in the ocean, while neighbouring Hon Tam has an organised beach with café and deck-chairs. Closest to shore, and accessible by public ferry, is Hon Mieu (see main text). Tickets for daily boat-trips are sold in every hotel and tour agency.

Views Looking south from Po Nagar you will see a luminously white statue of Buddha rising above the roofline of the town. This is part of the **Long Son Pagoda▶**, located on 23 Thang 10 just west of the railway station. Rebuilt in 1963, the modern pagoda commemorates the hundreds of Buddhist monks who died opposing Diem's regime. Its colonnaded main hall is impressive, while above, dominating the surrounding landscape, sits the giant Buddha on his lotus flower. Access is via a staircase, often lined with beggars, starting on the right of the prayer-hall.

Equally panoramic views radiate from the site of **Bao Dai's villas**, which stand in a luxuriant garden on the promontory south of the town. The art deco complex now functions as a hotel, but even if you just stop for a drink or meal at the open-air restaurant here you will be rewarded with sweeping, breezy views across the harbour and islands beyond.

Museums In the town centre, the main monument is the **Yersin Museum▶** inside the Institut Pasteur (8 Tran Phu. *Open* Mon–Sat 1.30–4.30. *Admission charge* cheap). A visit takes you through the sprawling 1895 building to an upstairs section dedicated to the exceptional life of Alexandre Yersin (1863–1943; see panel on page 156). French and Vietnamese captions are written on panels arranged in his huge library, where surgical instruments stand beside astrological equipment. If you understand French, it is a fascinating place.

A few doors away is the **Khanh Hoa Museum** (16 Tran Phu), where ethnography rubs shoulders with Uncle Ho. Maritime interest is well catered for in the form of live and preserved specimens at the 1920s **Oceanographic Institute▶** (*Open* 7–11.30, 1.30–5. *Admission charge* cheap), located opposite Nha Trang's deep-water harbour south of town.

Drinks on the rocks at Hon Chong

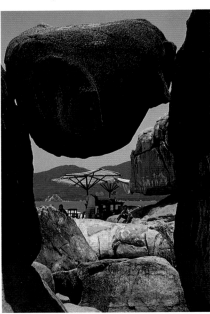

Waves If Nha Trang's surf and beach commerce become overpowering, there is welcome relief at **Hon Chong▶▶**, a lovely island-studded bay with calm, emerald waters, reached via a sandy turn-off from the highway about 500m north of Po Nagar. Small cafés line the beach, before the coast curves into a rocky promontory where steps lead up to more cafés, with fine views. A final sculptural point is created by a succession of smooth boulders where, inevitably, a drinks vendor lurks in the shadow of one rock that displays a gigantic and mysterious handprint. Less enigmatic are the four **islands▶▶**, which can be toured by boat from Nha Trang: inexpensive all-day trips include gargantuan lunches and make stops for snorkelling, sunbathing and visiting the **Tri Nguyen Fish-rearing Aquarium▶** or Hon Mieu, where close encounters with sharks and turtles are on hand

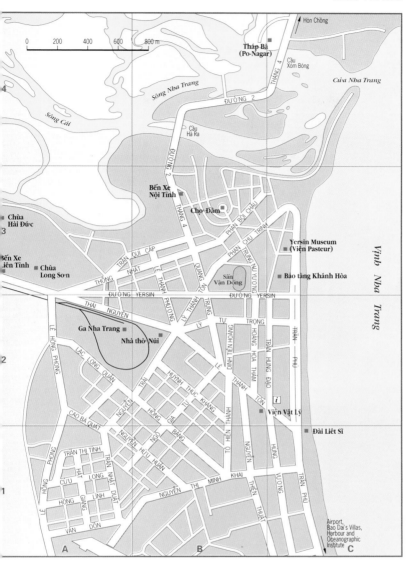

Private boats can be negotiated at the harbour for a few hours or a full day.

For a real escape head 40km north of Nha Trang, just beyond Ninh Hoa, to **Doc Let**▶▶▶, a stunningly beautiful swathe of white sand edged by feathery casuarinas and palms. A restaurant with changing-rooms and beach kiosks attracts locals at weekends, but otherwise it is idyllically unspoilt with a horizon interrupted only by basket boats. A large fishing village lies at the southern end, and there are some basic beach-huts for overnighting at the main beach entrance. It is possible to get to the beach by a slow, decrepit bus from Nha Trang, but as it is more difficult to leave, a car or motor bike is recommended.

Scuba-diving

Nha Trang's diving season is February–September. Local dive centres are:
● The Blue Diving Club, Coconut Grove Resort (opposite the Hai Yen Hotel; tel: 058 825390; fax: 058 824214).
● Triangle Diving Center, Bao Dai Hotel (tel: 058 881049; fax: 058 991471).

▶ **Phan Rang** *130B1*

The provincial capital of Ninh Thuan consists of the two adjoining towns of Phan Rang and **Thap Cham**, both situated on the banks of the Cai River about 5km from the sea. They lie in a flat, arid region supporting scrub, cacti and gaunt cattle, although euclaptus trees are making visible inroads. Onions, chilli peppers and grapes are the local specialities, often cultivated by the Chams who inhabit the region. Hot and dusty Phan Rang offers few amenities and should be treated as a daytime stopover. Far more attractive accommodation is available to the south at Ca Na Beach (see page 137).

The main reason for coming here is to visit the magnificent **Po Klong Garai towers**▶▶▶ (*Admission charge* moderate), 7km east of town near Thap Cham railway station on the road to Da Lat. Four towers remain of a group of six built in the late 13th century when the Chams were being pushed southwards by the Viets. Built on a granite hilltop that rises out of a barrage of dense cacti, they have been partly restored but still present a harmonious unity. The entrance steps pass under a stone arch before leading to the main pyramidal tower, rising 21m and dedicated to King Po Klong. A restored sculpture of a dancing, six-armed Siva stands over the entrance and in the antechamber is a statue of Nandin, the bull god which transported Siva and governed agriculture. At the heart of the tower stands a linga, painted with the face of a divinity. In front of this sanctuary is a beautiful example of a boat-roofed shrine which, in turn, fronts another shrine that formed the original entrance. During the French excavations, archaeologists found a number of gold and silver bowls as well as jewellery, proof that Champa still had resources despite its ailing civilisation.

Serious Cham fans should also visit **Po Ro Me**, the last temple to be built by Champa's last king in the late 17th century. It is located on one of a pair of hills about 16km south of town, and is reached by heading 5km west along a dusty track from the village of Hau San. The main, extremely simplified temple resembles a pagoda and has a bas-relief of Siva surrounded by gods.

Beach-lovers can head for **Ninh Chu Beach**▶▶, 6km east of Phan Rang, where 5km of

160

Geckos, a Phan Rang delicacy

Mui Ne sand-dunes

white sands and clear turquoise waters back on to groves of casuarina trees. The quality of the site is such that for years it was reserved for South Vietnam's government elite under President Nguyen Van Thieu, who was also chief of the province.

Phan Rang is also the beginning (or end) of the main road to Da Lat, over 100km to the north-west. About half-way, the road starts climbing steeply to reach **Ngoan Muc Pass►►** (known as Bellevue Pass in French colonial days), where fabulous views unfold over the rolling pine-clad hills. Temperatures drop noticeably here and landscapes change radically.

► Phan Thiet   130B1

If you are following the coast road between Ho Chi Minh City and Nha Trang, this is a logical place to stop if you fancy a break at the beach, and it is increasingly becoming a favourite escape for city expatriates. Phan Thiet itself is a pretty little fishing port straddling a river mouth, with some pungent *nuoc mam* (fish sauce) factories. Cham interest is present, too, in the form of **Pho Hai►**, an 8th-century tower located about 7km north-east of Phan Thiet near the beach. The very early triple-tower shrine displays strong Khmer influence and is the southernmost of the Champa towers.

Classic blue fishing boats cluster in Phan Thiet's central harbour and there is a beach right in town, but the main interest lies 22km to the east at **Mui Ne (Ne Cape)►►**. Spectacular undulating sand-dunes reach Sahara-esque proportions along this promontory, where clear, calm waters and a tiny fishing village have also attracted some limited up-market hotel development. This is likely to expand in the future.

161

Basket boats at Ca Na, a more scenic option for hotels than Phan Rang

My Lai massacre

■ In March 1968, when the world press was emblazoned with photos of the massacre at My Lai, public opinion was already turning against the Vietnam War. The infamous 'search and destroy' missions had razed thousands of hamlets and killed their inhabitants, but My Lai was the first time these activities were so graphically made public. ■

Inevitability

'Calley appears to have been a sadist, but his personality alone does not explain the massacre. What Calley and others who participated in the massacre did that was different was to kill hundreds of unarmed Vietnamese in two hamlets in a single morning and to kill point-blank with rifles, pistols and machine-guns. Had they killed just as many over a larger area in a longer period of time and killed impersonally with bombs, shells, rockets, white phosphorous and napalm, they would have been following the normal pattern of American military conduct... The military leaders of the United States, and the civilian leaders who permitted the generals to wage war as they did, had made the massacre inevitable.'
From *A Bright Shining Lie* by Neil Sheehan (1988).

Statue at the My Lai memorial

By 1965, Quang Ngai's coastal hamlets had already suffered hundreds of deaths from bombs and naval gunfire. The region, known to be staunchly supportive of the Viet Cong guerrillas, became a prime target for US attacks. In late 1967, Jonathan Schell, a *New Yorker* journalist, estimated that 70 per cent of an estimated 450 hamlets had been destroyed, and the annual civilian casualty rate was put at 50,000 by a British volunteer doctor. However, the My Lai massacre of 16 March 1968 was to kill 504 in one fell swoop.

War crime Colonel Henderson of the 11th Brigade was responsible for the operation, Captain Ernest Medina commanded the three platoons and Lieutenant William Calley headed the 1st Platoon. After initial bombing by helicopter artillery, the troops were landed in the ricefields of Son My, a group of four hamlets that included My Lai and Tu Cung. From then on unspeakable crimes took place. Sadistic, indiscriminate killings of unarmed old men, women, children and babies, mass executions, torture, rape and sodomy all took place in the space of a few nightmarish hours. Lt Calley headed 'operations' at My Lai, personally herding his victims into a mass grave and inciting his soldiers to more atrocities. Some refused, including the only American casualty of the manoeuvre, Herbert Carter, who shot himself in the foot to avoid participating.

Forgiven? Calley was eventually court martialled in 1971, the only soldier or officer to be convicted. He was found guilty of personally murdering 22 civilians out of an initial charge of 109, and sentenced to life imprisonment. For three years Calley remained under house arrest pending an appeal, but in 1974 President Nixon personally intervened and he was released. Yet 504 Vietnamese lay dead and many more remained psychologically damaged by the atrocity.

Plei Ku   130A4

High in the sparsely populated Central Highlands and often swathed in chilly mist is Plei Ku, a provincial capital that was the South Vietnamese command post for the entire mountain region. The surroundings were not only doused in Agent Orange, but also underwent repeated B52 bombing, particularly during the Americans' 'last stand' in 1972 when the North Vietnamese Army was closing in. When President Thieu finally ordered his troops out of Plei Ku, a panicking and partly fatal exodus of some 100,000 inhabitants followed.

Plei Ku was deliberately burned down by the retreating soldiers to destroy anything that might be of use to the Viet Cong, so most of today's town consists of charmless Soviet-style concrete structures, terminally depressing in the frequent mist and rain. Visits to minority villages in the area are the only reason to come here, and for these a car and guide are essential. The crater lake of **To Nung►**, 6km north, offers some tranquil scenery as well as abundant freshwater fish.

Quang Ngai   130B5

This Viet Cong stronghold, with a long history of resistance, was a major battleground and today is capital of one of Vietnam's poorest provinces, sugar and salt being the economic mainstays. It sprawls unattractively along the highway to Tra Khuc River, inland from some beautiful unspoilt beaches. Visitors come here for one reason only: to visit the memorial ground of **Son My►►►** (*Open* daily 7–5. *Admission charge* cheap), where the terrible My Lai massacre took place on 16 March 1968 (see opposite). A turn-off immediately north of the bridge runs 14km east past paddy-fields, a lively village market and tiny hamlets before reaching the enclosed site of the massacre, now a landscaped garden and graveyard with neo-realist monumental statues and a small museum. This is perhaps Vietnam's most moving war memorial and, inevitably, highly disturbing, heightened by its isolation and absence of visitors. The museum houses a graphic display of detailed and captioned photos, domestic relics and rusting mortar shells. In the grounds outside, grave markers list the names and ages of occupants at the site of each torched hut and the mass grave of a Mrs Thong and seven others, while coconut palms still bear bullet holes.

Latex being transported from a rubber plantation near Plei Ku

Jungle of Screaming Souls
'That was the dry season when the sun burned harshly, the wind blew fiercely, and the enemy sent napalm spraying through the jungle and a sea of fire enveloped them, spreading like the fires of hell. Troops in the fragmented companies tried to regroup, only to be blown out of their shelters as they went mad, became disoriented and threw themselves into nets of bullets, dying in the flaming inferno… No jungle grew again in this clearing. No grass. No plants… From then on it was called the Jungle of Screaming Souls.'
From *The Sorrow of War* by Bao Ninh (1991), referring to an area north of Plei Ku.

The very 20th-century altar at Quy Nhon's Long Khanh Pagoda

Tourist office
● Binh Dinh Tourist Company, 10 Nguyen Hue, Quy Nhon (tel: 056 822524/822753/822329; fax: 056 821162).

▶   **Quy Nhon**   *130C4*

Yet another pummelled victim of the war, Quy Nhon has nevertheless risen above its past and is now a relatively prosperous port that straggles for 10km between the highway and the harbour. The port is the end of the line for trucks bringing timber down from the Central Highlands, and much of the local economy stems from this outlet, as well as from wood-processing. Shops selling hi-fis, sewing-machines and jeans are visible signs of its dynamism, also reflected in the numerous modern hotels. The municipal beach is not the cleanest, and nor are there any sights other than the **Long Khanh Pagoda**▶, dating from the 1720s, remodelled in the 1950s and now fronted by a gigantic Buddha. Not far from here is the market and, at the end of the beach, a rather odd zoo containing animals that were plundered from Cambodia by the Vietnamese Army.

Cham route Quy Nhon's interest lies more in its environs, rich in Cham relics and transient pastoral scenes. First on the agenda are the 'twin towers' of **Thap Doi**▶ on the outskirts of town. Symbolising male and female forces, these 11th-century towers rise 20m and 18m respectively out of the backstreets of town, and are now being extensively restored.

Some 20km to the north, off Highway 1, stand the four 'silver' towers known as **Banh It** (or **Thap Bac**)▶▶. Their isolated hilltop site dominates a valley between two branches of the Kon River, with paddy-fields stretching to the distant hills. The towers date from the early

12th century, and their limited ornamentation includes graceful bas-reliefs, Siva statues and decorative friezes, while the boat-roofed tower structure (edicule) is particularly impressive. At the northern base of the hill stands the Nguyen Thieu Buddhist Seminary, one of the largest in Central Vietnam.

Former capital A few kilometres further on, a turn-off west from the highway leads along a track past a Buddhist cemetery to **Canh Tien (Brass Tower)▶**. This and the neighbouring Do Ban ramparts are the only surviving relics of Tra Ban, the Cham capital from the late 10th to late 15th centuries. Crudely restored and almost invisible in a eucalyptus grove, it reflects the end of a glorious kingdom.

A fascinating extension of this site lies near by at the **Thap Thap Pagoda▶▶** (close to the highway 27km north of Quy Nhon). This was built in 1665 with the old Cham ramparts using bricks from the abandoned towers – hence its name, meaning 'Ten Towers'. The 30 resident monks still use Cham wells in the grounds. Although the pagoda is Buddhist, some of the interior motifs are distinctly Cham. The main sanctuary contains some beautiful *arhat* (saints), while the lotus-pond and carved tombs add to the tranquillity. About 10km further on is the group of three early 13th-century 'ivory' towers known as **Duong Long▶▶**. Their lintels imitate the Khmer Bayon style, and their façades incorporate some remarkable animal gods and intricate bas-reliefs.

A 13th-century Cham stone-carving at Duong Long

165

▶   Sa Huynh   130B4

This large fishing village, with a harbour and half-moon beach, makes a scenic lunch stop on the Quang Ngai–Quy Nhon stretch of Highway 1. There is one reasonable hotel at the southern end of the beach which also arranges boat-trips to nearby Genh Nhu Island. Family seafood restaurants, boat-building, fishing and salt production constitute the activities here, a far cry from the Iron Age Sa Huynh civilisation of 2,500 years ago. Numerous Iron Age graves containing some precious artefacts have been excavated in the region but there are no sites to visit.

▶▶   Song Cau   130C3

Located about 40km south of Quy Nhon, this beautifully sited village looks out over Xuan Dai Bay towards a small peninsula. Seafood restaurants on stilts creep into the water, making it a perfect place to stop for lunch, and there is also an attractive waterside hotel. Boat-trips around the bay can be arranged and lazing on the beach is always another option. Apart from its fishing, Song Cau is a basketware centre, while immediately to the north are salt-ponds and, beyond these, some of Vietnam's most idyllic, picture-postcard paddy-fields.

Tay Son Rebellion
The Tay Son Rebellion of 1771–89 (see page 38) erupted 45km inland from Quy Nhon. Three brothers led the peasants against their exploitative mandarins and the ruling Trinh and Nguyen lords, and in 1788 the eldest brother, Nguyen Hue, proclaimed himself emperor under the name of Quang Trung. At the same time, the Chinese, sensing an ideal opportunity to invade Vietnam, sent in their massive army. On the 5th day of Tet 1789, the brothers made a surprise attack on the Chinese, routed their army and subsequently reunified the country. A museum dedicated to the brothers lies on the road from Quy Nhon to Plei Ku.

Vietnam on screen

■ **Few countries have supplied such abundant cinematographic source material as Vietnam. From French colonial days to the GI experiences of the Vietnam War, a stream of films has played on the entire range of human emotions, usually in highly realist fashion. With American catharsis possibly complete, attention should now turn to young Vietnamese directors.** ■

Gallic nostalgia
Jean-Jacques Annaud's film *L'Amant* (*The Lover*) was based on the semi-autobiographical novel by Marguerite Duras (1914–96) recounting her adolescent experiences in Saigon. Asked by Annaud to rework the book to form the basis of a film script, this prodigious writer produced *L'Amant de la Chine du Nord* (*The Lover from North China*), which she declared was an improved version. The completed film, imbued with aesthetic excesses and high on explicit sexual scenes, was not popular with Duras, but this did not stop the French edition of her original novel selling over 2 million copies.

Robert De Niro in The Deer Hunter

French connection Despite their 70-year Indochinese presence, the French have only recently started exorcising their nostalgia in films such as Jean-Jacques Annaud's *L'Amant* (*The Lover*, 1992), based on Marguerite Duras' novel. In Régis Wargnier's syrupy *Indochine* (1992), Catherine Deneuve plays the title role, always impeccably turned out despite visiting rubber plantations and opium dens in her search for her Eurasian daughter. Whatever their quality, both these films do examine relationships between the colonisers and the colonised.

Anti-heroes Since the late 1970s, American military experiences in Vietnam have been indelibly recorded on celluloid, portraying troops sweltering in the mud and jungle of the Central Highlands, hiding in the waterways of the Mekong Delta or leaping from helicopters. In the aftermath of anti-war demonstrations and America's eventual retreat, Hollywood concentrated on marginalised cases of deserters or veterans unable to reintegrate into society, so underlining the absurdities of war. Elia Kazan's *The Visitors* (1972), Martin Scorcese's *Taxi Driver* (1975) and Michael Cimino's *The Deer Hunter* (1978) all painted portraits of a fractured society in which veterans struggled with their consciences. Then came the ultimate tableau of the horrors of the Vietnam War, Francis Ford Coppola's *Apocalypse Now* (1979), a descent into a hellish, neo-Conradian world where LSD and insanity take over.

After a short period of glorifying its heroes, Hollywood turned to exploring the daily realities of war and its psychological implications, as in Oliver Stone's *Platoon* (1987) and *Born on the Fourth of July* (1989), or Stanley Kubrick's *Full Metal Jacket* (1987). There was even enough distance to treat the entire national trauma with humour, as in Barry Levinson's *Good Morning Vietnam* (1988). In the late 1990s, over 20 years after the US retreat, Vietnam War films are a fading phenomenon. One of the few more recent releases was *Between Heaven and Earth* (1993), the last of Oliver Stone's trilogy, in which he bravely put himself into the skin of a Vietnamese peasant family. This intimate account of village relationships and hardships spanned an ambitious historical sweep of 40 years.

Home produce The Vietnamese themselves have been churning out productions since 1948, when Ho Chi Minh's Viet Minh started making propaganda films. Until the 1980s, government-controlled domestic cinema was solely concerned with films of combat and 'liberation', stirring the

patriotic spirit with titles such as *Deserted Field*, *The Great Victory of 1975* or *Fairy-Tale for a 17-Year-Old*, all made with antiquated technology. However, by 1992 *doi moi* (open-door policy) had led to deregulation and the mushrooming of independent film production companies, all after the 15–22-year-old audience (70 per cent of cinema admissions). Kung Fu and melodramatic romances imitating those of Bollywood (Bombay's 'Hollywood') dominate production, attracting only these young audiences and so creating yet another generation gap. Censorship remains omnipresent, prohibiting violence, sex and subversive content (a nebulous category).

After Tran Anh Hung shot *Cyclo* (1995), a surrealistic Franco-Vietnamese co-production portraying corruption, prostitution, protection rackets and gangsters in contemporary Saigon, he was banned from returning to his country and now works in France. His first, much-acclaimed film, *L'Odeur de la Papaye Verte* (1993), was shot entirely in French studios due to the unhelpfulness of the Vietnamese authorities. This was not surprising, as the film centred on the household of a bourgeois Saigon family in the 1950s, depicting in minute and sensitive detail the feudal customs that still prevailed. The world may have to wait a little longer to see home-made Vietnamese perspectives on screen.

Apocalypse Now *(top)*, Catherine Deneuve *in* Indochine*, Adam Baldwin* in Full Metal Jacket *and (bottom) Charlie Sheen in* Platoon

HO CHI MINH CITY (SAIGON)

Ho Chi Minh City may be Vietnam's most westernised city, but pigs still mean pork for supper

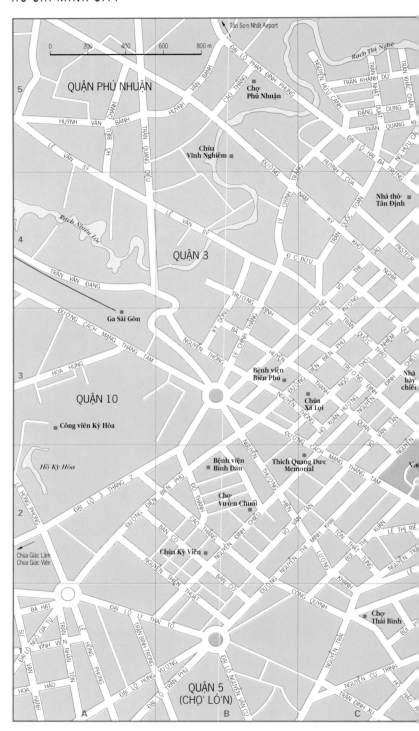

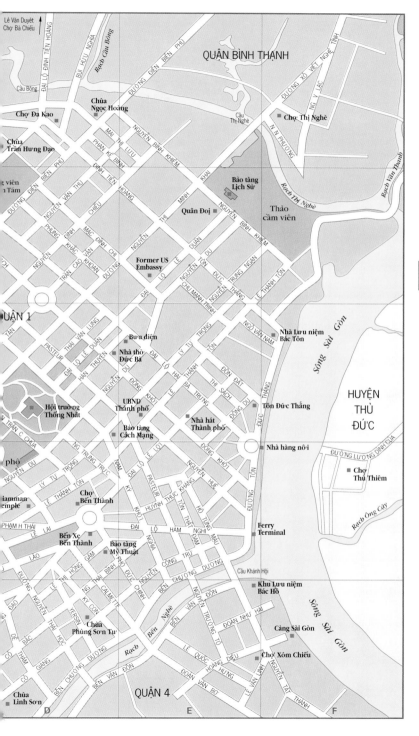

HO CHI MINH CITY

Pham Ngu Lao, Ho Chi Minh City's backpackers' hub

Ho Chi Minh City Insolent, brash, free-wheeling and fast-paced, Ho Chi Minh City has more recently been called Vietnam's Los Angeles in contrast to the century-old label of Saigon as the Paris of the East. Yet the two are not incompatible: enterprising dynamism coexists with a relaxed café society; soaring postmodern blocks rub shoulders with graceful colonial mansions and monuments; and daytime commerce gives way to a frenetic nightlife that is spiked by drugs and prostitution. Despite these socio-cultural imports, Ho Chi Minh City remains resolutely Vietnamese – the cyclos and noodle-soup stands spell this out, while corruption flourishes less visibly in the wings.

Saigon Less entrenched in tradition and more cosmopolitan than Hanoi, Ho Chi Minh City sets its sights forwards and outwards. This is partly due to the fact that as a port it has always been open to outside influences, and pre-18th century was part of the Khmer Kingdom. The French arrived 150 years later and Saigon became the capital of Cochinchina, the only French Indochinese possession to achieve colony status as opposed to being a protectorate.

For over 50 years Saigon revelled in a decadent *belle époque*, while the French administrators set about clearing filthy canals, planting trees along wide avenues leading to the river, and building docks, warehouses, official mansions and elegant private villas. Meanwhile, Chinese immigrants had established themselves in Cho Lon, where brothels, secret societies and opium dens flourished, a seedier tradition that the government still has not managed to erase. And nor has the old name of Saigon been eradicated, except in the realms of officialdom.

District layout Business, cultural and tourist life is concentrated in the central District 1, bordering the Saigon River, while the adjoining District 3, more residential and with some fine old villas and gardens, follows a close second. To the far west lies District 5, the Chinese quarter of Cho Lon (see pages 182–5), while south of the canals are the less prosperous and often decidedly impoverished Districts 4 and 8. Most short-term visitors will rarely emerge from Districts 1, 3 and 5.

Colonial style Relics of the colonial period abound in the centre, from the pretentious red-brick **Notre Dame Cathedral (Nha tho Duc Ba)**, dated 1880, to the far more imaginative **Central Post Office (Buu Dien)►**, just across the street, built in an eclectic style in 1891 with an iron and glass ceiling designed by Gustave Eiffel Looming over the city's central commercial crossroads is the **Ben Thanh Market**, a domed 1914 edifice Saigon's architectural symbol remains its **Hôtel de Ville►**, a town hall lifted

The Gallic curves of the Central Post Office

...traight out of the French provinces, and which dominates the main crossroads of Le Loi and Nguyen Hue boulevards. Immaculately restored, its pristine façade gazes down on a small park where food-vendors, shoe-shiners and motorbike taxis all tout for customers.

Vying in structural splendour with the Hôtel de Ville is the **Municipal Theatre▶**, located 100m to the east. It was inaugurated in 1900 and put on inimitably Parisian shows for an expatriate population of only 3,000, later becoming the seat of the South Vietnamese National Assembly. From here, lively **Dong Khoi▶▶** leads down to the river. Flanking the theatre are the historic Continental and Caravelle hotels, with the Rex situated beside the Hôtel de Ville. This, too, is where weekend evening cruising revolves, when the entire population of Saigon seems to adopt two wheels and hits the town.

Outdoor life Ho Chi Minh City lives outdoors, except when tropical downpours are in progress. Much of its attraction lies in exploring the backstreets, stumbling across a pagoda, weaving through a market, sampling the food at a roadside stall or simply soaking up the atmosphere on a café-terrace. Taxis, cyclos and motorbike taxis are at the ready, but if you plan to explore on foot you must first learn how to cross a traffic-choked road: walk, weave, but do not stop. To escape this cacophonous nightmare, negotiate a boat-trip from the wharf at the base of Ham Nghi Boulevard, best undertaken towards late afternoon.

Saigontourist offices
For years Saigontourist monopolised Ho Chi Minh City's tourist infrastructure. Today, numerous private tour agencies have jumped on the bandwagon, making prices more competitive and offering a wider variety of tours. In response, in 1996 Saigontourist opened up a 'backpackers' branch, where staff are more helpful and prices more reasonable than at the central office. (See page 238 for addresses of private agencies, which also operate tourist buses throughout the country.)
● Saigontourist, 49 Le Thanh Ton (tel: 08 829 5834; fax: 08 822 4987).
● Saigontourist, 187 Pham Ngu Lao (tel: 08 835 4535; fax: 08 835 4533).

HO CHI MINH CITY

Desperate Diem
The man who fashioned the Reunification Palace, Jean Baptiste Ngo Dinh Diem, was a 53-year-old Catholic mystic when he returned from exile to become the US-backed prime minister of South Vietnam in 1954. On gaining a suspicious 98 per cent support in a referendum, Diem deposed the absent Emperor Bao Dai and named himself President of the Republic of Vietnam. For the next eight years until his assassination, he lived in a state of permanent paranoia, his only trusted cronies being his despotic brother, Ngo Dinh Nhu, and sister-in-law, Madame Nhu (see panel opposite).

History lies in wait beside the Botanic Gardens

Museums

▶ Art Museum (Bao tang My Thuat) 171D2
97A Pho Duc Chinh, District 1
Open: Tue–Sun 7.30–4.30. Admission: free.
This light, spacious colonial building, with an exceptional antiquated lift, is a meeting point for Ho Chi Minh City's artists, who exhibit at a small gallery opening on to the garden. On the first floor, a variable collection of contemporary art includes lacquerwork, woodcuts, carved wood panels and numerous depictions of the Vietnam War. The second floor displays a more inspiring collection of antiques, including Buddhist statuary (above all a very beautiful gilded statue of Quan Am, the Goddess of Mercy), porcelain, carved architectural fragments, inlaid boxes and hardwood furniture.

▶▶ History Museum (Bao tang Lich Su) 171E4
2 Nguyen Binh Khiem, District 1
Open: Tue–Sun 8–11.30, 1–4.30. Admission charge: moderate.
This attractive pagoda-style museum was built by the French in 1929 at the entrance to the Botanic Gardens and Zoo. Exhibits displayed in rooms ranged around central garden courtyards offer good coverage of early Vietnamese history, namely Stone Age tools, Dong Son bronze drums, artefacts from Oc Eo (including an extraordinarily pure wooden *c.* 5th-century Buddha over 3m high, some fine gold jewellery, and a Roman coin dated AD 180 which proved Funan's extensive trading links), and finally Cham and Khmer sculptures. Vietnamese dynastic history takes over with ceramics, incense-burners, imperial robes and accessories, inlaid furniture and models of historical battles. A further room is devoted to minority cultures and, opposite the main entrance, a hall displays Buddhist statuary from all over Asia.

Outside, the **Botanic Gardens (Thao cam vien)**▶ are reasonably well maintained but the Zoo is decidedly neglected. The garden was created in 1864 to bring new crops – such as sugar cane, indigo and cotton – to Vietnam, but suffered from a long period of neglect during the war years.

▶▶ Ho Chi Minh Museum (Khu Luu niem Bac Ho) 171E1
1 Nguyen Tat Thanh, District 4
Open: 7.30–11.30, 1.30–4.30. Admission charge: cheap
Housed in the shuttered, colonnaded old French customs house, this museum has the added attraction of manicured gardens and an outdoor café with strategic river views. The museum itself gives a fascinating outline of Uncle Ho's life. The chronological display enters into endless details (with English captions) which are often very telling, juxtaposing memorabilia with photographs, models and documents (some of these are originals, such as handwritten letters from Ho to American friends and typewritten reports by the French secret service on his activities). Uncle Ho's rubber-tyre sandals, pith helmet, cane, bush-jacket and portable Hermes typewriter are all included.

►►► Reunification Palace
(Hoi truong Thong Nhat) *171D3*

Nam Ky Khoi Nghia, District 1
Open: daily 7.30–10.30, 1–4. Admission charge: expensive. Guided tour.

This less-than-impressive example of Vietnamese 1960s architecture has enormous historical significance. It was by crashing through these gates that a North Vietnamese tank put the final seal on the South Vietnamese regime on 30 April 1975. Earlier on, the site was occupied by a palatial 1873 edifice, the seat of Indochina's governor-general, but in February 1962 an attempted *coup d'état* by two of South Vietnam's top pilots bombed most of it into ruins. President Diem survived the *coup*, but a new palace had to be built, this time with 95 rooms.

What visitors see today is a place where the clock stopped in 1975. Although occasionally used for top-level functions, it remains a remarkable time capsule of the 1960s and represents a true reflection of the self-aggrandisement and hypocrisy of South Vietnam's rulers. English-speaking guides troop visitors around vast, richly draped halls packed with antiques, hand-made carpets and modern Vietnamese craftwork, and along marble-clad corridors dripping with chandeliers to end at the third-floor casino and helipad. From here, stairs descend directly to the basement operations centre, an underground labyrinth crammed with military maps, transmitters, the president's emergency bedroom and extensive bomb-proof tunnels. A recent addition to the palace is a music room for demonstrations of traditional instruments, while another option is a crackly old French television documentary about the 1945–75 war period. Outside in the garden stands one of the 30 April tanks in verdant glory.

Madame Nhu

The sister-in-law of South Vietnam's President Diem was the insidious 'power behind the throne', revelling in her Parisian-style opulence at Saigon's Reunification Palace and repeatedly pronouncing Vietnamese versions of 'let them eat cake' (Marie Antoinette's infamous words as the revolutionary hordes descended on Versailles). In an attempt to be remembered in a more positive light, Madame Nhu had a statue of the heroic Trung sisters (see page 96) erected on Saigon's riverfront with Trung Trac's face mysteriously resembling her own. In 1963, after the assassination of Diem and his brother Nhu, the statue was torn down. However, the wily Madame Nhu, already out of the country, escaped sharing their fate and today continues to eat *pâtisseries* in her French Riviera home.

175

Reunification Palace

Street-names

Since French colonial times, Saigon's street-names have been 'Vietnamised', a process that evolved yet again in 1975 with the expurgation of non-politically correct names. Louis Pasteur, the French chemist and father of bacteriology, is an exception, although his name was removed for a time in the years before *doi moi* (open-door policy). Thus, for a while Duong Pasteur, a major axis in District 1 and 3, became Nguyen Thi Minh Khai in honour of a woman martyr executed by a French firing squad in 1941. For readers of pre-Independence literature, the following transformations may be relevant: rue Catinat, now Dong Khoi; Boulevard Charner, now Nguyen Hue; Boulevard Bonnard, now Le Loi; Boulevard de la Somme, now Ham Nghi; and Quai de la Marne, now Ben Van Don.

Food sign at Ben Thanh Market

► ### Revolutionary Museum (Bao tang Cach Mang) *171D3*

65 Ly Tu trong, District 1
Open: Tue–Sun 8–11.30, 2–4.30. Admission charge: cheap.

One of Saigon's most striking stuccoed colonial mansions, originally designed in 1885 for trade exhibitions but subsequently used as the governor-general's residence, now illustrates Viet Minh and Viet Cong struggles. The ground floor shows photos, maps and statues relating the resistance against the French, but all captions are in Vietnamese only. At the back is a music room where students perform fascinating instrumental demonstrations every afternoon. Up the sweeping *grand escalier* are exhibits covering the Vietnam War, including a cross-section of the Cu Chi tunnels, numerous weapons, field equipment, photos and documents. The lovely garden packs in a South Vietnamese Air Force fighter jet, a Huey and an A37 Cessna.

► ### Thich Quang Duc Memorial *171C2*

Corner of Nguyen Dinh Chieu and Cach Mang Thang 8, District 3

A visit to this modest memorial is a pure act of homage to the Buddhist monk Thich Quang Duc, who in June 1963 set off a spate of self-immolations in Vietnam when he publicly set fire to himself (see panel opposite). This corner is where he sat in meditation, the little grey Austin in which he had driven from Hue parked a short distance away. Photos of the heroic act shocked the world, drawing attention to Diem's arbitrary persecutions of Buddhists. Madame Nhu, Diem's infamous sister-in-law, referred to the monk's action as a 'barbecue'.

► ### US Embassy (Former) *171E4*

Corner of Le Duan and Mac Dinh Chi, District 1

Half-way between the History Museum and Reunification Palace stands a seven-storey concrete stronghold with rooftop helipad that was once the US Embassy. After the original embassy was bombed in 1967, this heavily guarded bunker became the think-tank centre for plotting war operations. What could ironically be called its finest hour came in the last days of April 1975, when the North Vietnamese Army was rolling into Saigon. Thousands of panicking Vietnamese attempted to fight their way in to join the desperately retreating Americans, who were being shuttled by helicopter to aircraft-carriers at sea. Finally, at dawn on 30 April, the US ambassador carried his nation's flag into a helicopter and took off. Since then the embassy has remained closed, although it may reopen again as a consulate.

►►► ### War Remnants Museum (Nha trung bay toi ac chien tranh) *170C3*

28 Vo Van Tan, District 3
Open: daily 7.30–11.45, 1.30–4.45. Admission charge: expensive.

Wherever one's sympathies lie, this museum is an eye-opener on both the atrocities of war and on the manipulative language of propaganda, and as such inspires powerful sentiments. Beyond the courtyard bazaar (selling anything remotely military in spirit) lies a display that some visitors may find uncomfortable, so be warned. Fronting the exhibition halls are rusting war trophies that include fighter jets, tanks, artillery, howitzers and bombshells, a fitting introduction to the display of photographs, diagrams, maps, objects and information panels that are found inside.

Although the museum's name has now been changed from its original 'Museum of American War Crimes', the essential focus remains on atrocities committed by US forces and their South Vietnamese allies. Captions (in Vietnamese, English and Chinese) spell out the official attitude, accompanying graphically horrifying photos of destruction, torture (including paintings of barbaric treatments carried out at Con Son Prison), massacre (with much emphasis put on the horrors that took place at My Lai in March 1968 – see page 162), and the victims of napalm and white-phosphorous bombs. Many of the photos were taken by international press photographers, yet another unique aspect of the Vietnam War which has had repercussions in subsequent wars. A small section shows photos of American peace demonstrations.

One entire room is devoted to the environmental ravages wrought by defoliants such as Agent Orange (see page 204), backed up by detailed statistics, and another, the Hostile Forces Room, recounts the backgrounds, actions and fates of reactionary forces in the South post-1975 – a thinly disguised warning? Two more rooms are filled with weapons used by both sides. Outside, at the back, there is a replica 'tiger cage', the pigsty-style prison cell used on Con Son Island (see page 203).

Buddhist crisis
The Buddhist crisis was inspired by another of President Diem's *faux pas*, when he banned the flying of the Buddhist flag to celebrate Buddha's birthday, a major festival. The edict, issued in 1963, stimulated a protest in Hue that saw nine people killed by the Civil Guard. This, plus nine years of discrimination by the Catholic-led government, was the final straw. On the morning of 11 June 1963, a 73-year-old monk by the name of Quang Duc seated himself in the lotus position of meditation at a crossroads just a few blocks from the US ambassador's residence. Another monk poured a jerrycan of petrol over him, then Quang Duc lit the fatal match.

177

The Vietnam War is long over but no one is allowed to forget

Pagodas

For pagodas in Cho Lon, see pages 182–5.

▶▶▶ Giac Lam Pagoda (Chua Giac Lam)   170A2

118 Lac Long Quan, Tan Binh

Although situated out on a limb north-west of Cho Lon, this pagoda should not be missed as it is arguably Saigon's finest and certainly the oldest. It was built in 1744 and has been twice restored since (most recently in 1906), but still exudes architectural and decorative harmony. The obligatory Quan Am statue stands outside in the partly cultivated garden near some elaborate tombs with Chinese inscriptions. Inside, 98 pillars and 113 statues emerge from the atmospheric gloom of a hardwood hall lined with rows of ancestral tablets, the only anomaly being the plastic cloths on the monks' refectory tables. In the main altar room stands a 'tree of wandering souls', as well as tiny Bodhisattvas and a vast pantheon of Buddhist statues.

▶▶ Giac Vien Pagoda (Chua Giac Vien)   171A2

247 Lac Long Quan, District 11

Slightly closer to Cho Lon and very similar in style to Giac Lam is this lavish pagoda. Dating from 1805 and rebuilt in 1899, it is located down an unsurfaced rural lane near Dam Sen Lake (Khu du lich Dam Sen). The grounds are used by the monks as a vegetable garden and bonsai and plant nursery. The pagoda itself unfolds behind an army of potted plants and numerous carved dragon-heads into a succession of halls that are punctuated by solid teak pillars, funeral tablets and over 150 expressive statues. Right at the back is the main, stepped altar with a gilded A Di Da (Buddha of the Past), backing up an intense crowd of statues. Here, too, is a striking 'tree of wandering souls'. Monks and nuns are friendly and will identify the statues.

Above: a Buddhist monk lights incense at the Giac Lam Pagoda, the oldest in Ho Chi Minh City
Right: a host of smiling Buddhas and arhat at the Giac Vien Pagoda

▶▶▶ Jade Emperor's Pagoda (Chua Ngoc Hoang)   171D5

73 Mai Thi Luu, Da Kao, District 1

This theatrical 1909 pagoda, built by Saigon's Cantonese community, successfully unites most of the Buddhist and Taoist iconography – no mean feat. A paved courtyard with turtle-pond, shaded by a generous banyan tree and fragrant frangipanis, fronts the pink-washed building. It is dedicated to the Taoist Jade Emperor, Ngoc Hoang, whose draped statue presides over the inner sanctuary, flanked by his four Guardians of the Great Diamonds and watching over six Taoist gods. At the back on the right is the 18-armed Mother of the Five Buddhas of the North, South, East, West and Centre, and on the left is the sword-grasping Ong Bac De, reincarnation of the Jade Emperor.

Leading off this hall is a side room filled with wood panels that represent the 1,000 torments of hell and, adjoining this, a room dominated by Thanh Hoang, the Ruler of Hell, and his red horse. Equally fascinating are the rows of 12 ceramic female figures surrounded by children, each symbolising a Chinese lunar year and a vice or virtue.

The Taoist supreme god, the Jade Emperor, is a key figure in Vietnamese worship

► Le Van Duyet Temple (Den Le Van Duyet)

171D5

126 Dinh Tien Hoang, Binh Thanh District

The temple and tomb of Marshal Le Van Duyet (1763–1831) and his wife is another of Ho Chi Minh City's bizarre monuments, hardly aesthetic but a much-visited memorial to a national hero. It stands at a major cross-roads north of the centre on the site of the old citadel, and can be combined with a visit to the nearby Ba Chieu Market. Extensively renovated in 1937, although much neglected since, the interior harbours an extraordinary hotchpotch of personal memorabilia: crystal goblets stand alongside a stuffed tiger, carved elephants and weaponry. Pilgrims throng here on the 30th day of the seventh lunar month (August) and during Tet.

► Phung Son Tu Pagoda (Chua Phung Son Tu)

171D1

338 Nguyen Cong Tru, District 1

Not one of Saigon's oldest pagodas, but nevertheless conveniently sited in the centre, Phung Son Tu is very much a Chinese temple and was built in the 1940s by the Fujian community. Its modern brick exterior frames original main doors, these beautifully painted with warrior images. Ong Bon (Guardian Spirit of Happiness and Virtue) dominates the main altar, while numerous incense urns and spirals testify to the pagoda's popularity.

Alternative worship

Buddhism and Taoism are not the only religions catered for in Ho Chi Minh City. Hindus (most of whom are ethnic Chinese) have their own temple, the recently restored Mariamman, at 45 Truong Dinh (a few blocks away from Ben Thanh Market). Islam has its own rather elaborate mosque on Dong Du, just off Dong Khoi, built in 1935 by a wealthy Muslim. It is frequented by a mixture of Indians, Chams and Vietnamese. Christians have several churches to choose from, the most frequently visited being Notre Dame. More appealing and modest in scale is the Tan Dinh Church at the northern end of Hai Ba Trung.

■ **Joyous, exuberant and noisy, Tet is Vietnam's biggest calendar event and brings with it three days of non-stop revelry. Firework displays, concerts, street theatre and endless partying welcome in the new lunar year – whatever its zodiac symbolism. ■**

Cosmic trees

One week before Tet, bizarrely decorated bamboo canes start appearing. These are *neu*, whose odd appendages are intended to chase away evil spirits. A bunch of pineapple leaves, cocks' feathers, a handful of red paper and a lantern are all attached to a bamboo stick complete with sprouting leaves, which is then planted in the ground. Buddhist legend has it that this will intimidate the devil, but *neu* is thought to be a tradition that existed long before among Southeast Asia's animist societies. Some of Vietnam's ethnic minorities practise the same tradition, hanging up fake drums (representing thunder), animal sculptures, strips of red silk (symbolising the sap of life) and cocks' feathers (a call to the sun).

Tet commerce

The Vietnamese may spend several months' salary on imported food and drink for Tet, but in 1995 a new outlet found a way to reverse the season's trade and announce the coming Year of the Rat. A nursery garden in Ben Tre province shipped over a thousand ornamental rats fashioned out of bonsai trees to Singapore.

Although firecrackers were banned in 1994 because of the countless accidents they cause, the Vietnamese, with their outstanding knack for improvisation, have circumvented this and now throng the streets armed with cassette-players instead – any noise will do so long as the decibels are in keeping with the joys of Tet. Today's manic celebrations are a far cry from the first historical description, when 'Young men and women observed the rules of Buddhist abstinence and made incense and flower offerings to Buddha. People played with balloons, sang and danced…' (from an 11th-century Chinese text by Cao Hung Trung). Nor do any of today's activities reflect another less happy connotation of Tet, the 1968 Tet Offensive, which spelled the turning-point in the Vietnam War (see opposite).

Traditions Tet really starts a week before New Year when absent family members start the journey home, as this is the one time in the year when everybody should be reunited. Buses and trains are swamped and hotels taken by storm. This period also marks the departure of the Tao, or household god, who takes off to report back to the Jade Emperor on the past year's goings-on. Traditionally, each home erects a small altar for the Tao, laden with suitable offerings (including a live carp for his celestial transport) and aimed at culling his favours. Trips are then made to the cemetery to invite the spirits of dead relatives home, *neu* (bamboo mast offerings – see panel) are erected, and houses are thoroughly cleaned and filled with flowers.

One tradition that is alive and kicking is that of the dwarf mandarin tree, the Vietnamese equivalent of the Christmas tree, which joins sprays of peach or apricot blossom (North and South respectively). Shopping continues in local markets at stalls laden with rare festive goods: Russian caviar and champagne, Bulgarian wine, Scotch whisky, French brandy and cheeses. Prices soar, but this is Tet after all.

Midnight A few hours before midnight, ceremonial offerings are made at domestic ancestral altars, filial piety being a cornerstone of family life. As midnight strikes and the old year becomes the new, fireworks light up the skies and family banquets are consumed. A knock on the door at 1am announces the guest of honour, a respectable and, if possible, prosperous and influential citizen who will determine the family's luck for the following year.

After this, it is time to visit the pagoda. By now the city streets are packed with family motor bikes, and the pagodas filled with worshippers and clouded with

Tet

Tet in Ho Chi Minh City lasts a whole week, and sees dragon-dances on the streets of Cho Lon and spectators dressed to kill

sphyxiatingly thick incense smoke – to he extent that some pagoda attenants don diver's goggles. Parks, iscos, restaurants and bars are the ll-night venues, while street photographers with specially painted backrops depicting mythical creatures do roaring trade. Cho Lon sees dragonances, fire-eaters and street heatre, while music – both rock and raditional – takes to every street of ietnam. In Hanoi celebrations last three days, while in Ho Chi Minh City they go on for an entire week.

he offensive In contrast, the Tet Offensive of January 968 left little to celebrate. An estimated 35,000 troops on oth sides were killed, and an even greater number of ivilians died in the weeks that followed. This impressively hasterminded attack started a week before Tet with a hajor offensive at Khe Sanh. Then, on the evening of 1 January, while the entire country was involved in its raditional celebrations and firecrackers were exploding, he North Vietnamese forces launched a simultaneous ttack on over a hundred towns. Saigon was included in his, and a Viet Cong commando team even took over the JS Embassy and held it for six hours.

Although the offensive did not attain its target of a popuar and generalised uprising, and Viet Cong control lasted nly a few days in most towns, it nevertheless succeeded h dealing the final blow to American public opinion. From hen on, the US government was fighting a losing battle.

Chinese/Vietnamese zodiac
Each lunar year, represented by an animal, is part of a 12-year cycle. The coming cycle is: Buffalo (1997), Tiger (1998), Cat (1999), Dragon (2000), Snake (2001), Horse (2002), Goat (2003), Monkey (2004), Rooster (2005), Dog (2006), Pig (2007), Rat (2008).

To calculate the animal that governs your life, take your birth year and add a multiple of 12 to arrive at one of the above totals – for example, 1960 + 48 = 2008, so someone born in 1960 is of the Year of the Rat.

182

An elephant's rescue
A strange tale is associated with the Phung Son Pagoda, located a short distance north-west of Cho Lon at the end of Hung Vuong. It was built in the early 19th century on the site of Khmer temples which, in turn, covered ancient structures from the Oc Eo civilisation. It was perhaps because of these historical antecedents that an attempt to move the pagoda failed dramatically. After the temple contents were loaded on to an elephant, the animal slipped, letting its priceless burden tumble into the pond. As a result, the pagoda stayed put. Today, with its large garden peopled by glistening new statues of Buddha and Quan Am, the pagoda attracts a motley local crowd who sleep, chat or play checkers on the steps.

Lavish decoration at Nghia An Hoi Quan

Cho Lon

Some 4km west of central Ho Chi Minh City is the no less enterprising and buzzing Chinese quarter of Cho Lon. Its name (meaning 'Big Market') once denoted a separate settlement, but Cho Lon has now been engulfed in Saigon's urban spread to form District 5. Pre-1975, it had a population of 1 million, the majority of whom were of Chinese origin (the Hoa), but this number has since halved despite a considerable influx of North Vietnamese immigrants. Much of its Chinese charm still lingers, however, in the form of ideograms, street markets, old men with wispy beards playing mah-jong, numerous glitteringly decorated pagodas and the stuccoed early 20th-century shophouses that line the main roads.

Bordering Cho Lon to the south is the dirty Ben Nghe Canal, edged by warehouses and decrepit stilt-houses. Although a boat-ride back to the city centre can be arranged here, care should be taken in this rougher and visibly poorer area. Two main boulevards – Tran Hung Dao and Hung Vuong – connect Cho Lon with central Ho Chi Minh City. When one of Cho Lon's numerous festivals is in progress, incorporating dragon-dances and processions, traffic along these routes comes to a standstill.

▶ Binh Tay Market (Cho Binh Tay) 184A1
Hau Giang
This bustling, two-storey market building, in the far west of Cho Lon, revolves around a central courtyard, with market-stalls spilling out into the muddy backstreets. Huge stone water jars, basketware, plastic goods from China, aluminium containers, caged birds, elbow-length gloves (worn by Ho Chi Minh City's motorcycling beauties) and endless fresh produce (which arrives straight from the Mekong Delta by canal) is piled up in impressive quantities. Vendors mainly ignore tourists, so it makes for a stress-free wander, but be wary of pickpockets.

▶▶ Minh Huong Gia Thanh Pagoda (Chua Minh Huong Gia Thanh) 184B1
380 Tran Hung Dao
This rare Confucian temple dates from the 19th century but was rebuilt in 1901. Only 25 of the Ming families that once practised ancestral worship here remain, descendants of those who left China for Vietnam in the 1820s–40s. As a result, the pagoda has a neglected feel but the roof displays impressive tile- and ceramic-work and the interior has some beautiful inlaid furniture, including a dragon-backed chair destined for the king, brass-headed spears and three superb portraits of the founders. Three altars are dedicated to the Ming Dynasty, while a separate hall on the left honours the Goddess of Fertility. The pagoda's guardian, whose job is hereditary, loves practising his French on visitors.

▶ Nghia An Community Hall (Nghia An Hoi Quan) 184B1
678 Nguyen Trai
This community hall is dedicated to General Ong Quan Cong of the Three Empires, whose stern countenance

*Another stopover on
Cho Lon's temple tour*

dominates the altar. He is flanked by his assistants, the civil and military mandarins and, to the right, by Thien Hao, Goddess of the Sea. At the entrance is an enormous statue of Quan Cong's red horse and groom with, on the opposite side, a statue of a rod-carrying Ong Bon, the Spirit of Luck and guardian of the temple. There is some impressive gilded woodwork, but the pagoda has been heavily restored over the years. The huge courtyard in front is used for theatre performances.

▶▶ Phuoc An Community Hall (Phuoc An Hoi Quan) 184B1
184 Hung Vuong

Behind its modernised façade and tacky rock garden topped by a laughing Buddha lies an intimate, atmospheric community hall full of remarkably carved wood panels, beautiful inlaid mahogany furniture and antique cult objects. The hall was built in 1902 by the Fujian congregation and has preserved most of its original decoration, with the odd addition of some aquariums and a more obvious cluster of incense spirals. The superb brass-headed spears fronting the altar are weapons for entering the world of the immortals, while behind the altar is a statue of Quan Cong, to whom the temple is dedicated.

▶ Quan Am Pagoda (Chua Quan Am) 184B1
12 Lao Tu

Stone dragons guard the beautiful old lacquered doors of this much-frequented pagoda, founded in 1816 by the Fujian community though extensively renovated since. The roof decoration is a delight: a riot of ceramic figures, boats, houses and mythical creatures relating traditional Chinese legends. Inside, three elaborate central altars wink with fairy lights, while incense coils cloud the air. A gilded statue of A-Pho, the Holy Mother, stands behind the main altar, while another representation of her presides over the altar at the back.

A pantomime set
'In Cho Lon you were in a different city where work seemed to be just beginning rather than petering out with the daylight. It was like driving into a pantomime set: the long vertical Chinese signs and the bright lights and the crowd of extras led you into the wings, where everything was suddenly so much darker and quieter.'
From *The Quiet American* by Graham Greene (1955).

*Rival headgear at the
Thien Hao Pagoda*

► **Tam Son Hoi Quan (Chua Ba Chua)** *184B*

118 Trieu Quang Phuc

Dedicated to the Goddess of Fertility, Me Sanh, this Fujia
pagoda attracts a flow of childless women who mak‹
offerings in front of an ornate showcase where th‹
goddess sits beside her daughters. In front, the centr‹
covered courtyard is squeezed between recent concret
extensions housing numerous shrines and a room full c
urns of ashes and photos of the dead. On the righ
stands the ferocious Quan Cong, flanked by his mandarin
and red horse.

►► **Thien Hao Pagoda (Chua Pho Mieu)** *184B*

710 Nguyen Trai

The inner courtyard of this large pagoda gives a fabulou‹
close-up on its most outstanding feature: the intricat‹
ceramic bas-relief that faces the roofline. Built in the earl

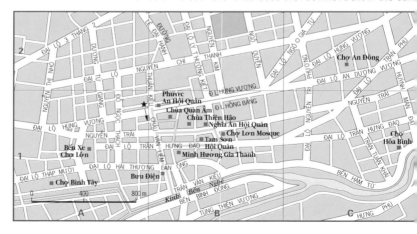

1800s by local Cantonese, it is dedicated to the Goddess of the Sea, Thien Hao; three statues of the goddess flanked by guardians stand on the main altar, with her bed on the left and a scaled-down boat on the right. She became the object of particularly fervent worship in the late 1970s when throngs of aspiring boat-people came to pray before escaping. Gratitude from overseas survivors is evident in the pagoda's high levels of maintenance and renovation.

Walk Cho Lon

See map opposite.

This short circuit meanders through the heart of Cho Lon, taking in the main pagodas and typical roadside sights and aromas. It takes about half an hour to cover the ground, but you should allow longer if you wish to explore the pagodas.

Start by visiting the **Phuoc An Hoi Quan** on Hung Vuong. From here, cross the boulevard to Chau Van Liem and take the next street on your left, Lao Tu; there is an excellent Chinese restaurant on the corner (Com Ga Vinh). The street is packed with little cafés, and incense- and bird-vendors soon announce the **Quan Am Pagoda**. At the end of the street turn right, then take the first left into Nguyen Trai. Both the **Thien Hao Pagoda** and the **Nghia An Hoi Quan** are located on the left-hand side.

From here, cross to the Cho Lon Mosque, which stands beside a small food market (Cho Xa Tay), and walk down the side lane. Food-stalls alternate with *pho* kitchens before the lane reaches Tran Hung Dao. Facing you is a good example of some partly restored colonial shophouses, with wrought-iron balconies, decorative columns and French wooden shutters.

Turn right along Tran Hung Dao past tailors' shops and opticians (where, if necessary, spectacles can be made up in under 30 minutes), before making a short detour to the **Tam Son Hoi Quan** on Trieu Quang Phuc; ornate cakes, Chinese scissors and some restaurants lead you there. Tran Hung Dao continues, with an imposing colonial building on the left

(now a police station), to **Minh Huong Gia Thanh Pagoda**.

From here, take the next right on to Luong Nhu Hoc, where embroiderers and banner-makers are concentrated, and which brings you back to Nguyen Trai. Turn left past a row of sandal shops and an ageing rubber-stamp and seal maker at No 787, before returning to the Chau Van Liem crossroads. You can now choose between turning right for sustenance at the restaurant mentioned above (Com Ga Vinh), or turning left towards the ornate post office (Buu Dien) and walking down to the canal.

185

Plants, birdcages and laundry among Cho Lon's peeling façades

■ **Love of music has always been deeply ingrained in the Vietnamese soul, but before *doi moi* (open-door policy) traditional tunes and sentimental love songs were regarded as reactionary and had to be performed on the quiet. Today, Vietnam resounds again to harmonies that range from bamboo xylophones and monochord lutes to home-grown hard rock.** ■

North–South vocals

The complex tonal inflections of the melodious Vietnamese language make for an easy transition from poetry to a wide repertoire of songs. Varying in mood from North to South, their lyrics are often expressions of simple emotions, nature, village or family life, or the seasons. Northern songs, not surprisingly, often express patriotism, developed against continual invasions over the centuries, but also more melancholic moods revolving around absent or dead family and friends. In the Centre, Hue's rowing songs express a love of river landscapes and an admiration for local heroes (see panel on page 102). Satirical and joking songs are more widespread in the South, while drinking and card-playing songs are universally reserved for men.

Bamboo creates an astounding range of sounds

More than any other source of music, the most commonly encountered throughout Vietnam is that of the ice-cream man. Suddenly, in the middle of nowhere, melodious strains waft through the air and from around the corner comes a man on his bike, speaker bound to the handlebars, car battery strung to the crossbar and an ice-box on the back. This is just another indication of how much the Vietnamese are drawn to music, above all to syrupy popular melodies, love songs and even funeral dirges. More sophisticated classical music is played by 40-piece orchestras (*Hat A Dao* in the North and *Ca Hue* in the South), while *Cheo* (popular opera) synthesises folk-songs, dances and narration. However, this youthful nation is also into rock 'n' roll in a big way, despite attempts by the authorities to suppress such 'infectious cultural germs', and Vietnamese rock groups are ever increasing in number.

Heavy-metal history 'The history of Vietnam is truly rock 'n' roll, synonymous with war and with human dramas' announces Tran Quang Thang, vocalist with the Saigon band Atomega. After his father died in a post-1975 re-education camp, Thang, like thousands of other children, spent years sleeping rough. His lyrics reflect Vietnam's tragic ambiguity: the enormous fracture between rampant capitalism and the hard reality of life on the streets. Most Vietnamese bands in Saigon and Hanoi sing in Vietnamese, as in this way they can communicate their existential anguish directly to the hordes of teenagers who fill nightclubs and pubs when ephemeral concerts are staged.

The classics Traditional music continues a style that arrived with the Chinese in the 2nd century, along with archery, horse-riding, literature and calculus. Every self-respecting poet, philosopher or painter played an instrument in order to strengthen his life force and longevity: music was held to have a magical influence on both body and soul.

The five classical instruments are the *nhi*, a type of two-stringed lute played

Regained confidence in national identity is stimulating the next generation

vertically on the knees; the *dan tranh*, a 1m-long zither with 16 strings raised on bridges (while plucking with one hand, the musician uses the other to regulate pitch and vibrations); the *dan nguyet* or *kim*, a two-stringed long-necked type of guitar; the *ty ba*, a pear-shaped four-stringed lute; and, finally, the *dan tam*, a three-stringed banjo. These were used to create the ceremonial court music of Hue that accompanied imperial anniversaries or deaths, formal audiences and royal banquets, but this disappeared with Bao Dai, the last emperor, in 1945. Today, however, the instruments have made a radical comeback.

Enterprising sounds Apart from these five instruments, known as the five 'perfects', there are numerous indigenous instruments. The passion-inspiring *dan bau* is a monochordal lute whose tone is altered by twisting a flexible projecting plate (said by musicians to produce a range as complex as the Vietnamese language, and that is saying something), while the *sao truc* is a bamboo transverse flute. *Sao truc* made of terracotta have been unearthed in ancient burial sites, proving the instrument's long history, and numerous variations are found among the ethnic minorities of the highlands, including the *to rung*, a bamboo xylophone whose sound is said to evoke the running water of mountain waterfalls.

Ingenious as ever, the Vietnamese have never let material shortcomings limit their imagination: the *klong put* is a set of suspended bamboo tubes that are played quite simply by cupping the hands around one end, an acquired but effective technique. Last but far from least are bronze gongs, an integral part of any music performance. These date from the Dong Son culture of over 2,500 years ago, which also produced huge, elaborate drums engraved with dancing figures. Superb examples of gongs hang in pagodas, while ethnic minorities hoard them as precious heirlooms.

Wartime interlude
'The fog rolled across the ground, seeped into my armpits, crawled up my neck. I heard, as if in a dream, the strains of a flute. It was a song from the countryside, an evening song:
The moon has risen over the hillside
River water glistens, eternal
Slowly, the water buffaloes return from the fields
Never had this music sounded so beautiful to me.'
From *Novel Without a Name* by Duong Thu Huong (1995).

Accommodation

Five O'Clock Follies
This was the derisive term coined by the press for the military briefings held every afternoon on the ground floor of the Rex Hotel: by the mid-1960s, most reporters were well aware of the propaganda directed at them. The hotel dates from 1961, when a Vietnamese couple transformed a garage into a six-storey hotel, just in time for the US Information Service to move in downstairs and officers upstairs. By 1973, it was renamed the Rex Trading Centre and incorporated three cinemas and a dancehall. After reunification in 1975 the Rex slumbered, but since the late 1980s it has been extensively overhauled, expanded and redecorated, with its symbolic crown spinning in the breeze above its inimitable rooftop restaurant.

The Rex Hotel, queen of the night and king of the central crossroads

In recent years Ho Chi Minh City's accommodation has become optimistically top-heavy with luxury hotels. In 1995, 815,000 visitors came to the city, although about a third of these were *Viet Kieu* (overseas Vietnamese) who stay with relatives. Add to this a steady flow of backpackers, and clients for luxury hotels became thin on the ground. The light is now dawning, however, and the number of mid-range hotels is increasing.

Old guard The city's venerable institutions are all concentrated in District 1, around Le Loi and Dong Khoi, with new luxury hotels invading Nguyen Hue. Here stands the atmospheric **Rex Hotel**, with its unique roof terrace and memories of wartime US army occupancy (see panel). Steps away is the clinically refurbished **Continental Hotel**, run by Saigontourist and now bereft of the pavement café so loved by Graham Greene and his drinking pals during the last days of French rule. Opposite stands another old French favourite, the **Caravelle**, recently enlarged and refurbished to move into de luxe class. At the bottom of Dong Khoi facing the river is the elegant but noisy **Majestic**, also managed by Saigontourist. On the west side of the city centre is a relative newcomer and modern landmark, the **New World Hotel**.

Budget ghetto Backpackers all head for a maze of streets and lanes running off Pham Ngu Lao, immediately southwest of Ben Thanh Market. Countless mini-hotels and guest-houses, backed up by travellers' cafés and tour agencies, offer excellent value but a ghetto-like atmosphere. Moving up a notch on the price ladder, there are increasing numbers of well-kept mini-hotels in the sidestreets between Dong Khoi and Hai Ba Trung. The modern **Saigon Hotel** on Dong Du is a pioneer in this category and neighbourhood, and maintains consistent standards. Similar in spirit but smaller is the **Orchid Hotel**, handy for Ho Chi Minh City's main concentration of bars.

Restaurants and nightlife

Foodies will enjoy Ho Chi Minh City as it offers Vietnam's best selection of restaurants and international cuisine in all price ranges. Street food-stalls abound, making a quick noodle-soup an easy option (the best are located at the northern end of Pasteur Street), while the numerous ice-cream parlours will provide your dessert. For a look-and-sample lunch, little can beat the stands in Ben Thanh Market.

The Hammock Bar, a cool spot for watching Mekong life go by

Restaurants with sophisticated interiors include **La Bibliothèque**, with an exclusive, rococo-style library setting; **Vy Restaurant**, an arcaded garden-restaurant with chamber music tinkling in the background; and the very elegant **Vietnam House**, with its piano-bar and traditionally dressed staff. French cuisine naturally keeps a high profile, considered best at **La Camargue**, a restored colonial villa, or at the equally ritzy **Mékong**, which concocts some subtle taste combinations. Meanwhile, pasta enthusiasts cannot go wrong by frequenting **Guido's** in the Continental Hotel.

Vietnamese imperial cuisine comes into its own in the magnificent setting of **Tib**, on Hai Ba Trung, while several more reasonably priced Vietnamese restaurants spill out onto the pavement of Ngo Duc Ke, just off Dong Khoi. The latter is home to the popular **Lemon Grass** and **Liberty** restaurants, both of which serve reliable local specialities.

Hot cocktails True to tradition, Saigon nightlife is hot and long. Bars monopolise a network of streets at the lower end of Hai Ba Trung, where the pioneering and high-decibel **Apocalypse Now** has been doubled in size to include a beer garden. Next stop is the **Buffalo Blues**, where live jazz and blues accompany billiards, darts and pub food. Thai Van Lung has **Sa Pa**, a more tranquil bar-restaurant in romantic Indochinese style. New to the scene is **Globo**, a hip bar-restaurant decorated in African style located on a narrow street off Dong Khoi: *tapas* and pricey cocktails are the way to go here. A perennial after-midnight favourite with the young expatriate crowd is the **Q-bar**, easily located under and outside the Municipal Theatre, while the theatre's other flank is home to the more sedate **Saigon Headlines**.

River food

Bach Dang Wharf on the Saigon River is lined with floating restaurants which untie their ropes to cruise the river every evening. Saigontourist operates its own 500-seat boat which leaves at 8pm for a 90-minute trip, with shatteringly loud music and an unspectacular dinner on offer (for information and bookings, tel: 08 823 0393). The Siren is more restrained, and the seafood not bad. If you are after a beer and a steak, try the Hammock Bar; moored next to the Saigon Floating Hotel, this converted two-storey barge offers a pleasantly relaxed and breezy setting, closing at midnight.

Shopping

Books
Every street-hawker displays them: photocopied English-language books that cost a third of the original. Copyright laws are non-existent in Vietnam, and the practice of selling photocopies also makes books eminently affordable, catapulting the *Oxford Dictionary* to the top of the bestseller list. Ubiquitous is Graham Greene's *The Quiet American,* closely followed by Duong Thu Huong's *Paradise of the Blind* and Bao Ninh's *The Sorrow of War.* For a wider selection, go to Quoc Su Bookstore at 20 Ho Huan Nghiep (off Dong Khoi), where art, architecture and history are well covered in old French, English and Vietnamese originals as well as photocopied versions. The Pham Ngu Lao backpackers' area is also a good source of relevant travel reading: try Tiem Sach at 251 De Tham.

Lacquerware, silk, Zippo lighters, Rolex watches, army surplus, ceramics, table linen, geomancers' compasses, very ecologically incorrect tortoiseshell and ivory carvings, jewellery, fake antiques...these are some of the eclectic offerings on sale in Ho Chi Minh City's markets and shops. Commerce is what the city was built on, after all, and it continues to be its leitmotif. Hard bargaining is, of course, part of any transaction.

Central shops The obvious starting point is **Dong Khoi,** which displays the full gamut of tourist-oriented articles. In the 'antique' shops, neo-Cham statues rub shoulders with gleaming lacquerware, inlaid boxes, old pens and some truly awful paintings (art lovers should concentrate on Hanoi instead – see panel on page 72). Raw silk clothes make a good buy, and some shops offer a 24-hour tailor service, though don't be overambitious with designs. American watches, compasses and military paraphernalia are still on sale, but it is doubtful whether these are all genuine.

The block of streets surrounding the Hôtel de Ville is the place to buy hand-embroidery, while camera equipment, cassettes and hi-fis are reasonably priced at **Cua Hang Bach Hoa** (135 Nguyen Hue), a cornucopia of Asian and

Western goods including some interesting handicrafts. Several wholesale emporia that price their goods reasonably also sell to individuals: **My Thuat** (160 Pasteur Street) displays a vast selection of new traditional-style furniture, lacquerware, ceramics and inlaid articles. Shipping can also be arranged.

Markets Specialised markets kick off with **Ben Thanh,** where food, textiles, toys, basketware, shoes and clothes are all sold under one domed roof. Luggage vendors do

If fake Rolex watches do not fit the bill, head for Ben Thanh's multifarious offerings

a roaring trade, but don't expect their bags to last long. More up-market is **Le Cong Kieu** (opposite the Art Museum), lined with antique and bric-à-brac shops that sell anything from carved Buddhas to 1960s telephones. What was once a landmark on every tourist itinerary, the **Army Market (Cho Dan Sinh),** at 104 Yersin, has obviously run out of goods and now concentrates on practical work clothes, raincoats, leather jackets, tools and kitchen equipment. Finally, head for Cho Lon to buy that dragon-mask you've always hankered after.

Practical points

Getting mobile Travelling around Ho Chi Minh City is no problem, although your mode of transport will depend on your budget. Radio taxis are now widely available and most use their meters, although some do take circuitous routes (see panel). Next step down are the *Honda om*, motorbike taxis that zip around the city with customers riding pillion. Prices are always negotiated in advance and, once you have unearthed a reliable *Honda om*, it is worth hiring it by the hour or day (count on US$10–15 per day). English-speaking drivers gather in front of the big hotels.

A third option is the cyclo, a nostalgic pedicab that creaks gently around the backstreets – ideal for soaking up the

atmosphere and a budget delight. Cyclos are now banned from the central grid but loiter at street corners near by; again, fares should be negotiated in advance. The limited public buses are hardly worth investigating, although Ben Thanh bus station (opposite the market) operates half-hourly airport buses and another service to Cho Lon. As a suicidal alternative, bicycles and motor bikes can be rented in the Pham Ngu Lao area.

Road sense Newly arrived tourists are often daunted by Ho Chi Minh City's dense traffic. The solution when crossing a road is to be purposeful. Spot a gap, start crossing and weave through oncoming vehicles to reach safety at the opposite kerb. Above all, don't hesitate, slow down or stop.

Beyond the city Brave souls who intend to explore Vietnam by public bus should head either for the western bus station, **Ben Xe Mien Tay**, which serves the Mekong Delta, or the eastern bus station, **Ben Xe Mien Dong**, where buses leave for the North. A smaller bus station called **Ben Xe Van Thanh** runs shorter-distance routes to north-eastern destinations such as Da Lat and Vung Tau.

Budget travellers who appreciate some comfort should investigate the private-bus routes operated by **Kim Café** at 270 De Tham (tel: 08 835 9859; fax: 08 829 8546) and **Sinh Café** at 179 Pham Ngu Lao (tel: 08 835 5601; fax: 08 835 7722). Economic tickets are available covering the entire route to Hanoi, with designated stopovers, but this puts you firmly on a well-trodden tourist trail.

Ga Sai Gon, the railway station where the Reunification Express starts its long, slow ride to Hanoi, is at 1 Nguyen Thong in District 3. Private chauffeur-driven cars can be hired through tour agencies (see page 238), with rates ranging from US$35 to $50 per day.

Radio taxis
● Airport Taxi
(tel: 08 844 6666).
● Cho Lon Taxi
(tel: 08 822 6666).
● Gia Dinh Taxi
(tel: 08 822 6699).
● Saigon Taxi
(tel: 08 844 8888/842 4242).
● Vina Taxi
(tel: 08 842 2888).

Even torrential rain cannot stop the flow of traffic

THE MEKONG DELTA

REGION HIGHLIGHTS ◄◄◄◄◄

The Mekong melts into a fiery sunset

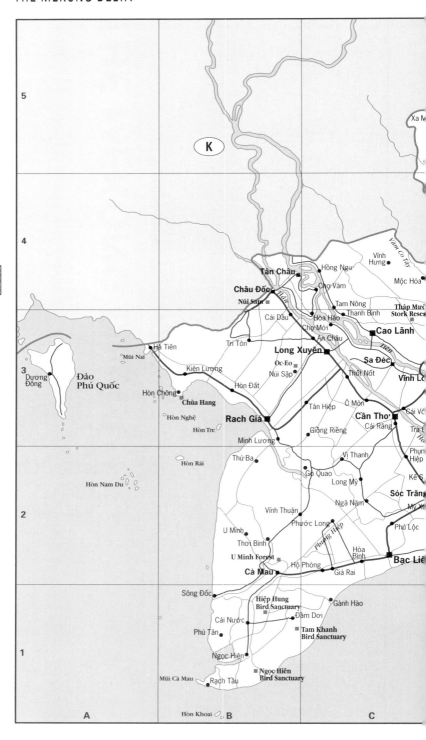

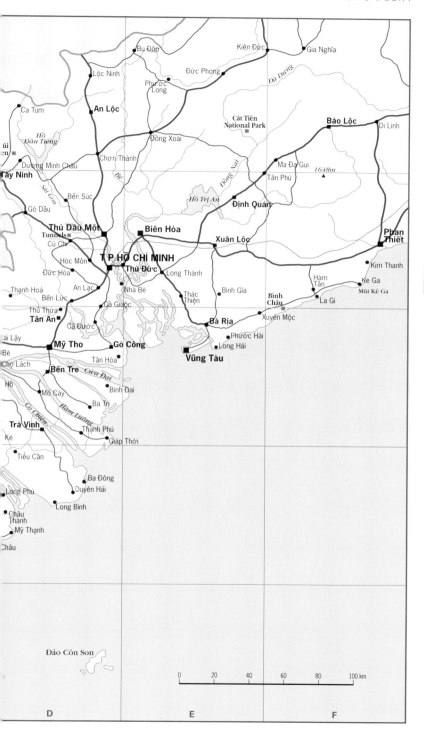

THE MEKONG DELTA

Mekong River
Starting its 4,400km course high in the Himalayas, Asia's third-longest river cuts through the mountains of Yunnan in southern China before flowing through Myanmar (Burma), Laos, Thailand, Cambodia and Vietnam. Its Vietnamese name, Cuu Long ('Nine Dragons'), refers to the nine estuaries of the delta where it flows into the South China Sea. The Mekong River is responsible for creating the entire delta region through the slow build-up of silt deposits over the millennia, a sedimentation process that continues today. During the rainy season (May–October) the Mekong reaches its highest level, and although in the past floods were avoided by drainage into Cambodia's vast Tonle Sap Lake, ecological changes are now provoking them in the delta region.

Diversification
Rice may be perceived as 'white gold' by the Mekong farmers whose production has soared since co-operatives and forced quotas were abandoned in the late 1980s, but a few ingenious souls are striking out in new directions. Frog farming is one of them (a French relic on Vietnamese menus?), led by an inhabitant of Soc Trang who optimistically predicts exporting up to 10 tonnes of frogs per year. In Can Tho, a local fish farmer started breeding hybrid golden catfish in 1988 and now produces some 25 million annually. The Mekong waters have also proved fertile breeding grounds for pearl oysters, originally raised for food consumption but soon expected to enter the cultivated-pearl market.

The Mekong Delta Superficially at least, the Mekong Delta is a land of milk and honey, or rather water and rice: this fertile 'rice basket' of Vietnam accounts for 90 per cent of the country's rice exports. Not only this, but its central region abounds in exotic fruits, the offshore waters teem with shrimps and fish, and the northern region claims hectares of sugar cane. Quintessential images of Vietnam abound in this maze of waterways, be they canals laid out by the Funan Kingdom nearly 2,000 years ago or the hundreds of tributaries of the mighty Mekong River. Sampans, fishing boats, houseboats and car ferries win hands down over any land-based mode of transport, thereby making the Mekong Delta a difficult region to tour. However, as Vietnam develops, roads in the region are being rebuilt and new bridges are appearing.

Luminous heart This chapter includes several destinations that lie immediately north of the Mekong Delta as they, too, share a water-based economy and are accessed via roads radiating from Ho Chi Minh City.

The heart of the region is the south, where bamboo, coconut and majestic nipa palms line the arroyos, narrow dikes crisscross luminous-green rice-fields, and a checkerboard of flooded fields mirrors the skies. Rice, incense and rice-cakes dry beside the road, herds of ducks waddle or swim by, water-buffaloes pull ploughs, floating and land markets display every imaginable tropical fruit, and old men walk pigs on leads in the mellow evening light.

Although rural life rules here, the prosperous towns of Can Tho, My Tho, Long Xuyen and Rach Gia show other less idyllic facets when commerce takes over. Beyond, in the drier and hillier north-western region bordering Cambodia, or in the swampy southern peninsula, are smaller, quieter-paced towns. Ha Tien, Chau Doc, Soc Trang, Ca Mau and, out on a limb, Tra Vinh offer both natural and spiritual interest, the latter relating to the Khmers, rulers of the Mekong Delta until the 18th century.

Minorities The Khmer population is concentrated south and west of Can Tho, in some cases accounting for 30 per cent of the population, and was responsible for the hundreds of spectacular pagodas in the region. Their finely carved, winged roofs soar above large peaceful gardens, while monks in saffron robes can be glimpsed as they disappear into a monastery or through the trees. Khmer pagodas are usually locked, but there is always a monk present who speaks a few words of English and will let visitors in. Cambodia's more recent incursions into Vietnam left a rather different legacy, when Khmer Rouge troops regularly attacked villages along the border, thereby provoking Vietnam's invasion. On another religious note, flamboyance reaches fantastic heights at the Caodaist cathedral in Tay Ninh and is repeated to a lesser extent in the sect's temples throughout the south.

The other noticeable minority is the Chinese, although their numbers dropped radically after 1975 when thousands fled. The tragedies of the boat-people's sea journeys have been well recorded (see pages 48–9), but countless other incidents took place in Vietnam itself, such as at Tra Vinh in 1979, when over 1,000 died in a boat accident after being chased by police.

War reminders Intense and protracted fighting took place in the Mekong Delta during the Vietnam War, and relics of this merciless period abound in the nameless graves, huge war cemeteries, the Cu Chi tunnels, Xeo Quit and the prisons of Con Son and Phu Quoc. Since the French war, the Viet Minh (reincarnated as the Viet Cong) had established strongholds and training camps in the region, often using the abundant natural cover of mangrove forests and man-high water-reeds for camouflage. Frustrated and irate at their inability to overcome 'Charlie', the Americans waged war on the land, blasting it with bombs, searing it with napalm and Agent Orange, torching its hamlets and massacring its inhabitants. Today, the environmental effects are not over, but nature reserves have replaced guerrilla bases in the vast mangrove forest of Ca Mau and in the 'Plain of Reeds' near Cao Lanh, storks and cranes standing in for the dove of peace.

Although the Mekong's waterways create agricultural abundance, they also make road transport problematic

Tourist offices
● Hai Tourist Office (branch), 2 Hoang Van Thu, Bac Lieu (tel: 078 822623).
● Ben Tre Tourism, 65 Dong Khoi, Ben Tre (tel: 075 829867/829618).
● Minh Hai Tourist Services, 17 Nguyen Van Hai, Ca Mau (tel: 078 831464; fax: 078 834402/835075).

► **Bac Lieu**   194C2

Some 10km inland from the delta's marshy southern coast lies Bac Lieu, very much a Mekong backwater and well off the main trail. A few crumbling French colonial buildings provide atmosphere, but interest lies more in one of Vietnam's few bird sanctuaries, San Chim, 4km east of town where the immense mangrove forests begin. Numbers of birds have been falling lately due to an unidentified ecological imbalance that has reduced tree foliage.

The many Khmer inhabitants of the region have an impressive though relatively new pagoda, Chua Moi Hoa Binh, visible south-west of town on the road to Ca Mau. There are a couple of budget hotels in Bac Lieu if you are stuck for the night, but nearby Soc Trang has a much livelier atmosphere (see pages 212–13).

► **Ben Tre**   195D3

This provincial capital lies in the shadow of the larger My Tho, across the mighty Mekong and beyond four islands with names such as 'Turtle' and 'Phoenix'. Frequent car ferries link the two provinces in 30 minutes, and private motor boats can be hired at Ben Tre's jetty for reasonable rates (compared with My Tho's government rates) to make a tour of the backwaters. Narrow, muddy channels lined with huge nipa palms twist around the islands. Houseboats moored beside the orchards regularly make the nine-hour river trip to Ho Chi Minh City to sell the abundant and varied fruit that grows here. Most famed of the islands is **Con Phung►**, once home of the pacifist 'coconut monk' whose dilapidated sanctuary rusts away in the tropical humidity (see panel on page 207). Ben Tre has some decent hotels and a picturesque floating restaurant, so although it is difficult to get to it makes a reasonable alternative to touristy My Tho.

Boats are the transport staple for food, fuel and people, particularly in the almost roadless region around Ca Mau

► **Binh Chau**   195F3

If you are feeling the strain of touring Vietnam, this destination may revive you. Here, over 100 underground hot springs (bubbling up at over 80°C) are reputed to contain medicinal properties good for rheumatism and hepatitis, while acupuncture and massage treatments are also on offer. The springs complex includes a hotel and restaurant, and is located in a small valley near Xuyen Moc (about 60km northeast of Vung Tau), accessible from Highway 1 by a well-surfaced but less well-signposted road.

►► **Ca Mau** 194B2

The end of the line as far as roads in southern Vietnam go is at Ca Mau, the centre of a peninsula of mangrove swamps covering over 1,000sq km, making it the largest inundation forest in the world outside the

Amazon basin. Despite suffering severe damage from chemicals during the Vietnam War, the region is now recovering and is consequently a haven for birds and animals – as well as mosquitoes and slithering reptiles. The latter can be seen caged at Ca Mau's market before they are transported to Ho Chi Minh City's top restaurants. Other points of interest in town include a typically technicoloured Caodai temple and several restaurants that specialise in shrimps (these are raised in farms throughout the peninsula).

Several nature reserves can be visited in the area: **Ngoc Hien Bird Sanctuary**, located in the far south of the peninsula and accessible only by boat; **Tan Khanh** (said to harbour bears, monkeys, snakes and storks); **Hiep Hung Bird Sanctuary**; and, above all, the **U-Minh Forest**▶▶, which starts 16km north-west of Ca Mau. Many species of trees have been identified here; most of those fringing the waterways are mangroves, which tolerate the brackish or salt-water conditions. This enormous expanse was a favourite refuge for the Viet Cong, who destroyed many US patrol boats by mining the waterways; as a result, it attracted planeloads of defoliating Agent Orange from the Americans. Today, environmental problems continue with the destruction of the mangroves for use as firewood. This short-sighted approach overlooks the invaluable service the mangroves provide in preventing coastal erosion.

All the reserves are accessible by boat or by four-wheel drive, but despite the area's unique status in Vietnam, the infrastructure has not yet caught up and Ca Mau's hotels are optimistically overpriced. Boats can be hired at the canal jetty behind the market.

Big and wild
'It was during a ferry-crossing over a tributary of the Mekong between Vinh Long and Sa Dec, in the vast plain of mud and rice in the south of Cohinchina, the Plain of the Birds. I get out of the bus. I go to the bulwarks. I watch the river. My mother sometimes tells me that never again in my life will I see rivers as big and as wild as the Mekong and its tributaries descending towards the sea, these territories of water that disappear into the cavities of the oceans. Across the flatness, as far as the eye can see, these rivers run quickly, flowing as if the earth was sloping.'
From *L'Amant* by Marguerite Duras (1984).

199

Bountiful fruit and vegetables on sale near Ca Mau

Hard negotiating pays off when the boatpeople lead you to the backwaters

Tourist offices
● Can Tho Tourism, 20 Hai Ba Trung, Can Tho (tel: 071 821854; fax: 071 822719).
● Dong Thap Tourist, 2 Doc Binh Kieu, Cao Lanh (tel: 067 851343/851547; fax: 067 852136).

▶▶▶ Can Tho 194C3

The hub of the delta's land, air and water routes is Can Tho, an animated, outgoing town that is used to foreigners. Here, visitors will find quintessential images of southern Vietnam without encountering the infrastructural headaches of more far-flung places. One unresolved problem stemming from Can Tho's crossroads position is the ferry across the Hau River (a distributary of the Mekong), which transports cars, buses, trucks, bikes and people to and from the Ho Chi Minh City highway. Long waits wear patience thin, but plans are afoot for a Japanese-financed bridge, due to be completed by the turn of the century.

Riverside Life centres on the landscaped riverfront (Hai Ba Trung), where the main hotels are located between the Mekong's largest market at the southern end and a floating restaurant to the north. Canoes and motor boats tout for custom while garden cafés lining this strip buzz with life late into the evening. Clients are not allowed to forget Uncle Ho, embodied in a giant silver statue, while in a similar spirit Can Tho's People's Committee runs a very audible public-address system which kicks off the day at 5am. Inhabitants are friendly and ever-ready to practise their English on tourists (many are students at the local university), so the opportunity is ripe for finding out more about life in the delta.

Sights Running virtually parallel to the river a few blocks inland is the stately Hoa Binh boulevard, along which are located government buildings, the Vietcombank, the post office, a museum and, at No 36, the imposing **Munirangsyaram Temple▶▶**. This colourful pagoda was built by the local Khmer community in 1946 and is now home to seven monks. Among its Buddha statues, the endearingly kitsch altar harbours an idiosyncratic collection of fans, plastic flowers, clocks and toys – all in high contrast to the surrounding simplicity.

The **Museum of the Ninth Military Zone** is, obviously enough, concerned with military matters, announced by an American helicopter and odd pieces of artillery adorning the front courtyard. On the right is a room devoted to Ho Chi Minh (*Open* afternoons only) and, to the left, an anomaly – an orchid and bonsai nursery garden.

Floating produce Can Tho's main attraction lies in its boat-trips, either to nearby fruit orchards or to the floating market at **Cai Rang►►** beyond the deep-water harbour. An early morning ride offers views of people washing in the river, market boats laden with produce, sampans being rowed by foot and fishing boats trawling nets. At Cai Rang itself, business is carried out entirely on the water, be it a breakfast bowl of rice or major negotiations.

Cao Lanh   194C3

Possibly one of the ugliest towns in southern Vietnam, Cao Lanh is tipped for greater things as the newly designated capital of Dong Thap province, paradoxically a scenic region with some outstanding nature reserves and plains of lofty reeds that were once a favourite hide-out for Viet Cong guerrillas. The only sight in town is an elaborately laid out war cemetery containing over 3,000 graves of North Vietnamese sympathisers. Otherwise, Cao Lanh's concrete buildings and shadeless boulevards have no charm, but naturalists will have to pass through here to arrange trips to the **Thap Muoi Stork Reserve►** (35km north-east) or to the **Tam Nong Crane Ground►** (50km north-west), the latter a breeding ground for sarus cranes (see panel). Due to its distance from Cao Lanh, entailing a rough road journey or a long boat-ride, it is advisable to spend the night at Tam Nong itself.

Nearer Cao Lanh, about 15km to the south-east, lies the historically and ecologically significant **Xeo Quit►**, a swamp sheltered beneath soaring canopies of trees and vines that once concealed a top-secret underground base for Viet Cong generals. Boat tours can be arranged from Cao Lanh and may include the Thap Muoi Stork Reserve, but beware as the stagnant swamp waters breed aggressive, malarial mosquitoes.

Sarus cranes
Several species of crane are rare but regular visitors to Vietnam. Of these, the sarus crane is the most regular and even breeds in small numbers at certain locations such as Tam Nong. Although these tall, elegant birds are widespread and common in many parts of the Indian sub-continent, their status elsewhere in Southeast Asia is sufficiently precarious to cause concern to conservation bodies. Sarus cranes have largely grey-brown bodies, long necks and heads which show a considerable amount of red. When standing alert, they are nearly as tall as a man. The birds pair for life and couples often engage in ritual displays accompanied by loud, trumpeting calls.

201

Cao Lanh's concrete memorial to the Viet Cong fighters who died here during the Vietnam War

Thoai Ngoc Hau
Once a mandarin and now a major icon at Sam Mountain, Thoai Ngoc Hau (1761–1829) deserves his revered status. In his role as a high-ranking adviser to the Nguyen lords and dynasty, in particular under Minh Mang, he was responsible for reclaiming much of the wilderness in the basin of the Mekong to build villages. He also ordered the digging of the Vinh Te and Thoai Ha canals for drainage purposes. Shortly before his death, he had his tomb built close to the Tay An Pagoda on the path of one of his canals. This stands in a forecourt flanked by the tombs of his two wives; the elaborate temple behind houses a carved wooden bust of this enlightened man.

▶   **Chau Doc**   *194B4*

Chau Doc's confluence position near the Cambodian border makes it another of the Mekong Delta's great trading centres, but this does not alter the poverty of the region. Until 1995 vast profits were made by smuggling goods in over the border, but a government crackdown has since tamed this lucrative business.

A sprawling central market backs on to the main square, a hub for nocturnal socialising and home to an ornate pagoda. Chau Doc's Chinese, Cham and Khmer minorities have all left their mark in the town. The Chinese-style **Chau Phu Pagoda**▶ (1926), a brilliant yellow stuccoed building with a tiered roof, dominates the main riverfront junction and was built to worship Thoai Ngoc Hau (see panel), while the Cham community's modest mosque is reached by taking a small ferry across the Hau River south of the Hang Chau Hotel to Chau Giang. Boat-trips offer a close-up on Chau Doc's floating raft-houses and on the ramshackle water-village.

Pilgrimage time A canal-trip or taxi ride 5km west takes you to the thronging pilgrim site of **Sam Mountain (Nui Sam)**▶▶, rising dramatically out of the rice plains and riddled with temples and tombs. First on the circuit is the

Rising abruptly out of the plains only a few kilometres from the Cambodian border is Sam Mountain, not surprisingly crowned by a military outpost

Tay An Pagoda▶ (1847, extended 1958), whose garish neo-Mogul exterior belies a more sober interior containing 200 statues. Continuing to the right, the next and most crowded stop is **Mieu Xu Than (Chua Xu)**, a temple dated 1821, though rebuilt since. It is dedicated to an ancient granite statue of Thanh Mau (Mother of God), which

attracts prolific offerings. More aesthetically pleasing is the tomb complex of **Thoai Ngoc Hau▶▶** (1829), further along on the left. The last stop is **Chua Hang (Grotto Pagoda)▶▶**, a cave-temple clinging to the mountainside. Monks in the main hall accompany visitors up more steps to the grotto shrines above.

Beyond Chua Hang, a turning twists up past boulders, craggy cliffs and the odd kitsch café to the summit where, at the sign for 'Am Buu Thanh', a path leads to a lookout point on a rock marked with two mysterious footprints. The views reach over the vast plains, the chain of seven hills, Chau Doc and distant Cambodia.

Three rivers converge at Chau Doc, making ferries an indispensable part of daily life

▶   Con Son Island   *195D1*

Idyllically flung out in the emerald waters of the South China Sea, this forested island and its superb beaches have been awarded national park status. The museum points to a grim past, firstly under the French as an exile colony with a notorious reputation for mistreatment, and then, after 1954, as a detention and torture centre for prisoners of the Saigon government. The infamous sunken 'tiger cages', barred across the top and measuring a mere 2.7 x 1.5m, held up to 14 detainees.

Today, Con Son Island envisages a brighter future with a projected US$290 million Korean joint venture for two large hotels, a water park, a golf course and a fast boat service from Vung Tau. Until this materialises, facilities remain limited and the present boat journey takes 12 hours; the alternative is to fly by small plane.

▶   Cu Chi   *195D4*

The tunnels of Cu Chi (*Admission charge* moderate) are Vietnam's most visited war exhibit and are easily seen on a half-day tour from Ho Chi Minh City. Over 250km of tunnels dug over a period of ten years and on three levels (up to 7m deep) created an ingenious underground habitat for some 16,000 resistance fighters, initially in the war against the French and subsequently against the Americans. Although the ancient film screened at the visitor's centre helps little with understanding the importance of this site, the military guides are well trained in reciting its glorious past. The tour passes an outdoor gallery of booby traps and other lethal devices before entering the tunnel zone, showing kitchens, meeting rooms, a trick minefield and a bomb crater.

Tunnel rats
For the US army, the sensitive area 35km north of Ho Chi Minh City where Cu Chi is located was known to be rife with Viet Cong; the local resistance record dated from the days of the French rubber plantations when workers were so abysmally treated that they were only too ready to fight for the communist cause. Endless attempts were made by the Americans to dislodge the relentless guerrillas from their tunnels, by dropping bombs from B-52s or sending in squads of 'tunnel rats', specially trained, slimly built members of the chemical platoon accompanied by hunting dogs. The tunnel dwellers countered this by changing their tactics, even using American shaving-cream and cigarettes to disorientate the dogs.

■ **Not an undercover spy but a destructive chemical herbicide, Agent Orange was liberally sprayed over southern Vietnam by the US army. Its effects are still highly visible today in the Central Highlands and in parts of the Mekong Delta. Although some vegetation has recovered, the pernicious side-effects live on.** ■

204

Weakened soil

'There were still bomb craters all over the place, each an arduous task to fill in, and the villagers were convinced that the defoliants, usually referred to as Agent Orange after the most common one, had permanently weakened the soil. All the older people in the room nodded assent when Mr Liem said that in prewar years no fertilizer had been necessary for rice growing. The silt from the Saigon River had sufficed. Now fertilizer was necessary, and fruit trees were said to bear less than before.'
A visit to Ben Suc, near Cu Chi, recounted in *Two Cities* by Neil Sheehan (1991).

The use of Agent Orange (named after the orange stripes on the canisters that contained one of the most toxic forms of dioxin) began in 1962 when President Kennedy and Secretary of Defense McNamara, encouraged by President Diem, sought radical solutions to dealing with Viet Cong guerrillas. Their aim was to destroy crops and defoliate forest in order to deprive the Viet Cong of both their food supply and hide-outs. By 1967, 600,000 hectares were being doused annually, ravaging rubber and coconut plantations as well as half the Mekong Delta's mangrove forest, and inadvertently hitting fruit orchards due to wind drift and vaporisation. In total, an estimated 72 million litres of the defoliant were sprayed from planes, helicopters or armoured cars.

Side-effects Laboratory studies made in 1969 established a link between Agent Orange and birth defects, and two years later the use of chemical defoliants was stopped. But it was too late. By then some 2 million hectares of forest had been defoliated, half of which remains unrestored today. Dioxin accumulated from repeated spraying entered the ecosystem of Vietnam, while tens of thousands of troops on both sides had been exposed to the chemical. Not least, Vietnamese birth defects are now double those of neighbouring countries. Scientific surveys continue to uncover side-effects, the latest (1996) documenting the high proportion of children with spina bifida born to Vietnam veterans.

The devastating effects of Agent Orange continue to cause concern

Other spin-offs of Agent Orange include nerve and urological disorders, skin diseases and soft-tissue cancers. In 1984 a US$240 million settlement was made to Agent Orange victims in the US, New Zealand, Australia and Canada (excluding South Korea, the second-largest foreign contingent), but many are still fearful of long-term reproduction in their children.

▶▶ Ha Tien 194A3

The 'Town of the Beautiful Angel', situated right on the Cambodian border, is another end-of-the-line place sheltered by hills and bordered by a beautiful coast, but has long been isolated because of its atrocious access road (this is now being rebuilt). Fishermen, lontar palms, shrimps drying in the sun and some attractive Malay-style houses adorned with fretwork eaves introduce this small town, which lies clustered around a harbour. The hotels are reasonable, although the restaurants and market are limited in choice.

The main historical sight is **Lang Mac Cuu▶▶**, an atmospheric hillside west of the centre dotted with 46 tombs of the Chinese family that ruled here in the 18th century (see panel). These tombs (called Nui Lang by locals) are elaborate examples of Chinese horseshoe graves and are decorated with dragons, tigers and phoenixes. The largest belongs to Mac Cuu himself and was built by order of Emperor Gia Long in 1809. Access is through a brightly coloured pagoda fronting the hill. Both **Tam Bao Pagoda▶** and **Phu Dung Pagoda** in the town centre were founded by Mac Cuu. Some 3km towards the border is the **Thach Dong Cave-temple▶**, containing several shrines and with lookout points to sea. At the entrance is a memorial to a 1978 atrocity, when 130 villagers were massacred by the Khmer Rouge.

From Thach Dong onwards the landscape picks up in pastoral beauty as the road passes the border post, a crumbling tower and a toll-gate before reaching the lovely cape of **Mui Nai▶▶**. Palm-fringed beaches, seafood restaurants and colourful fishing boats more than make up for the tepid, silty water.

▶▶ Hon Chong 194B3

About 20km south of Ha Tien lies Hon Chong, reached via a long and dusty road dominated by two huge cement factories, a Chinese joint venture that has successfully blighted the horizon. Sharply sculpted limestone outcrops rise out of mangroves and shrimp ponds before the road eventually reaches Hon Chong village. Here, lovely views unfold over a mini-Ha Long Bay that is dotted with countless limestone islands. A few kilometres further on, the road ends at **Chua Hang**, a Buddhist cave-temple which gives access to **Duong Beach▶**, a popular local destination lined with seafood restaurants and cafés. Boats tour the bay and visit **Nghe Island▶**, a two-hour trip justified by unspoilt beaches and clear waters.

> **Mac Cuu**
> Until 1708 the fishing village of Ha Tien belonged to Cambodia, but after repeated attacks by the Thais it was seized from the Khmers by Mac Cuu, a Chinese adventurer and former governor. On Mac Cuu's death in 1736, his son Mac Thien Tu took over, but repeated invasions from Siam prompted him to switch his 'capital' to Can Tho. The Tay Son Rebellion of 1771–89 finally ended Mac rule, and the family fled to Thailand.

The Mac Cuu tombs, partly engulfed by vegetation, are still respected by locals

THE MEKONG DELTA

Tourist office
● An Giang Tourism, 83–5
Nguyen Hue, Long Xuyen
(tel: 076 844718/841036).

Hoa Hao
The Hoa Hao religious sect
was founded in 1939 by
Huynh Phu So. The name
derives from Huynh's home
village, Hoa Hao, situated
half-way between Long
Xuyen and Chau Doc.
Despite Huynh's aversion
to temples, a number were
built in An Giang province;
these still function today
for the approximate
1.5 million followers. The
Hoa Hao were also known
for their private militia of
10,000–15,000 men, trained
by the Japanese during
World War II and who
subsequently sided
with the French. Because
of this, Huynh was
assassinated by the Viet
Minh in 1947, although
Diem's short-sighted
policies subsequently
prompted many sect
members to join the Viet
Cong from 1955.

*Photos of the Coconut
Monk are set into this
ceramic-encrusted urn*

▶ ■■■ **Long Hai**   *195E3*

This growing coastal resort north of Vung Tau makes an
easy escape from Ho Chi Minh City provided you have
your own transport. Two adjoining beaches, Long Hai and
Phuoc Hai, boast long stretches of palm-fringed white
sand and calm waters that are trawled by local fishing
boats. Accommodation is nothing special, but fine for a
short break from the city. Beach life is also picking up at
nearby **Thuy Duong▶**, where a resort complex offers
beach bungalows, changing-rooms, parasailing and water-
skiing, although new hotels will soon change the skyline
here. Real escapists should head 40km away to **Ho
Coc▶▶**, a rustic fishing village with a few beach
bungalows and restaurants.

■■■ **Long Xuyen**   *194C3*

There is little of interest in this prosperous crossroads
town, the capital of An Giang province and once the fief of
the Hoa Hao, a militaristic religious sect (see panel). Sights
are limited to a towering 1960s Catholic church that can
accommodate some 1,000 worshippers, and a renovated
museum (77 Thoai Ngoc Hau) displaying relics from Oc
Eo. Otherwise, Long Xuyen offers a good choice of
comfortable, reasonably priced hotels, so is best treated
as a staging post.

▶ ■■■ **My Tho**   *194D3*

My Tho offers classic glimpses of the rural beauty of the
Mekong Delta, and its proximity to Ho Chi Minh City
makes it a favourite with day-trippers. Add to this a particularly forceful People's Committee, and you have a
perfect example of tourist-fleecing. This is especially
noticeable in the control and (high) pricing of Mekong boat
tours by local authorities. Yet free-market forces are
responding, and subterfuge techniques by local boatmen
are becoming quite an art – stroll or cruise along the
streets beside the river and they will come to you. Their
trip may include a return by ferry which docks down-
stream to avoid detection; in this case make
sure they arrange transport back to the
centre of My Tho.

Most **boat-trips▶** circle around the fabulous patchwork of fruit orchards on Dragon,
Turtle, Lion and Phoenix islands (the latter
home to the Coconut Island monk's strange
sanctuary – see panel opposite) that lie
midstream between My Tho and the
province of Ben Tre (see page 198), or go
further afield to Cai Be floating market. Fruit-
tasting (longans, rambutans, mangoes,
durians, sapodillas and guava) should be on
the agenda.

Inheritance Back on land, My Tho offers
interest in the *hoi quan* (community halls) of
the old Chinese quarter, which dates from
the founding of My Tho in the late 17th
century by refugees fleeing the Manchu
invasion. When the French conquered the
delta in the 1860s, they enlarged the town
into a military, commercial and administrative

centre; their influence is still visible in some fine colonial architecture (including a yellow stuccoed Catholic church). In contrast, the heritage of the large American army base is noticeable in the Amerasian features of some locals.

From the church, Nguyen Trai runs east across a bridge to reach the unusual **Vinh Trang Pagoda**▶▶ (*Open* 7.30–12, 2–5), an 1849 construction rebuilt in 1907 in elaborately stuccoed and imposing style. Lotus-ponds, tombs and gardens create a peaceful setting for the richly gilded carvings and 60 statues inside, including 18 *arhat* (saints). Further on still, about 12km from My Tho on the road to Vinh Long, is the **Dong Tam Snake Farm**▶, where pythons and cobras are raised for research into snake-based medicines. Other fauna on show here are monkeys, crocodiles, deer, birds and some strangely deformed turtles and fish, thought to have been affected by toxic Agent Orange.

Oc Eo   194B3

The archaeological site of Oc Eo, which flourished in the 1st–6th centuries, may be highly significant in historical terms (see page 34) but is actually of no great interest to visit, nor is it easy of access. It lies half-way between Long Xuyen and Rach Gia in a grid of canals dug by the Funan Kingdom, and can only be reached from Rach Gia by four-wheel drive in the dry season or by boat. Only the foundations remain, although numerous artefacts (coins, utensils, tools and stilts) have been excavated and are exhibited at Ho Chi Minh City's History Museum (see page 174), at Long Xuyen's small museum (see opposite) and at the museum in Rach Gia (see page 211).

The immaculate Vinh Trang Pagoda

Coconut Island monk
The extraordinary sanctuary built on Con Phung (Phoenix Island) vaguely resembles a 1950s fairground, with dragon columns, a giant ceramic urn and meditation tower. It was created by Nguyen Thanh Nam, who in 1945 chose a monastic existence in the pursuit of peace in Vietnam. Seated on a stone slab, he meditated day and night for three years, nourishing himself only with coconuts. At the same time, he founded a religion based on Buddhism and Catholicism that combined icons of Buddha and Jesus. However, his pacifist activities led to constant harassment by the authorities, including repeated imprisonment. He died in 1990, leaving a unique though sadly neglected legacy.

Tropical fruits

■ **Mountains of temptingly succulent fruit fill the markets of southern Vietnam, some of them bizarre to Western eyes and taste-buds. The Mekong Delta's island orchards send their vitamin-packed tropical produce to Ho Chi Minh City, where it no doubt helps fuel the population's manic energy, while Da Lat reigns supreme over higher-altitude fruit such as strawberries and mulberries.** ■

Tropical temptations, top from left to right: rambutans, coconuts, papaya and mangoes, starfruit and jackfruit

Coconuts
This tropical classic can be found throughout most of the South and Centre, its endless swaying palms sure indications that a good sandy beach is close by. Large, smooth and green (the brown, hairy nut seen in the West is the small inner casing), the coconut is both multi-functional and highly nutritious. Stands selling *nuoc dua* (coconut juice) line every ferry queue and beach in the Mekong Delta; vendors hack the top off the coconut, so creating a scoop to spoon out the young, jelly-like flesh after the juice has been drunk. Coconut also finds its way into countless candies and numerous meat dishes.

Durian (*sau rieng*) The king of fruit and the most controversial, being either hated or loved, has a strange Vietnamese name meaning 'one's sorrows'. Some people may well regret hacking into the tough thorny skin of a durian as the pervasive sewer-like aroma strengthens. But indulge in the creamy dense flesh and the rewards are great, its ambiguous flavour combining avocado, nuts, gorgonzola cheese and honey. This gigantic and very expensive fruit is in season May–August.

Guava (*oi*) High in vitamins A and C, and in the minerals iron and calcium, the granular pink flesh of the guava is encased in a thick green pear-shaped skin. It is eaten raw or used for juices.

Jackfruit (*mit*) These giant pear-shaped fruits contain chewy yellow segments, potent sources of vitamins A, B and C. The wood of the *jak* tree is often used for pagoda carvings.

Longan (*nhan*) These tiny fruits grow in the Mekong Delta and in the North. Smooth, light brown skin coats translucent white pulp encasing a large black seed. The thicker the pulp, the juicier and more fragrant it becomes.

Lychee (*vai*) Sprays of dark red, bumpy-skinned lychees are a common sight in the North, where connoisseurs of these fruit home in on Hung Yen province for the juiciest, sweetest variety (known as *vai thieu*).

Mango (*xoai*) The fibrous orange flesh of this familiar tropical fruit comes in several varieties, the sweetest being the large rounder ones with a bright yellow skin (*xoai cat*), weighing up to 500g. The most sought-after grow at Cao Lanh in the Mekong Delta, and are in season March–June.

Mangosteen (*mang cut*) A typically illusory tropical fruit, the deep purple, apple-sized mangosteen looks totally uninspiring. However, peel it and slice the transparent white flesh and you can indulge in a delicious sour-sweet flavour, considered by Chinese as a perfect *yin* balance to the durian's *yang*.

Papaya/papaw (*du du*) There are 45 species of this fruit, indigenous to Latin America and brought to Southeast Asia in the 16th century. High in vitamins A and C, the

large, oval fruit has a refreshing though bland orange flesh, best eaten with a squeeze of lime juice.

Pineapple (*dua*) Vietnam's pineapples grow mainly in the Mekong Delta region but are often disappointingly ropey and dry. The juice is sometimes made into a liquor or mixed with egg yolk to produce an energising drink.

Pomelo (*buoi*) Huge pomelos with thick skins and pith yield a sweeter, less acidic flesh than the grapefruit. The coast of Central Vietnam grows the best varieties and the season is August–November. Pomelos are a favourite on train journeys, and are much touted by child vendors.

Rambutan (*chom chom*) The tough, hairy red skin of rambutans encloses a tender white flesh whose cool sweet flavour matures during the rainy season (May–October). It is distantly related to the lychee.

Soursop/custard-apple (*mang cau*) A smaller, more civilised version of the durian, the soursop is apple-sized with a bumpy green skin that blackens as it overripens. The subtly flavoured creamy flesh is best scooped out with a spoon, which will bring with it numerous black pips.

Star-apple (*vu sua*) With a Vietnamese name meaning 'milk from the breast', it is hard to be less than rhapsodical about this smooth-skinned fruit which grows suspended from the trees of Can Tho's orchards. The ritual of eating it involves squeezing the fruit before piercing a hole through the skin; the fragrant white juice, by now mixed with the flesh, is then sucked out.

Starfruit (*khe*) The English name for this fruit refers to the star shape of sliced segments. The crisp white flesh is more refreshing than sweet, and is a favourite for juices.

Tamarind (*me*) Originally brought from India, these brown seedpods contain a tart fruit. Its high acidic content is used mainly for flavouring savoury dishes and desserts, or the fruit is crystallised.

Lontar-palm fruit
The lofty lontar palm grows prolifically in An Giang province in the south-western corner of the Mekong Delta. Great clusters of round aubergine-coloured fruit are sliced open for their flesh, a mushy, tasteless affair, or their juice, a much more inspiring product that is sold by women vendors from large bamboo containers that are suspended from a yoke. Sugar is also made from the syrupy juice.

209

A pile of crisp rose-apples, a Mekong speciality

Nuoc mam
This pungent fish sauce is an integral part of the Vietnamese diet as it contains high levels of protein and replaces salt in flavouring dishes. It is made by fermenting specific types of fish with large quantities of salt in huge wooden vats for anything between four and 12 months. The resultant high-protein paste (*nuoc lot*) is diluted with salt water before being bottled and then placed on every Vietnamese dinner table. As usual, there is no waste: the fish residue left in the vats is used as a fertiliser.

▶▶　　**Phu Quoc Island (Dao Phu Quoc)**　　*194A3*

This 560sq km island (Vietnam's largest), situated about 120km west of Rach Gia in the Gulf of Thailand, is another of Vietnam's 'ready-to-boom' destinations. Idyllic white-sand beaches, scenic mountains, mineral springs, low-key villages, a transparent turquoise sea rich in tropical fish and dense background forest all lie in wait for future development. The downside is a lack of infrastructure, the presence of military bases (Cambodia also claims this island) and an all-pervading aroma of *nuoc mam* (fish sauce), the island's main product along with black pepper (see panel). Phu Quoc's past was no less repellent: 30,000–40,000 prisoners were held here by the Saigon regime. Access is either by daily boat from Rach Gia, an uncomfortable nine-hour trip, or by plane from Ho Chi Minh City. Both arrive at the main port town on the west coast, Duong Dong, where accommodation is concentrated.

▶　　**Phung Hiep**　　*194C2*

Half-way between Can Tho and Soc Trang is the boat-building village of Phung Hiep, a picturesque stopover for a visit to the floating market (*Open* dawn–around 11am). Note the poles with attached produce specialities swinging aloft which allow easy identification of your chosen

Freshly built and ready to paddle: boats at Phung Hiep (right) and the floating market (below)

vegetable from afar. The market spills over into roadside stalls which operate all day, but these are no different from any other in the Mekong Delta. Sawmills are plentiful, as are the builders of local wooden boats, painted in blue with red and white eyes on the prow to frighten away river spirits.

Tourist offices
● Kien Giang Tourist Office, 12 Ly Tu Trong, Rach Gia (tel: 077 862081/863824; fax: 077 862111).
● Branch office in Duong Dong, Phu Quoc (tel: 077 846318; fax: 077 847125).

▶   **Rach Gia**   194B3

Visibly prosperous, the dynamic and friendly capital of Kien Giang province is an inevitable stop on the appalling road to Ha Tien (see page 205). This important fishing port, straddling two arms of the Cai Lon Canal, abounds in opticians, tailors, billiard halls, hi-fi shops and prostitution, all sure signs of the wealth that is derived from local rice and fish production. Evening strolls around the city centre – squeezed into an island in the canal – also offer glimpses of interiors packed with antiques and cafés in grand old French mansions. Naturally enough, Rach Gia is known for its excellent seafood, and this, combined with a handful of reasonable hotels, makes it an enjoyable place to spend the night.

Sights Apart from the colourful market and wharf area, try investigating the **museum** in its heavily stuccoed colonial edifice (21 Nguyen Van Troi; often closed), where Funan artefacts excavated at nearby Oc Eo (see page 207) are displayed. Several pagodas are worth visiting, mainly to the north of the canal. Those along Quang Trung represent all three local ethnic groups: Chinese worship at Chua Ong Bon, where incense spirals smoke in a pretty open courtyard; Vietnamese frequent the more modern Chua Phat Quang; and the Khmer community is catered for by the 18th-century **Chua Phat Lon (Big Buddha Pagoda)**▶▶ about 1km up the road. Set in a large park with a lotus-pond, this terraced Theravada Buddhist pagoda displays some fine roof carving and a brilliantly painted hall with murals depicting the life of Buddha. The overgrown garden contains cremation towers and stupas where former monks are buried; today, some 30 monks inhabit the buildings at the back.

Resistance Fronting the northern canal and a small park is the **Nguyen Trung Truc Pagoda**▶, built in the 19th century to honour a resistance fighter of this name who was executed by the French in Rach Gia in 1868 after he had helped destroy the battleship *Espérance*. This colourful pagoda has evolved much over the years and underwent its most recent modernisation in 1986; a portrait of Nguyen Trung Truc hangs inside. In the town centre at 14 Nguyen Du stands the ornate Chinese pagoda of **Hoi Tuong Te Nguoi Hoa (Ong Bac De)**▶, over a century old and with a central altar devoted to the Jade Emperor's reincarnation, Ong Bac De. Rach Gia also claims a Caodai temple and a Protestant church, both located south of the centre on Nguyen Trung Truc.

A spiritual shower in front of burial stupas at the Phat Lon Pagoda

A worthy witness to the large Khmer community in Soc Trang is its museum, where exhibits range from model long-boats to a bonze's funeral casket

Ba Den legend
A certain Ly Thi Thien Huong is the subject of several versions of a legend that inspired the pagoda on Black Lady Mountain. Her fame stems from her devotion to her fiancé, a poor peasant sent away to fight in a war. During his absence, her beauty attracted the advances of a wealthy and powerful local mandarin whom she was ordered to marry. To escape this fate, she threw herself from the mountain. Another version describes her worshipping piously at a mountain shrine when she was attacked by a gang of thugs; to escape dishonour, she threw herself over the cliff.

▶▶   **Soc Trang**   *194C2*

Few foreign visitors reach Soc Trang, yet it has plenty of sights, numerous festivals, and is the lively, friendly capital of a province that has the largest Khmer and Chinese populations of the Mekong Delta (28 per cent and 7 per cent respectively). Recent prosperity is symbolised by a replica Eiffel Tower, the new telecommunications mast dominating the central bus station and market area. The town, crossed by canals, has some peeling old colonial buildings and an interesting Khmer flavour.

Dating from the French period is the small **Khmer Museum**▶ (*Open* Mon–Sat 7–11, 1.30–4. *Admission* free), at the corner of Mau Than 68 and Nguyen Chi Thanh. Sculptures, musical instruments, costumes, architectural models, caskets and domestic utensils are displayed. Opposite stands the impressive **Khleng Pagoda**▶▶, built at the turn of the century to replace an ancient bamboo structure. The extensive gilded woodcarvings in the richly worked interior are well maintained, and a superb tiered Buddha throne is reflected in a mirrored wall. The surrounding garden is shared by the adjoining school, so is far from being a haven of peace. Continuing east, Mau Than 68 leads to the 200-year-old **Dat Set Pagoda**▶, entered down a narrow alley. Inside is an incredible hotch-potch of banners, chandeliers, clay sculptures (it is also known as the Clay Pagoda), lanterns, sequinned parasols and plastic flowers – altogether a glittering visual feast wreathed in incense smoke.

On the road About 10km on the road to Bac Lieu is **Xa Lon**▶, a huge pagoda founded in 1815 that was bombed in 1968 and slowly rebuilt. Faced in a bizarre juxtaposition of bathroom tiles, it harbours garish friezes and a techni-coloured main altar flanked by dragon statues. Monks and a Buddhist school are housed near by. A decorative exam-ple of a dragon-boat used in Khmer festivals is stored here.

In contrast, **Chua Doi (Bat Pagoda)**▶▶ is a more harmonious 400-year-old temple with some fabulous ornamentation, including intricately painted shutters, a subtle ceiling mural and a beautiful gilded Buddha. It stands in a large monastery compound planted with trees that have inspired an added attraction – fruit-bats! Thousands of these creatures hang from the trees before taking off on nocturnal sorties; sunset is a favourite visiting time for local children. Chua Doi lies about 5km south-west of Soc Trang along a potholed turn-off near the post office.

► **Tay Ninh**   195D4

Some 100km north-west of Ho Chi Minh City lies the centre of the weird and wonderful Caodaist sect (see page 214), easily visited on organised tours that take in Cu Chi *en route*. Tay Ninh is otherwise an unattractive sprawl, its only interest found 11km north-east at **Nui Ba Den (Black Lady Mountain)**►. The peak looms 900m above the paddy-fields and is adorned half-way up by **Van Son Pagoda**, dedicated to a legendary heroine (see panel opposite). A trek to the pagoda takes under two hours, passing count-less cave-temples and offering sweeping views, but you will not be alone: some half a million pilgrims visit the mountain annually and there are guest-houses at its base. The mountain was the focus of intense fighting during the recent wars and attracted heavy US bombing and defolia-tion. Tay Ninh's population also suffered from murderous Khmer Rouge incursions in the late 1970s.

The **Caodai Great Temple**►►► stands in twin-towered, polychromatic splendour within a vast area of related structures. Neighbouring villages are all Caodaist, and followers can be spotted in their white robes. Visitor reac-tions invariably include astonishment at this flashy hybrid of Singapore's Haw Par Villa and Disneyland: riotous pastel-coloured stuccowork, a glittering star-spangled ceil-ing, gaudy curtains, an acrobatic statue depicting Jesus, Lao Tse, Confucius and Buddha standing on each other's shoulders, and everywhere the Caodaist symbol, a trian-gle containing a holy eye. Masses are held at 6am, noon and 6pm, when vigilantes herd visitors upstairs to the gallery. Women enter on the left, men on the right, and shoes are removed. Although visually fantastical, the cere-mony is rather disappointing, consisting of repetitive genuflexions and monotonous chanting.

A candy palace
'From a distance this structure could have been dismissed as the monstrous result of a marriage between a pagoda and a Southern baroque church, but at close range the vulgarity of the building was so impressive that mild antipathy gave way to fascinated horror... It was a palace in candy from a coloured fantasy by Disney; an example of fun-fair architecture in extreme form... But the question was, what had been Pham-Cong-Tac's intention in producing a house for this petrified forest of pink dragons, this hugger-mugger of symbolism, this pawnbroker's collection of cult objects?'
From *A Dragon Apparent* by Norman Lewis (1951).

213

A dazzling riot of colour and form inside Soc Trang's Dat Set Pagoda

■ **Of the many idiosyncratic spiritual sects of the South, Caodaism is the longest lasting and certainly the most eccentric. Buddhism, Islam, Christianity, Taoism and Confucianism are all rolled into one tinsel-wrapped package, at its technicoloured best in the ritualistic masses held at Tay Ninh's Holy See.** ■

214

Exhaust-pipes
'A Pope and female cardinals. Prophecy by planchette. Saint Victor Hugo. Christ and Buddha looking down from the roof of the Cathedral on a Walt Disney fantasia of the East, dragons and snakes in technicolour... How could one explain the dreariness of the whole business: the private army of 25,000 men, armed with mortars made out of exhaust-pipes of old cars, allies of the French who turned neutral at the moment of danger?'
From *The Quiet American* by Graham Greene (1955).

Some 2 million Vietnamese are followers of Caodaism, a syncretic sect founded in 1926 by Ngo Van Chieu, a civil servant who saw the light on Phu Quoc Island. Doctrine has altered over the years, but includes 'revealing to men the posthumous consequences of the acts by which they assassinate their souls' and basically aims to fuse Eastern and Western philosophies. Spiritualism plays a major role and conferences are held with a motley pantheon of saints, including Joan of Arc, Victor Hugo, John the Baptist, the Jade Emperor and Sun Yat-sen. Communication with the beyond is through a *corbeille à bec*, the Caodai equivalent of an ouija board.

Divine eye The all-seeing holy eye set in a triangle, the Cao Dai ('Great Palace') that first instructed the founder, was adopted as the religious symbol and appears between the twin towers of every Caodai temple, said to number over a thousand. Ceremonies are conducted by male and female

Disneyland? Or the Cao Dai Great Temple?

priests, who are dressed and who worship according to a specific hierarchy. Prescribed Caodai rites include monotonous chanting, fruit offerings, burning of incense and oriental-style prostrations.

Military quest Caodaism gained popularity rapidly, mainly because it was perceived as a truly Vietnamese religion. Military power followed, aided by Japanese training during World War II, so that by the 1950s the Caodai pope held sway over much of the populated region north of Saigon and in large enclaves further south. The French-sponsored Caodaist army of over 20,000 men played an opportunist role, later supporting the Viet Minh but never quite entering the Viet Cong fold. In retaliation, the North confiscated all Caodai land in 1975, and although the Holy See was restored ten years later even today the front gate remains symbolically locked.

▶▶ Tra Vinh

195D3

Tra Vinh lies well off the main Mekong circuit, requiring a 67km detour from Vinh Long, but it certainly justifies the effort as the local Khmers (about 30 per cent of the population) have produced some remarkable Theravada Buddhist pagodas. *Xe loi* (motorised carts, for carrying people or pigs) are common, as are flocks of bicycling girls in fluttering white *ao dai*, all set against an idyllic backdrop of coconut palms, water-buffaloes and endless rice-fields. To the south at the river mouth lies the magnificent unspoilt **Ba Dong Beach▶▶**.

Pagodas In a shady garden about 4km from the town lies **Som Rong▶**, fronted by carved stupas and statues; a cremation tower stands across the road. Hidden down a twisting dirt-road at a turn-off some 300m back lies **Chim Pagoda▶**, home to some 40 monks who pray in an immaculate stone construction with a whitewashed, partly decorated interior.

Back on the main road by a cemetery, a turning leads south to **Ba Om▶**, a large lotus-pond rife with legends and today rimmed by small cafés and *cho den* trees with their knotted, tentacular roots. In the far corner a new structure, slowly being built and financed by overseas Khmers, is destined to become a Khmer museum. Behind this stands Tra Vinh's jewel and the main pagoda of the province, the **Ang Pagoda (Chua Kho Me)▶▶▶**. Set behind a pretty lotus-pond and stupa towers, and surrounded by lofty trees, the pagoda displays some magnificent painted woodcarvings on its sweeping, winged roof. One of the 20 monks will open the temple to show a raftered interior entirely faced with murals, a huge gilded Buddha, and over 100 *arhat* (saint) statues.

Centre The sleepy, tree-lined streets of Tra Vinh harbour a market, a miniature French château that is now a military headquarters, a French cemetery and Catholic church, the flashily painted Chua Ong Chinese temple, and even a Caodaist temple. About 5km south-east at Long Duc is Den Tho Bac, an incongruous and elaborate memorial to Uncle Ho standing inside a moat. This site was apparently chosen because a previous shrine was repeatedly destroyed by the South Vietnamese Army.

Tourist office
● Tra Vinh Tourist Office, Cuu Long Hotel, 999 Nguyen Thi Minh Khai, Tra Vinh (tel: 074 862559/862491; fax: 074 863769). Little English is spoken here, but staff may help with canal trips or directions to Chua Co (also called Chua Chim, leading to confusion with its namesake described in the main text), a Khmer pagoda that doubles as a stork sanctuary about 40km south of Tra Vinh. In the same direction lie archaeological excavations in the Funan ruins of Luu Cu, and from here you can continue to the sand-dunes of Ba Dong.

215

Tra Vinh's large Khmer community has financed some striking pagodas

Tourist offices
● Cuu Long Tourist, No 1, 1 Thang 5, Vinh Long (tel: 070 823616/822494; fax: 0170 823357).
● Ba Ria-Vung Tau International Tourist Company, 40/5 Thu Khoa Huan, Vung Tau (tel: 064 852385; fax: 064 859860).

▶ **Vinh Long**   194C3

The main interest of Vinh Long lies in its **boat-trips▶▶**, economically arranged at the central wharf opposite the main hotels and busy market. As at My Tho, local authorities try to monopolise the tourist business, so if you hire a private boat subterfuge tactics may include a return by public ferry. Boats follow narrow, meandering channels through a network of lush islands, passing endless monkey bridges, simple palm-thatched houses and grander new brick houses, shrines, sampans, kingfishers, coconut palms, and trees laden with mangoes and rose-apples. Another common sight is the water hyacinth, a weed that gradually chokes the waterways. Cai Be floating market lies to the north.

South of the centre is the unusual Confucian **Van Thanh Mieu Temple▶**, now sadly neglected and full of bats, although the fairy lights adorning Confucius's portrait in the rear hall function perfectly. At night fairy lights also festoon the garden cafés of Vinh Long's riverside tourist triangle, a good spot to watch families promenading on motor bikes and to enjoy the gentle breeze from the Mekong. An Australian-financed bridge projected for the end of the century will certainly change the town's mellow atmosphere.

▶ **Vung Tau**   195E3

Under the French, Cap St-Jacques (Vung Tau's colonial name, chosen by 16th-century Portuguese missionaries) became the fashionable place for escaping Saigon's heat and it has not looked back since. Some 15km of peninsula coastline have been developed into four main resorts encircling a mountain. Elegant French villas now stand in the shadow of Soviet-built concrete constructions, many linked to the offshore oil fields. There is also a noticeable Russian expatriate community, often seen glued to mobile phones, as well as numerous North Vietnamese immigrants. Weekends are best avoided as Vung Tau fills up fast with city crowds.

The sometimes fatal currents of Vung Tau hardly deter weekend hordes

Central sights Bordering the town centre is **Bai Truoc (Front Beach)▶▶**, a picturesque bay lined with kiosk cafés, restaurants and shops, and with views of fishing boats and, on the horizon, oil-tankers. At the northern end of the bay on the hillside is **Bach Dinh (White Villa)▶▶** (*Open* daily 7–11.30, 1.30–5. *Admission charge* moderate), built in 1898–1916 as a summer residence for the then governor-general of Indochina, Paul Doumer. Emperor Thanh Thai was kept here under house arrest in 1907, and in the 1960s–70s President Thieu, the South Vietnamese head of state, used it as a holiday home, as did government officials post-1975. Today, the villa functions as an eclectic museum, with exhibits ranging from exquisite Qing Dynasty Chinese ceramics rescued from a local shipwreck to a Dong Son drum, Oc Eo artefacts and Khmer bronzes. The drab nylon furnishings are of a more recent date but the furniture is resolutely French art deco.

Beach tour Some 3km to the north lies **Bai Dau▶**, a less frequented and less developed beach where Lon Mountain plunges into rocks and sandy coves. Palm-fringed and with several budget guest-houses, the beach makes a relaxing escape from Vung Tau's main catchment area. To the south of the centre a corniche circles past two pagodas high above, both tasteless recent constructions, although Niet Ban Tinh Xa houses a 12m-long reclining Buddha. Dominating the headland (and reached by a path from Back Beach – see below) is a 28m statue of Jesus, erected in 1971. An interior staircase leads to lookout points on Jesus's shoulders. Within view is the tiny island temple of Hon Ba, lying just offshore and only accessible on foot a few times a year.

On the eastern side of the peninsula the corniche reaches windy **Bai Sau (Back Beach)▶**, a motley concrete mess of unattractive tourist facilities. The undertow off this 8km beach can be dangerous and drownings occur regularly despite a flag system. At its northern end is the Paradise Marina Club, an expat hang-out offering a decent restaurant, changing-rooms and a reasonable beach.

Beyond the hotels and water-babies, life is still about survival

Vung Tau access
Minibuses to Vung Tau leave Ho Chi Minh City regularly from Dong Du and take about 2½ hours. A faster, more comfortable air-conditioned express bus is now in service, leaving every half-hour from Van Thanh bus station in Binh Thanh district from 6am. Those with dollars to spare can take the twice-weekly Vina Express hydrofoil that skims over the waves in just over an hour, although it is not a particularly comfortable ride (Ho Chi Minh City tel: 08 825 3888; Vung Tau tel: 064 859515/854522). Getting around Vung Thau itself is easy, either by cyclo or bicycle (the latter can be hired at hotels).

Khmer culture

■ **Khmer culture is symbolised by the extravagantly winged roofs of their *wat* (temples), rimmed by fragrant frangipani trees and highly visible in the southern Mekong Delta. Despite recent persecution, saffron-robed bonzes (Buddhist monks) flourish and now flock to their spiritual epicentre of Angkor.** ■

Haunting horns
'… [the pagoda's] roofs, faced in golden tiles, have horns at every corner, but very very long horns, that bow, rise and threaten in every direction! In comparison the horns of Chinese pagodas seem really rudimentary, hardly grown; you would think that several giant bulls have been shorn to decorate this strange temple. The various peoples of the yellow race have been haunted for centuries by this concept of horned roofs on their religious structures, but it is the Cambodians who beat them all by their extravagance…'
From *A Pilgrim to Angkor* by Pierre Loti (1912).

Elaborately winged and carved roofs embody a typically Khmer rhythm

Until the late 18th century the Mekong Delta was part of Cambodia, and today, with some areas claiming Khmer populations of up to 30 per cent, it represents a transitional region between the old rivals of Vietnam and Cambodia. There are visible differences between the two people, the Khmer being of Mon-Khmer stock and with physical similarities to the Indians, and the Viets keeping their Chinese features and work ethic. Their paths cross in Buddhism, as well as in an agrarian economy of rice and fish, making settlement across the border relatively feasible. Prior to the Pol Pot years there were some 200,000 Vietnamese living in Cambodia, although this number halved during the massacres, while Khmer communities in the delta account for over half a million inhabitants. The 1960s–70s was a terrible period for Khmer bonzes, who first suffered in Vietnam at the hands of the Catholic President Diem and then subsequently in Cambodia when the Khmer Rouge massacred an estimated 62,000 of the 64,000 monks. Yet reincarnation is cyclical, and the monasteries and *wat* are living again.

Origins Until recently, every Khmer man (including the king) had to spend a year of his life as a begging novice in a Buddhist monastery. This pacifist religion has its origins in the Indianised kingdom of Funan, which developed along the lower reaches of the Mekong River from the 1st to 6th centuries. Animism, Brahmanism and Hinduism were joined in the 5th century by Buddhism, creating a unique synthesis that was to colour the philosophy of Angkor, the Khmers' greatest monument.

Fresh start Radical change and a new identity came in AD 802 when Jayavarman II declared himself king and established his court at Angkor (meaning 'Capital') by the great lake of Tonle Sap. Jayavarman's enigmatic past included a long period at the Javanese court of the Sailendra Dynasty who were then starting their fabulous temple of Borobudur. Jayavarman eventually settled his capital at Roluos (see page 231), where he installed the *devaraja* cult, that of the god-king, an omnipotent protector of his subjects. From then on, every Khmer ruler identified himself with a deity and constructed a temple-mountain to symbolise Mount Meru, the Buddhists' sacred mountain. Within this were housed superb statues, including the phallic linga, the ultimate emblem of power and symbol of Siva.

Water economy Under Indravarman I (877–89), the foundations of the prosperous Khmer economy were laid in the form of complex irrigation systems. Canals, ponds and reservoirs were developed over the centuries to embrace the temples and irrigate the fields. These were perfected by Udayadityavarman II (1050–66), who also built the grandiose Baphuon and developed the cult of Vishnu. The Eastern and Western Baray, the two huge reservoirs that flank Angkor, probably also served to moor royal barges and to breed fish, a multi-functionalism that evolved again when King Sihanouk water-ski'd here in the 1960s.

Rise and fall Despite internal revolts and attacks by the Chams and the Thais, Angkor reached a second peak of glory, influence and creativity in the 12th–13th centuries. During this period Suryavarman II (1113–50) masterminded the beauty and complexity of Angkor Wat, and in a 30-year period Jayavarman VII (1181–1219) built as many temples as all his predecessors put together. These temples were concentrated in and around Jayavarman's palace, Angkor Thom, and include the 52 staggering towers of the Bayon. At the same time, the kingdom's boundaries were extended to Burma, Laos and the Malay Peninsula, and Hinduism was ousted by Mahayana Buddhism. However, Buddha did not help when the Thais sacked Angkor, first in 1353 and again in 1431. For the next five centuries, Khmer culture underwent a strong Siamese influence, the capital moved to Phnom Penh and Angkor was left to the jungle.

Mad about saffron
The colour of the familiar saffron robes of the bonzes was prescribed by Buddha himself. Its distinctive, unfadeable shade comes from boiling coarse cotton cloth in a preparation made from woodchips of the *jak* tree (of jackfruit fame). Each monk has three robes which he wears simultaneously, accessories to his shaven head and eyebrows. Monks are prohibited from inhaling flowers, listening to music, stretching legs when sitting, riding on an elephant, making gifts to women, eating seeds, washing in the dark and winking.

219

Left: the 11th-century ruins of Prah Vihar on the Cambodian–Thai border
Below: part of the Royal Palace in Phnom Penh

ANGKOR

*The activities of the
Khmer Rouge and
local bandits make a
visit to Banteay Srei
(left), 25km from
Angkor's main site,
a hazardous
undertaking*

Money matters

The Cambodian currency is the riel, but US dollars are widely accepted in taxis, hotels, restaurants and shops. Keep US$15 for airport tax on international departures and US$5 for domestic flights. Motorbike taxis can be hired in Siem Reap to tour the site of Angkor at about US$8 per day, cars with drivers cost about US$30 per day, and English-, French- or Chinese-speaking guides can be hired for US$20 per day. Bicycles or motor bikes can be rented cheaply through your hotel or guest-house.

Tentacular roots merge with stone at Ta Prohm

Visas

One-month visas are issued on arrival at Phnom Penh's Pochentong Airport. Two passport photos and US$20 are the current requirements. There are no specified vaccinations, but anti-malarial prophylactics are advisable during the rainy season.

Angkor Southeast Asia's greatest artistic and spiritual feat swelters in its Cambodian jungle setting near the immense lake of Tonle Sap. A visit to this evocative ancient city is the highlight of any itinerary in the region and easily justifies the special effort required. For six centuries from AD 802 until 1431, the Khmer royal capital rose in bricks, laterite and stone to create one of the wonders of the world. This mesmerising network of palaces and temples incorporated not only astonishing statuary, carving and construction skills, but also an incomparable vision and scale.

Yo-yo history Angkor's long period of glory ended when Cambodia became a virtual vassal state of Thailand, with alternating control from Vietnam. Things changed again when Cambodia became a French protectorate from 1884 to 1953, but at independence, engineered by King Norodom Sihanouk, cracks started appearing in the country's neglected socio-economic fabric. The situation was further exacerbated by the Vietnam War, which saw North Vietnamese troops taking refuge in Cambodia, consuming much of the basic rice supply and using Angkor as a military base.

Genocide Discontent and an increasingly fractured society in Cambodia culminated in the military coup of 1970, the growth of the Khmer Rouge and the intervention of the US, whose secret bombing of the communist threat escalated into full-scale carpet bombing in 1973. An estimated 500,000 deaths ensued, and millions of peasants fled from the ravaged countryside.

Internal chaos took a new turn in 1975, when Pol Pot's Khmer Rouge entered Phnom Penh and put into motion its regime of terror, starvation, purges, torture and executions – in short, genocide (see page 230). The temples of Angkor became the Khmer Rouge's ammunition dump and the terrain was laced with mines. In 1979, the Soviet-backed Vietnamese invaded Cambodia, announcing more violence and tragedy and leaving an unresolved situation when they withdrew in 1989.

Finally, in 1991, the four rival factions signed a peace agreement that entailed the deployment of 22,000 UN peacekeepers to demobilise militia, resettle refugees and generally oversee the road to democratic elections. In 1993 elections took place in a climate of unrest and intimidation, resulting in Prince Sihanouk reclaiming his throne and Hun Sen (an authoritarian Vietnam-backed communist) assuming the reins of Cambodia's new liberal coalition government.

Hazardous travel Much of the above explains the problems of travelling in Cambodia. In the last few years the democratic path has been littered with attempted coups, assassinations, sporadic attacks and kidnappings in the countryside. Although today's situation is relatively calm, is subject to sudden change, and prospective visitors are strongly advised to make enquiries before travelling here. Road travel is definitely not recommended, although the bus journey from Ho Chi Minh City to Phnom Penh is usually safe. Beyond that route and particularly in the north-west, where rebel strongholds are located, buses should not be used as they are subject to attacks by the Khmer Rouge and/or bandits. Express boats travel up the Mekong River to Tonle Sap, a relatively secure and scenic itinerary. Safest of all is to take to the air: there are several flights a day between Phnom Penh and Siem Reap, making for easy connections. Also beware that Angkor was heavily mined by the Khmer Rouge, and that although much clearance has occurred there is still plenty of ground to cover. To be safe, pay attention to warning signs and do not wander off the main paths.

To Siem Reap This pretty little town straggles along a tree-lined river, and offers plenty of family guest-houses, good mid-range hotels and small restaurants. Projects for four 300-room luxury hotels on the theoretically off-limits 7km road between Siem Reap and Angkor have recently stirred fiery controversy, with the World Heritage Fund threatening to remove Angkor from its list of protected sites. Old colonial buildings include the majestic Grand Hotel, while the area surrounding the new handicrafts market (selling fine textiles and jewellery) at the southern end of town has a wealth of stuccoed shophouses. Near by stands **Wat Prohm Reat▶**, a lovely old temple containing dozens of Buddha statues. Seventeen monks live in the *wat*, a contrast to the days before 1975 when there were over a hundred. A bank, post office, airline offices and numerous tourist shops complete the offerings.

Tourist services
Siem Reap's tourist office is on the right-hand side of the road to Angkor, just beyond the Grand Hotel. Guides and transport can be arranged here. Alternatively, contact one of the private tour agencies:
● Angkor Tourism, Street 6, Phum Sala Kanseng, Siem Reap (tel: 855 23 57466; fax: 855 23 57693). Also 178c Street 63, Boeung Keng Kong 1, Chamkarmon, Phnom Penh (tel/fax: 855 23 62169/27676).
● Siem Reap Tours, Phnom Penh (tel: 855 15 914283; fax: 855 23 366 526. Siem Reap tel: 855 15 914304; fax: 855 23 57990).

223

The continuous presence of monks in Angkor Wat saved it from the fate of other temples and from the ravages of time

ANGKOR

Each of Angkor Thom's entrance towers is crowned by four faces

Still functioning

Lost in the jungle a couple of hundred metres to the north of Phimeanakas is pretty little Preah Palilay, another Jayavarman VII relic, where Buddhist monks and nuns continue to worship. Only the central sanctuary remains intact, much of the rest lying scattered on the ground, but there are some interesting Buddhist scenes carved on the entry towers and *naga* balustrades frame the terrace. The large seated Buddha statue in front is of recent vintage. Closer to the road and the Terrace of the Leper King is Tep Pranam, a late 9th-century structure that is also much frequented by Buddhist monks.

Some 54 stone figures introduce Angkor Thom's South Gate

Climate

The rainy season is May–October, with temperatures at 35°C and humidity over 95 per cent. Exploring the sights of Angkor is most enjoyable in winter (November–April), although it is only slightly cooler and less humid at this time.

Main site

The 400 or so monuments of Angkor (*Open* daily 5–7. *Admission charge* expensive; one-, three- or seven-day tickets are valid for the whole site) cover an awesome 250sq km, and lie scattered between lofty hardwoods and rural hamlets. The most remote of the monuments, the exquisite 10th-century Banteay Srei, lies 25km to the north-east in an area that unfortunately is currently out of bounds, although this situation may change. Closest to the ticket office, about 7km north of Siem Reap, is Angkor Wat, followed by Angkor Thom and, to the east, a fascinating group of temples including Banteay Kdei and Ta Prohm. Structures continue to the north with the atmospheric Prah Khan and Neak Pean, while crowning the now waterless Eastern Baray is the East Mebon. To do the site any kind of justice, a minimum of three days is necessary.

▶▶▶ Angkor Thom

This colossal fortified city was built in the late 12th century by the last of Angkor's great rulers, Jayavarman VII, to enclose royal, religious and administrative structures. Its square layout puts the Bayon at the centre of a symbolic heaven and earth, the walls representing the mountains surrounding sacred Mount Meru and the moats (now dry) symbolising the ocean. Five elaborately carved entrance gates crowned with enigmatic faces lead into the city: arriving from Angkor Wat, the South Gate is introduced by 54 statues, demons on the right and gods on the left, all holding the sinuous bodies of seven-headed serpents (naga). As pillaging has been the bane of Angkor, many heads are copies; the originals are kept at Siem Reap's Angkor Conservancy.

Magic box The Bayon►►► easily vies with Angkor Wat in its ambitious conception. This maze of dark passages, terraces, steps and arches is dominated by the staggering force of 54 towering faces, their ambivalent expressions changing with the light. Bats, Buddhas and local mystical entrepreneurs inhabit the interior, and nor will you be alone as you emerge onto the upper terraces, where 200 stone faces await you. This pyramidal Buddhist monument was erected by Jayavarman VII at the turn of the 12th century, but may originally have been planned as a two-tiered structure dedicated to Siva. The characteristic faces and their 'smile of Angkor' are thought to be images of Jayavarman in the form of the Bodhisattva Avaloketsvara. Lively bas-reliefs of daily life, battles and processions, more deeply carved than those of Angkor Wat, face the outer gallery, which is punctuated by eight towers. Start at the eastern tower, turn left, and then work your way round to the southern tower to see the most accomplished examples.

Main complex Immediately north-west of the Bayon is the main complex. The temple-mountain of the Baphuon► (1060), lying at the end of a long causeway, is closed for restoration until 2003. Beside it, within the walled royal enclosure, stands Phimeanakas► (late 10th century), where Indonesian restoration continues until 1999. Once crowned by a gold pinnacle, this relatively unadorned Hindu temple rises on three levels to overlook laterite-paved ponds to the north, rampant vegetation and entrance gates that are now fully restored.

To the east, looking out over the royal square (home to two khleang, probably used for visiting envoys) on the north–south axis of Angkor Thom, is the magnificent 300m-long **Terrace of the Elephants►►►**, which merges into the **Terrace of the Leper King►►**. After immaculate French restoration, both have returned to their late 12th-century state. The Leper King statue is actually a copy (the original is at Phnom Penh's National Museum); one interpretation of this odd, sexless figure is that he represented the God of Death and so marks the site of the royal crematorium. He surmounts a double wall of superb bas-reliefs depicting garudas (mythical eagles), elephants, fish and multi-armed giants.

Temple plunder
Headless statues are legion in Angkor. One of the more illustrious plunderers was the writer André Malraux, later to become France's minister of culture. Henri Parmentier's archaeological team had been clearing the creepers from Angkor since 1898 when, in 1923, the young Malraux and his wife Clara turned up on an invented 'mission', their target being Banteay Srei. For two days the jungle echoed to the sound of saws as Malraux and his friend Chevasson (with Clara posted as lookout) hacked away some 800kg of priceless stone sculptures. A few days later, the trio was safely ensconced in a steamer about to leave Phnom Penh when customs officers knocked on the cabin door... Malraux was sentenced to three years' imprisonment, but managed to avoid this thanks to influential friends.

225

Elephants gather lotus-flowers at the south stairway while their bas-relief colleagues enact a royal hunt

Bas-reliefs

Following are the themes of the Gallery of Bas-reliefs, 'read' in an anticlockwise direction from the main western entrance: a *Mahabharata* battle; Suryavarman II riding an elephant into battle against the Chams; the judgements meted out in heaven and hell by Yama, the supreme multi-armed judge (seated on a buffalo); the churning of the Sea of Milk to generate the elixir of immortality, commanded by Vishnu (the most celebrated panel); a war between the gods, with Vishnu beating an army of demons (unfinished and of a later date); the victory of Vishnu (seated on a *garuda*) over the demon-king Bana (mounted on a rhinoceros); scenes from the *Ramayana*; and a *Ramayana* battle between Rama and the ten-headed demon-king Ravana.

Scaling the steps up the towers of Angkor Wat is a labour of love – and stamina

►►► Angkor Wat

The vast scale of this king of monuments makes it as confusing as it is breathtaking. Majestic causeways lead to a wonderland of towers, galleries, chambers, porches, courtyards and terraces, all on different levels connected by steep stairways. Above rise the temple's most prominent features: five seemingly encrusted towers (four in the corners and one in the middle), built in graduated tiers to resemble tapering lotus buds and once coated in gold. It took 30 years to construct this early 12th-century *chef-d'oeuvre*, whose role as funerary temple for Suryvarman II gave it a western orientation towards the setting sun, symbolising death. Unlike other Angkor monuments, the *wat* was saved from the ravages of vegetation by an almost continuous presence of Buddhist monks from 1432 until the present day.

The approach Surrounding the complex is a 200m-wide moat and a laterite wall stretching a total of 5.5km. Crossing the moat from the west, a wide sandstone causeway guarded by lions leads through a gate pavilion that is surmounted by three partly collapsed towers. Inside, colonnaded, vaulted galleries stretch in both directions, offering shade to pilgrims, vendors and statues. Finely chiselled *apsara* (celestial dancers) and *tevada* (heavenly brides) embellish the square columns. Twelve staircases lead down to join the next 350m of causeway, which crosses the main grassy expanse. Two libraries►►, ponds and *naga* balustrades lie on either side, while angled views from the lawns give fabulous panoramas of all five towers.

Bas-reliefs From the final cruciform **Terrace of Honour**, used for ceremonial dances and audiences, visitors penetrate the main sanctuary, introduced by the outstanding and unique **Gallery of Bas-reliefs►►►**. This incredible

feat of sandstone-carving continues uninterrupted around the entire sanctuary, its eight themes covering a total area of 1,200sq m. Remarkable detail, composition and quality of carving depict scenes from the Indian epics the *Mahabharata* and *Ramayana*, as well as Khmer battles. They were designed to be 'read' in an anti-clockwise fashion, so turn right on entering the gallery (see panel opposite for more details).

Beyond this lie the symmetrical **Hall of Echoes** and **Gallery of 1,000 Buddhas**, in turn flanked by ponds and libraries. Typical Khmer features such as corbel vaults, window balustrades carved to resemble turned wood, rosettes and a frieze of coquettish *apsara* are all contained in these cruciform halls. Most of the 1,000 Buddhas were plundered long ago, but those that remain are reverently worshipped with joss-sticks, wreaths and lotus buds.

To heaven From here, walkways and stairs enter the central pyramidal structure: three successive levels are crowned by towers on the second level, and on the final level rises the **Preseat►►►**, or supreme tower. The most staggering aspect is the mass of total sculpture: every inch of surface from lintel to architrave and cornice has been delicately chiselled to create a lace-like profusion of *tevada*, *apsara*, *garuda*, *naga*, flowers, foliage, birds and lotuses. Twelve slippery staircases (sloping at a vertiginous 70 degrees) lead to the final level, where only the king and priests were admitted to worship the sacred image dedicated to Vishnu. Around you the temple unfolds in all its 800-year-old glory and refinement; as the sun sinks opposite, bats squeak and bullfrogs and cicadas break into their insistent chorus. Heaven on earth?

Angkor Wat seen from the south across the moat

 Bakheng

Just over 1km to the north-west along the grand tree-lined avenue leading to Angkor Thom is this turn-of-the-9th-century hilltop temple, built for the Sivaite Yasovarman. Access demands an arduous, mainly stepless climb, eventually paid off by the stupendous 360-degree views from the summit. These are in part marred by a radio mast and the fact that few of the original 109 towers symbolising the cosmos remain intact, having suffered during Cambodia's recent wars. However, it is from here that the visitor grasps the immense expanse of jungle canopy, concealing endless temples and pierced only by the towers of Angkor Wat.

Tentacular nature
'Overgrown? Embosomed, rather; strangled in python coils. Trees, a hundred feet high, straddle the groaning roofs; their roots trail down on either side like the tentacles of immense white octopuses sucking nourishment from the earth, wrapping obscene arms about the carven goddesses. Seeds have grown to saplings, saplings to trees, and in swelling forced ton-weight blocks asunder, bursting walls out and roofs open. Banyans have dropped a network of slender air-roots about whole buildings and, waxing, crushed them as one would a matchbox. Dynamite could do no more. Ruin! Ruin!'
From *The Dragon and the Lotus* by Crosbie Garstin (1928).

Angkor's most evocative temple, Ta Prohm, purposely left in a state of vegetal embrace

▶▶ Banteay Kdei

This unrestored, ruined sandstone temple was begun in 1131, the first of Jayavarman VII's prolific creations (although it was later altered and extended). A *naga*-edged causeway leads through the Hall of Apsaras and a pavilion gate to the main sanctuary, introduced by a seated Buddha and rich *apsara* and foliage carvings. Scattered lichen-covered stone, roofless sections, libraries and towers add to the mystery of this intimate, often-deserted labyrinth. In front lies the Sra Srang ablutions pond, with steps flanked by *naga* and lions.

▶ Mebon (East)

Once only accessible by boat across the waters of the Eastern Baray, now dry, this island temple today merges into the rural landscape. Completed around 952, it is a Sivaite temple dedicated to the parents of Rajendravarman II and is designed in the same style as neighbouring **Pre Rup▶** (961). Three terraced enclosures, with battered elephants at each corner and seated lions flanking the stairways, culminate on the top level with five finely carved brick towers – look for Siva on his sacred bull Nandin on the southern lintel of the central tower. After this, brick was abandoned in favour of laterite and sandstone.

▶ Neak Pean

Imagination is required to envisage the princesses of the late 12th century depositing their offerings of gold and perfumes at this Buddhist temple, which is dedicated to the Bodhisattva Avalokitesvara. Four square ponds radiate from a larger central one that focuses on the circular island temple, its tiny base ringed with *naga* and once guarded by small elephants. Three walled doors of the central sanctuary display carved images of the Bodhisattva, while the pediments illustrate the life of Buddha. The most arresting feature is a sculpture of a swimming horse, a manifestation of the Bodhisattva rescuing Simhala and his shipwrecked companions.

▶▶▶ Prah Khan

Dedicated to Jayavarman VII's father as an incarnation of Lokeshvara, the atmospheric and complex Prah Khan (1191) served as the royal base while Angkor Thom was being completed. Four causeways (some bordered by gods and demons holding a *naga*, as at Angkor Thom) lead through the 3km perimeter walls surrounding this semi-ruined edifice, overrun by the jungle and now undergoing restoration. A wander through its extensive and confusing sanctuaries, galleries, dancehall, two-storey library and outer chapels offers fabulous close-ups on delicately chiselled floral designs, deities, *garuda* and a frieze of Buddhas, as well as tumbled blocks and sculptural vegetation.

▶▶ Prasat Kravan

This unique structure of five aligned towers built entirely of brick served as a Vishnu temple and was erected and dedicated by members of the nobility in 921, proof of the prosperity of the Khmer Kingdom. The inner walls of the main sanctuary display a series of carvings incised into the brick that depict Vishnu in his many forms, while the north tower houses reliefs of Vishnu's wife, Lakshmi. More carvings embellish the exterior, which stands in a pristine restored state.

▶▶▶ Ta Prohm

Miraculously preserved in its jungle-embraced state by enlightened French archaeologists, Ta Prohm (1186) represents a leap back to a time when the entire lost city of Angkor was wreathed in creepers, asphyxiated by strangler figs, cloaked in lichen and wrapped in banyan roots. This jungle-explorer's dream find was built to honour Jayavarman VII's mother, and like Prah Khan had a sumptuous and complex scale. Some 260 statues, 39 towered sanctuaries and 566 residences (including monasteries) were walled by a laterite rectangle over 3km in length. Today, Ta Prohm lies in supremely evocative ruins, its carvings and broken statues scattered through the undergrowth, and its tumbled blocks offering agile vistors some extraordinary vantage points.

▶ Takeo

The rather brutal forms of the late 10th-century Takeo result from the fact that the temple was struck by lightning while under construction; as this catastrophe was seen as a sign from the gods, the final touches of carvings and statues were never added and the temple was left unfinished. However, this means that all attention is focused on its imposing, three-tiered architectural structure, the first to be built in sandstone.

International restoration efforts continue at Ta Prohm

Maintenance funds
A rare Sanskrit stele found at Ta Prohm in 1939 relates the extreme extravagance engendered by the palace-temple before the decline of Angkor. Some 79,635 people were required to maintain it, including 2,740 priests, 2,202 assistants and 615 dancers. Its property (possibly exaggerated to glorify the king) included gold dishes weighing over 500kg, 35 diamonds, 40,620 pearls, 876 Chinese brocades, 512 silk beds and 523 parasols. To keep this little community ticking over in accustomed style, it needed the revenue from 3,140 villages. The maintenance of Prah Khan, built five years after Ta Prohm, escalated even further: 97,840 retainers were needed, financed by the revenue from 5,324 villages.

229

Pol Pot

■ From 1975 until the Vietnamese invasion of 1979, Pol Pot's regime of terror left an estimated 2 million Cambodians dead, along with hundreds of thousands of dislocated families, orphans, refugees and, indirectly, amputees. After rumours of his death circulated, in 1997 Pol Pot was sentenced by his followers to life imprisonment. ■

End of the Khmer Rouge?
Since operating in hiding from their bases along the northern border with Thailand, the guerrillas have supported themselves with revenue from gem mines and logging. Above all, it was China that for years furnished arms and aid to the rebels, mainly to fuel the guerrilla war against their Vietnamese foe. This officially ended in 1990, paving the way for the Paris Peace Accords. Mass defections have now reduced rebel-controlled areas to small pockets, and many observers see the Khmer Rouge as a fading anachronism of the Cold War, now replaced by the realities of the free market. Yet Pol Pot's trial by a dissident faction of Khmer Rouge, in July 1997, points to ongoing developements.

Skulls of Khmer Rouge victims

The infamous Killing Fields and their scenes of carnage and human tragedy were the creation of Pol Pot, born in 1928 as the peasant Saloth Sar and later known as Brother Number One amongst the Khmer Rouge. Inspired by the orthodox Marxism of the French Communist Party, which he observed while on a scholarship to Paris in 1949–53, Pol Pot was to target Cambodia's urban, foreign-influenced élite under his revolutionary battle-cry of *pativattana*, meaning 'return to the past'.

Growing control It was in the 1960s that Pol Pot emerged as a key leader of the Cambodian communist movement, which found popular support among the fractured rural population that had been ignored by Prince Sihanouk's corrupt regime. Deteriorating economic conditions were further exacerbated when President Nixon bombed Cambodia in 1973 in a last-ditch attempt to stem support for the North Vietnamese. In the subsequent power vacuum and chaos, Khmer Rouge control expanded to some two-thirds of the countryside, and on 17 April 1975 Pol Pot and his ragged men entered Phnom Penh in triumph.

Reign of terror For four terrible years, Pol Pot attempted to reshape the renamed Democratic Kampuchea into a self-reliant agricultural society of 'total communism', completely isolated from the rest of the world. City-dwellers were murdered or forced into the countryside, and the administration was run by torture, intimidation and barbaric executions. Pol Pot's methods were easily comparable to those of Hitler or Stalin, except that the death-toll was even higher.

In 1985, six years after his defeat by the Soviet-backed Vietnamese army, Pol Pot officially retired as military commander of the Khmer Rouge. However, in one of the manipulative vagaries of modern history, his movement was saved by the international powers, notably China and the US. Today, the Khmer Rouge still control 10–20 per cent of the country.

Side trip
▶▶ **Roluos**

Angkor's earliest group of temples lies about 13km east of Siem Reap along a picturesque rural road, and can also be reached circuitously from Angkor. After moving his capital several times, Angkor's founder, Jayavarman II, opted for the Roluos site and its role continued under the next three kings before Bakheng took over. Three Sivaite temples of brick, stone and stucco display similar characteristics in layout, decoration and construction, and are now joined by more recent *wat*, so bringing the entire setting alive.

Lolei and Prah Ko The remains of Lolei▶ (893) stand on an elevated terrace next door to a working monastery and *wat*, whose stone stupas rise in front while monks in saffron robes glide around behind. Four brick towers sprouting vegetation incorporate false doors cut from single blocks of stone, these carved with numerous figures. There is some fine carving on the lintels, including Vishnu riding his *garuda* and holding serpents on the south-eastern tower.

Opposite stands the elegant and compact **Prah Ko▶▶** (879), now undergoing restoration. Two rows of three tower-shrines stand on a raised platform, guarded by lions who watch Nandins (bull gods) on the grass below. Much of the lintels' superb stucco ornamentation has been restored, and they are supported by octagonal stone pillars with horizontal mouldings.

Temple-mountain More imposing in scale and majesty is Angkor's first temple-mountain, the Bakong▶▶ (881), rising steeply on five terraces in a moat-encircled enclosure that is reached by a causeway lined with *naga* and *garuda*. It was once the centre of Hariharalaya, established by Jayavarman II and named after the god Hari-Hara, a synthesis of Siva and Vishnu. As with Lolei and Prah Ko (see above), its construction methods and style inaugurated the 'classic' period of Khmer art. Elephants that diminish in size stand at the corners of the first three levels, pointing to the fact that this was the first temple to use stone, dragged here by the trusty creatures. Perforated square buildings in the eastern corners were used either as crematoriums or as forges for making weapons, while two sandstone buildings flanking the causeway may have been libraries. Beside Bakong stands a peeling 1921 *wat* and monastery buildings, with a stupa commemorating a 100-year-old monk who died in 1994. In 1975 the *wat* served as a prison for its monks at the hands of the Khmer Rouge.

231

Bakong, the most significant of the three Roluos temples

■ **A faithful constant throughout Asia for 2,500 years, Buddha thrives in multiple forms in pagodas and *wat*. Despite inroads from Islam over the centuries, Buddhism remains the world's most practised religion, whether in Himayana, Mahayana, Tantric or Zen interpretations.** ■

In a stupa
Although now seen as a classic Buddhist monument, the stupa has its origins in the tumuli (burial mounds) of the Bronze Age. Early Buddhist stupas were massive brick or stone constructions surmounted by pillars, and only gradually assumed the more characteristic conical bell-shape. They were originally designed to contain the ashes of a venerated Buddhist or even Buddhist relics: on Buddha's death a war nearly broke out between rival clans over who was to keep his bones, while legend maintains that the gods kept two-thirds and left only one-third to man. Some 230 years later, King Ashoka managed to divide Buddha's relics into 84,000 parts in order to facilitate the spread of *dharma* throughout his empire.

Buddhism originally developed from Hinduism and radiated from its native India to China, Indochina, Southeast Asia and Japan over a period of several centuries. It is thought to have reached southern Vietnam and, by extension, Cambodia (both sharing the Funan Kingdom) in the late 2nd century AD when Indian monks stopped here on their way to China; parallel to this, Buddhism entered northern Vietnam overland via China.

Siddhartha Buddha himself was born as Prince Siddhartha in 560 BC in present-day Nepal. History and legend merge in the accounts of his life, but his immaculate conception and horoscope all pointed to one thing: he was a Bodhisattva, a future Buddha come to earth to prepare his last birth and enlightenment. Although he married and even fathered a son, on his 29th birthday Siddhartha decided to renounce this easy life and pursue his true spiritual path. At this point the future Buddha made the symbolic gesture of shaving his head, so rejecting the privilege of his caste and creating the model for future Buddhist monks.

Ascetic For six years Siddhartha applied himself to studying Hindu philosophy, meditation, fasting (when he became the skeletal Sakyamuni portrayed in statues) and gathering disciples. Dreams and apparitions from the gods finally led him to the supreme awakening, attained on his 35th birthday at full moon while seated under a *bodhi* tree. Nirvana and Buddhahood were thus reached, and from then until his death aged 80, accompanied by his *arhat* (saintly followers), Buddha preached his doctrine: to escape the eternal cycle of reincarnation and attain nirvana, Buddhists must abstain from sin, practise goodness and purify their thoughts through meditation. A fundamental obligation is to spread the word, or Buddhist law, known as the *dharma*.

Left: Buddha rises at Quy Nhon's Long Khanh Pagoda Opposite: Phung Hiep floating market

Visas

Visitors to Vietnam should apply for a visa well in advance as processing can take at least two weeks. Apply to your local Vietnamese Embassy or, in some countries, to a private agency which makes the application for you (for a fee). There are different types of visa (tourism, business and professional) and regulations change constantly, so the following serves as a guide only.

Tourist visas (single entry or multiple entry) are issued for one month and can be extended at travel agents in Vietnam for a further 15 days. Two application forms need to be filled in and you must state your intended points of arrival and departure (for example, Ho Chi Minh City or Hanoi by air; Lao Bao if continuing by land to Laos; Huu Nghi or Lao Cai to China; Moc Bai to Cambodia); again, this can be amended inside Vietnam through a travel agent. You also need to supply two passport photos and a visa fee which varies from country to country (cheap in Southeast Asia, expensive in Europe and the US). The Vietnamese Embassy in Bangkok is particularly efficient in processing applications.

Customs and immigration procedure

After long waits on arrival you are given an immigration card which must be kept with your passport throughout your trip and surrendered on departure. Check that the length of stay stamped in your passport and on this card corresponds to your requirements. A customs form must also be filled in on arrival; again, keep the copy given to you for surrendering on departure.

Customs regulations

Firearms, explosives, narcotics, inflammable products, live animals and dong (the Vietnamese currency) are all prohibited imports. Allowances of 200 cigarettes or 50 cigars or 250g of tobacco, 1.5 litres of alcohol, foreign currency, perfume and jewellery for personal use all apply, but anything valuable (such as cameras or video cameras) should be declared to customs to avoid any problems on departure. The authorities are particularly finicky about the contents of video cassettes and books, so do not tempt fate by bringing anything of a political or pornographic nature, or that even could be construed as such.

Arriving by air

Air passengers will arrive at either Ho Chi Minh City's Tan Son Nhat Airport or Hanoi's Noi Bai Airport. Both have money-exchange facilities, tourist information, post offices, restaurants and duty-free shops, and are well supplied with taxis. Tan Son Nhat is less than 30 minutes from the city centre and meter taxis are relatively inexpensive. Budget travellers with only a small bag can look for a motor-bike taxi. In Hanoi it is a different story as the airport is about 50km from the centre and a taxi ride is not cheap. However, Vietnam Airlines runs an airport bus on a rather erratic timetable.

Arriving by land

There are currently four land entry points into Vietnam. The Chinese border has two official crossings at Dong Dang (near Lang Son in the north-east) and at Lao Cai (in the north-west). Dong Dang frontier, known as Huu Nghi Quan ('Friendship Gate'), can be crossed by train on the Beijing–Hanoi line, but Lao Cai is only traversed by bus and on foot. The border point with Laos is at Lao Bao (near Khe Sanh) and is another bus and foot crossing unless you are on the Da Nang–Savannakhet international bus. Buses from Phnom Penh in Cambodia cross at Moc Bai, although this is not always a safe route (see pages 222–3). If arriving or leaving by any of these points, it must be specified on your

Throughout Vietnam, ferry transport is the acceptable norm

visa and immigration card otherwise you will be turned back.

Arriving by sea
For the moment the only maritime route into Vietnam is by cruise ship. Enquire at your local travel agent.

Health and travel insurance
There are no health requirements for entry into Vietnam unless you are coming from a country where yellow fever is prevalent. Make sure you have a reliable travel insurance policy that includes repatriation for all accidents and emergencies as hospital treatment in Vietnam is not recommendable. Most travel agents supply reasonable policies.

Departure
Always reconfirm your international flight ticket at least 72 hours in advance. Have your immigration card and customs form ready to hand in, as well as airport tax (currently US$8 for international flights) if you are leaving by plane. If you have bought any antiques make sure you have the relevant documents, including, if necessary, an official export certificate.

Da Nang airport

Climate

Vietnam breaks down into three climatic zones: North, Central Highlands and South.

In the North there are four distinct seasons, with temperatures descending to around 10°C in drizzly wintertime Hanoi. If you visit mountain areas at this time you will need warm clothing and a saintly attitude towards the lack of hotel heating. Spring picks up in April/May when the infamous drizzle gathers strength and temperatures rise to 15–20°C. In summer, brilliant hot sun (temperatures averaging 30°C) alternates with heavy rain, the latter peaking with typhoons brought by the south-west monsoon in August and September. By October/November a calmer transitional autumn leads into the winter of December–February.

The Central Highlands have the highest rainfall in Vietnam, with most falling during the April–October rainy season. At this time roads become mudbaths, and the combination of heat, humidity and hot winds from Laos can make conditions very uncomfortable.

In the tropical South and along the central coast as far as the Hai Van Pass the weather pattern is more straightforward: either it rains or it shines. The rainy season gets going in April and patters on until October/November. From October to December the south-central coast becomes the target of typhoons. January–March is the driest period, although humidity remains high. Temperatures oscillate between 27°C and 33°C.

When to go

Vietnam's conflicting seasons and climates make it virtually impossible to have a rain-free holiday if you plan to travel all over. The best option is to aim for the transitional seasons of March–April and October–November, or to go for high contrast in February by experiencing a very cool North and a hot but dry South.

National holidays
● **New Year's Day** 1 January
● **Tet** Late January/early February

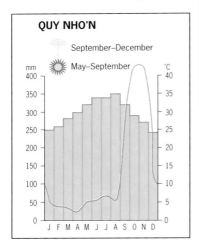

QUY NHO'N

September–December
May–September

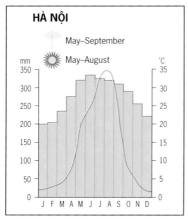

HÀ NỘI

May–September
May–August

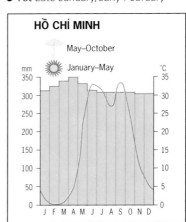

HỒ CHÍ MINH

May–October
January–May

- **Anniversary of the founding of the Vietnamese Communist Party** 3 February
- **Saigon Liberation Day** 30 April
- **Labour Day** 1 May
- **Ho Chi Minh's Birthday** 19 May
- **National Day** 2 September

Time differences

Vietnam is seven hours ahead of GMT, 12 hours ahead of Eastern Standard Time (New York) and 16 hours ahead of Pacific Standard Time (Los Angeles).

Money matters

The Vietnamese currency is the dong (VND), leading to the obvious Western epithet 'Once Viet Cong, now Viet Dong'. Coins are non-existent and notes range from VND200 to VND50,000 (the latter the equivalent of about US$5). This makes for bulky travelling, but US dollars are also widely accepted at hotels, travel agents, museums and tourist-oriented shops to the extent that prices are often quoted in dollars. Try to take a good quantity of US$20 and US$50 notes unless you are a really big spender. Be careful about confusing VND5,000 and VND20,000 notes as they are very similar. Always keep a stock of small notes for cyclos, beggars or minor purchases.

Traveller's cheques should also be in US dollars (these are exchangeable for either dong or dollars); some other currencies (French francs, sterling, Swiss francs, Deutschmark, yen, Australian dollars and Canadian dollars) can be exchanged only in the big cities, and even then there are sometimes problems. Dollar exchange is now quite easy as all large towns have a Vietcombank or equivalent, and transactions (needing a passport) are surprisingly quick once the scrum at the counter has been transcended. If payment is made in dollars, change is given either in dong or dollars.

Credit cards are still very limited in use and vendors often tack on a 4 per cent commission (anything more should be negotiated downwards). Top-range hotels, airlines and restaurants accept them without charging any extra but these establishments are not exactly widespread. Cash advances can be obtained with VISA cards (+ 4 per cent commission) or Mastercard (no commission) in large city banks.

Tips (euphemistically called 'souvenirs') are not expected except in top-range hotels and restaurants and by guides and drivers, but they are always welcome.

Counting dong is a national pastime, but notes burnt as offerings are resolutely fake

Opening times

Government offices are open Mon–Sat 7.30–4.30 with a variable one-hour lunch break, so avoid them between 11.30am and 2pm. Banks follow roughly the same pattern, opening Mon–Fri 8–11.30, 1–4 and closing one hour earlier on Saturdays. Museums are settling into the same generalised hours but close on Mondays. Major sights such as Hue's Imperial City or Da Nang's Cham Museum are open daily without any lunch break. Shops work hard for maximum business, opening around 8am and closing at nightfall around 7pm. Rail- and bus-ticket offices have idiosyncratic hours, sometimes opening in the morning only and/or corresponding to departure times.

Cars and motor bikes

Car rental Although it is not possible for foreigners to drive a car personally in Vietnam, there is no shortage of cars with drivers. Rates vary according to the type of car (jeep, Russian or Japanese make, air-conditioned or not), where it is rented, and the duration and distance of your journey. The average daily rate usually allows for 100km. Rates are lowest in competitive Ho Chi Minh City and highest in the North. Official tourist offices often charge exaggerated prices, but their drivers are reliable and often double up as informative guides. If renting a car with driver for several days, make sure that the fine points of the financial arrangement are clear (such as who pays for the driver's food, accommodation and petrol) and that he speaks at least some English or French, depending on your needs.

The following private travel agencies will supply cars and drivers at considerably lower rates than at government tourist offices:

Hanoi
● **Especen Center** 79e Hang Trong, Hoan Kiem (tel: 04 826 6856; fax: 04 826 9612).
● **Green Bamboo Travel** 42 Nha Chung, Hoan Kiem (tel: 04 826 8752; fax: 04 826 4949).

A brave tourist looks for the action in Hanoi

● **Vidotour** 28 Hao Ma (tel: 04 821 5682).

Ho Chi Minh City
● **Ann Tourist** 58 Ton That Tung, District 1 (tel: 08 833 4356; fax: 08 832 3866).
● **Asia Natural Travel (Bamboo Café)** 223 De Tham, District 1 (tel/fax: 08 835 6992).
● **Cam On Tour** 32 Dong Du, District 1 (tel: 08 829 8443; fax: 08 829 8169).
● **Fiditourist** 73–5 Dong Khoi, District 1 (tel: 08 829 6325; fax: 08 822 3571).
● **Kim Café** 270 De Tham, District 1 (tel: 08 835 9859; fax: 08 829 8546). Also runs a tourist-bus service throughout Vietnam.
● **Linh's Café** 235 Pham Ngu Lao, District 1 (tel: 08 836 0643; fax: 08 829 8540).
● **Sinh Café Office** 179 Pham Ngu Lao, District 1 (tel: 08 835 5601; fax: 08 835 7722). Also runs a tourist-bus service throughout Vietnam.
● **Vyta Tours** 52 Hai Ba Trung, District 1 (tel: 08 823 0767; fax: 08 824 3524). Well established, reliable.

Motorbike rental Many of the above agencies also hire out motor bikes, possibly the best way of seeing this country if you have the nerves to confront city traffic and rural road surfaces. Vyta Tours arranges guided motorbike tours for groups of a minimum of six people on 400cc Japanese bikes – a rarity in this country where 100cc is often the best you will find. For touring the North, the latter is the minimum power necessary to negotiate the bad, mountainous and often muddy roads. It is also possible to rent motor bikes with drivers, many of whom act as guides and can arrange accommodation with local people. As with car rental, make sure your driver speaks at least some English or French.

Driving conditions Highway 1, which connects Ho Chi Minh City with Hanoi, and the newly upgraded Highway 14 between Buon Ma Thuot and Plei Ku are, for the moment, the only Vietnamese roads in good (though sometimes merely passable) condition. There are plans to improve and widen Highway 5 between Hanoi and Hai Phong, one of Vietnam's busiest routes, and to upgrade the 160km stretch of Highway 1 between Hanoi and Lang Son on the Chinese border. Building also continues slowly on roads in the Mekong Delta which have been real endurance tests until now, but as little machinery is available, roadworks take a long and dusty time. Elsewhere, expect frequent potholes and rice laid out to be conveniently de-husked by passing vehicles.

The one advantage is that cars are still rare so there are no congestion problems except where ferries are involved: queues to cross certain rivers can last hours unless you have an officially rented car, which has priority. Avoid travelling during Tet, when the entire country seems to be out on the road.

Public transport
Buses Only a few courageous souls confront the public bus system. There are some remarkable variations in bus styles (from decrepit 1940s Citroëns to pick-up trucks, second-hand Chinese buses and some newer, faster minibuses) but all, without fail, break down. This pads out travelling

time considerably, although Vietnamese drivers seem to have an innate sense of mechanics and eventually get the vehicle moving again. Local buses also have a habit of picking up loads from backstreets (anything from coal to rice or sacks of cement), again lengthening the journey and often creating awkward seating arrangements (ever travelled with two mortar shells, a TV and a spare tyre under your feet?).

Seats are narrow and buses overcrowded, so for larger-scaled Westerners the best option is to buy two tickets each. Tickets for long-distance routes can be bought in advance at the bus station, where the normal Vietnamese price is charged; otherwise, when buying a ticket from

Vietnamese police are not to be trifled with

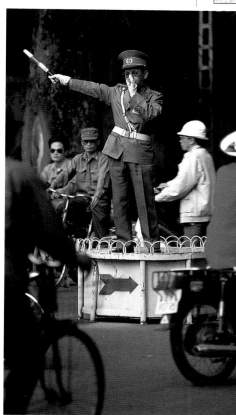

the conductor on the bus prices become negotiable.

Long-distance buses usually leave at 5–6am, adding yet another inconvenience to this form of transport. They can be flagged down on the highway but by then are often full. Keep your bag with you (another good reason to buy two tickets) as it may well disappear from the roof-rack or be squashed by other loads.

Trains One up on the bus network is Vietnam's railway. This French-built system, completed in 1938, starts at Ho Chi Minh City and runs 1,738km north along the coast to Hanoi, where it branches to connect with the Chinese border. Speeds average 45kph. The Reunification Express (with restaurant car, air-conditioning or fans, and hard or soft berths) runs daily between the two cities, takes 36–40 hours, and should be booked several days in advance. Depending on your starting point, departure times are not always convenient, but if time is short it is well worth taking the overnight train from Hue to Hanoi for example. First-class travel is obviously the most comfortable, with a second-class 'soft seat' a viable alternative for shorter hops. Ticket prices for foreigners are about five to six times those for locals, making the journey cost almost the same as travelling by plane. However, you are more than compensated by the sights, sounds and smells of daily Vietnamese life.

The morning after the night before

● **Hanoi Railway Station (Ga Ha Noi)** 120 Le Duan (tel: 04 825 3949).
● **Saigon Railway Station (Ga Sai Gon)** 1 Nguyen Thong, District 3, Ho Chi Minh City (tel: 08 844 3952/844 0218).

Air services Vietnam Airlines runs an extensive internal flight network, but this deprives the traveller of one of the country's greatest assets: landscapes and roadside sights. Only a few years ago this airline was notoriously unsafe and unreliable, but vast improvements have been made, notably an upgrading of the fleet of 30-odd planes and a gradual withdrawal of the old Soviet planes. Fokkers, Boeings and Airbuses (the latter for international flights and the Hanoi–Ho Chi Minh City line) will soon become the norm except for very obscure destinations.

With passengers increasing annually by an average of 37 per cent, service should also be improving, but this is not always the case. Always double-check any flight departure before heading out to the airport as flights may be delayed or even cancelled at the last minute. Remember to have cash available for the airport tax (currently VND15,000 on domestic flights).

Vietnam Airlines serves the following towns: Buon Ma Thuot, Can Tho, Da Lat, Da Nang, Dien Bien Phu, Hai Phong, Hanoi, Ho Chi Minh City,

Hue, Nha Trang, Phu Quoc, Plei Ku, Quy Nhon, Rach Gia, Vinh and Son La. Tickets are priced in US dollars and can be bought with international credit cards without any surcharge at the airline's main offices, listed below:

● **Hanoi** 1 Quang Trung, District 1 (tel: 04 825 0888/3842).

● **Ho Chi Minh City** 116 Nguyen Hue, District 1 (tel: 08 829 2118). Also at 15b Dinh Tien Hoang, District 1 (tel: 08 823 1483).

● **Da Nang** 7 Yen Bai (tel: 051 822808).

● **Hai Phong** Cat Bi Airport (tel: 031 847137/8).

● **Hue** 12 Hanoi (tel: 054 823249).

● **Nha Trang** 12b Hoang Hoa Tham (tel: 058 823797).

● **Quy Nhon** 2 Ly Thuong Kiet (tel: 056 823125).

● **Son La** San Bay Na San (Na San Airport) (tel: 022 843101).

● **Vinh** 28 Nguyen thi Minh Khai (tel: 038 847359).

Student and youth travel

There are no discounts on any internal transport for foreign students or young people, although certain international carriers may offer reductions. Check with your local student travel office.

Motor bikes? Trains? The choice is yours

An immaculate French post office watches over the changes

Post offices

Vietnamese post offices (*buu dien*) are usually easy to spot as most of them are elaborate stuccoed buildings dating from the French administration. Stamps are a philatelist's delight and also appeal to the low-paid post-office official: make sure that any letters or postcards are postmarked at the counter in front of you as the value of a stamp to Europe is also that of a good bowl of *pho*. Mail sent from top-range hotels can usually be relied upon.

Post is slow but eventually reaches its destination so long as it is not a suspicious-looking package; allow two weeks for most Western destinations, although it can be faster. EMS (Express Mail Service) offers delivery the next day to main towns in Vietnam and in two to ten days to foreign destinations. Hanoi and Ho Chi Minh City central post offices have international counters with efficient English-speaking staff.

Poste restante is reasonably reliable, particularly in Hanoi and Ho Chi Minh City: have your mail addressed to 'Poste Restante, Buu Dien' plus the name of town and province, but again avoid having parcels or bulky envelopes sent as these may arouse the suspicions of customs officers and delay matters.

DHL, Federal Express and TNT are all making inroads into larger cities.

Telephone and fax

Telecommunications have greatly improved in recent years and faxes are becoming quite run of the mill. However, the cost of telephone calls remains astronomical (one of the highest in the world), even when using a Uniphone Kad (phonecard) from one of the rare appropriate phones in Ho Chi Minh City. Public phones are virtually non-existent, making hotel rooms with private phones essential if you need to contact people, agencies or guides. It is, of course, cheaper to make trunk or foreign calls/faxes from the local post office, and services here are generally helpful.

● **International dialling code** 00
● **International operator** 110
● **Domestic operator** 101
● **Enquiries on socio-economic and cultural subjects** 108

Media

There is a surprising amount of foreign-language press in Vietnam, making it easy to keep abreast of developments even though contents are strictly censored. By far the best is the *Vietnam Investment Review*, a weekly newspaper with an excellent colour supplement and dynamic approach published in Hanoi. Apart from economic and business news, it offers interesting social insights, cultural listings and some wide-ranging features. Another weekly, the *Saigon Times*, produces more standard but nevertheless useful business information and features. The *Saigon Newsreader* is a third, very limited weekly alternative. The only English-language daily is the *Vietnam News*, a government mouthpiece.

Television and radio stations provide excellent regional coverage but remain firmly in Vietnamese. On top of this, many towns with strong People's Committees have a public-address system that feeds government propaganda from dawn to dusk (this includes, surprisingly, Nha Trang). Satellite television is becoming increasingly common, even in middle-range hotels, so visitors need not feel isolated from the rest of the world.

Language
Vietnamese is unfortunately an extremely difficult language to master as its tonal subtleties remain beyond the reach of the average traveller or even linguist. Add to this the wide variations in accents from north to south, and you realise that you are unlikely to make many communicative inroads. Luckily, English is widely spoken among the young in urban areas, while older educated people may speak impeccable French. Other than that, in the North there are numerous Vietnamese who worked in East Germany or the USSR, so it may be useful if you speak German or Russian.

Useful words and phrases

hello	chao
goodbye	tam biet
thank you	cam on
no thank you	khong, cam on
yes	co
please	xin
see you later	hen gap lai
good luck	chuc may man
I don't understand	toi khong hieu
quickly	nhanh
slowly	cham
where is...?	...o dau?
which way?	huong nao?
on the right	o ben phai
on the left	o ben trai
hotel	khach san
I want a room	toi muon thue phong
with a single bed	phong mot giuong
with a double bed	phong hai giuong
a room with a bathroom	phong co phong tam
how much?	bao nhieu?
that is too expensive	dat qua
toilet	ve sinh

Map features

district	quan
bay	vinh
island	dao
pass	deo
river	song
lake	ho
mountain	nui
bridge	cau
market	cho
museum	bao tang
pagoda	chua
temple	den
palace	dien
bus station	ben xe
railway station	ga xe lua
post office	buu dien
hospital	benh vien
police station	don cong an
church	nha tho
airport	san bay
street	duong/pho
gardens/park	vuon/ vuon hoa (cong vien)
north	bac
south	nam
east	dong
west	tay

Numbers

1	mot	8	tam
2	hai	9	chin
3	ba	10	muoi
4	bon	11	muoi mot
5	nam	20	hai muoi
6	sau	21	hai muoi mot
7	bay	100	mot tram
		1,000	mot ngan

Crime and police

Foreigners in Vietnam have to remain alert to pickpockets, particularly active on buses, trains and along the main avenues in Ho Chi Minh City, where another danger is fast-moving motorbike thieves. Apart from this it is a relatively safe country to travel in. Police are not the most helpful of breeds, so only contact them in extreme emergencies, when you will need a Vietnamese-speaker to accompany you. Always keep your traveller's-cheque numbers and/or credit-card numbers and contact telephone numbers separate, and avoid carrying large amounts of cash on you. If you put a good padlock on your bag, keep it locked when you leave your hotel room and do not lose sight of it on buses or trains, you should avoid any unnecessary trouble.

Lost property

If you lose anything there is little to do bar return to where you think you left it. In countries as poor as Vietnam it is unlikely that valuable items such as cameras will be diligently returned, so the answer is to keep a close tab on your belongings.

Emergency telephone numbers

- **Police** 113
- **Fire brigade** 114
- **Ambulance** 115
- **International Hospital, Hanoi (Bach Mai)** 04 869 3521/3515/4462
- **Swedish Clinic, Hanoi** 04 845 2464/821 3555
- **International SOS, Ho Chi Minh City** 08 824 2866
- **Emergency Center, Ho Chi Minh City** 08 829 6485/1711 (24-hour service)
- **Institut Pasteur, Ho Chi Minh City** 08 823 0352

Embassies and consulates

- **Australian Embassy** 66 Ly Thuong Kiet, Hanoi (tel: 04 825 2703; fax: 04 825 9268).
- **Canadian Embassy** 31 Hung Vuong, Hanoi (tel: 04 823 5500; fax: 04 823 5333).
- **New Zealand Embassy** 32 Hang Bai, Hanoi (tel: 04 824 1481; fax: 04 824 1480).

- **UK Embassy** 16 Ly Thuong Kiet, Hanoi (tel: 04 825 2510; fax: 04 826 5762). There is also a UK consulate at 261 Dien Bien Phu, District 3, Ho Chi Minh City (tel: 08 829 8433/820 0127; fax: 08 822 5740).
- **US Liaison Office** 7 Lang Ha, Hanoi (tel: 04 843 1500/1/2/3/4/5/6/7; fax: 04 843 1510).

Health

Vietnam does not present any worse health conditions than other Southeast Asian countries, so the usual precautions apply. Tap water should never be drunk; bottled mineral water is widely available and is worth drinking constantly during the hotter months to avoid dehydration. Hotels always provide boiled water, which is safe to drink. It is advisable to avoid ice (particularly as large blocks of the stuff are transported by motor bike) although some travellers do not seem to be affected by it. High-factor sunscreens should be used liberally as the tropical sun is fierce – bring them from home and invest in a hat (coolie or otherwise) when you arrive.

Fresh, unpeelable fruit should be well rinsed, but otherwise Vietnamese food is reasonably hygienic – although there are exceptions. Bring pills such as Lomotil for stomach upsets, and if struck with a bad dose of diarrhoea, take oral rehydration salts, rest and avoid eating anything other than boiled rice or bananas until the attack passes. Strangely enough, flat Coca Cola is found to be an efficient killer of stomach bacteria. If the problem continues for more than a few days, consult a doctor.

Before leaving home, make sure that your tetanus, typhoid and polio immunisations are up to date and, well in advance, invest in Havrix, a double jab against hepatitis A that is spaced over two weeks and needs a double booster after six months (this lasts ten years). Malaria is a danger and visitors should take precautions, whether by taking prophylactics (starting two weeks before arrival) or using abundant insect repellent with a high level of DEET. Mosquito spirals are easily purchased and nearly every hotel has mosquito nets. Insect bites can be treated with anti-histamine cream.

Another useful item to have in your first-aid kit is a treatment of general antibiotics for emergencies and an antibiotic ointment for bad cuts.

Vietnamese pharmacies, designated by a sign of an uncoiling snake, are common in all large towns, although pharmacists rarely speak a foreign language. An incredible range of medicines is available, many from former Eastern Bloc countries, and prescriptions are not required. English-speaking doctors can be consulted in Hanoi or Ho Chi Minh City (see **Emergency telephone numbers**), but for anything serious, including broken limbs, try to reach a

Urban Vietnamese are adopting Western sporting habits to keep fit

neighbouring country such as Singapore or Hong Kong for treatment. Vietnamese hospitals are understaffed, underfinanced and severely lacking in equipment and hygiene.

As is the case elsewhere in Southeast Asia, Aids is on the increase and is certainly not helped by the high numbers of prostitutes and junkies, above all in Ho Chi Minh City. A potentially useful extra for your first-aid kit is a sterilised syringe as many hospitals do not have them. Women should also bring a stock of tampons.

Camping and self-catering

Camping is not at all common even among the Vietnamese, and only a few national parks actually have facilities (notably Cuc Phuong). Self-catering accommodation is, on the other hand, available in towns such as Hue and Da Lat at government-run villas. Contact the local tourist office for further information.

Visitors with disabilities

As Vietnam is still a developing nation, facilities for disabled visitors are extremely rare. Some top modern hotels in Hanoi and Ho Chi Minh City are designed for wheelchairs, but as nearly every tourist sight – from museums to pagodas – involves flights of steps, Vietnam cannot be recommended as a destination.

Places of worship

Buddhists have no shortage of destinations for worship, while Christians, whether Protestant or Catholic, will also easily find a church in every large town. After 17 years of suppression, religious belief is on the rise and at some churches Sunday services are packed out.

The triple religion has bounced back after communist suppression

Toilets

Public toilets are just passable in airports, railway stations and museums, but elsewhere they assume a variety of guises ranging from pigsty annexes to mere holes in the ground (possibly with a view). Keep a supply of toilet paper on you.

Photography

Vietnam's sublime landscapes and attractive people together form another Asian photographic paradise. Supplies stores are excellent in Ho Chi Minh City (film prices are about 20 per cent lower than in Europe) and offer an increasing array of equipment. Colour-print film (Kodak, Fuji, Konica) is available throughout the country but slide film, usually Ektachrome, can only be found in the larger touristy towns. Always check expiry dates and storage conditions.

In Ho Chi Minh City several good camera and film-processing shops on Nguyen Hue, near the crossroads with Le Loi, include the Fuji shop at No 78, reliable for slide processing as well as prints. In Hanoi, photo-supply and processing shops surround Hoan Kiem Lake. Lithium batteries can be found fairly easily but keep a spare set if you are travelling to more remote places. X-ray machines at airports should be checked to see if they are film-safe before letting any film through – avoid this procedure if possible.

On the whole, the Vietnamese love being photographed, but do be sensitive, above all among ethnic minorities and at religious sites, and ask permission beforehand. Military buildings and subjects should not be photographed overtly. High fees are charged for using video cameras at major sights such as Hue's Imperial City and Tombs.

Electricity

Voltage is generally 220V, but in some places 110V is still in use: always ask before plugging anything in. In the South, sockets generally take US-style two-pronged plugs with flat pins, while in the North French-style two-pronged round pins prevail.

Etiquette and local customs

The Western handshake is now the accepted manner of greeting in Vietnam, but patting children's heads is regarded as inauspicious and pointing at someone is downright rude. To call someone's attention, beckon with your palm facing downwards.

Most Vietnamese are extremely courteous, and in small towns you may be approached by the local English teacher or students; be patient and give them some of your time. Avoid losing your temper, however irritating a situation may be, as this is not considered a sign of strength but quite the opposite. The answer at times such as these is to keep smiling.

When visiting minority villages, only enter a house if invited, be circumspect about photographing and bring small gifts such as pens or notebooks. In Khmer pagodas, remove your shoes in the main sanctuary, and in all pagodas leave a donation. Throughout Vietnam, if you are offered a cup of tea it would be considered discourteous to decline.

Clothing

Much depends on the region and season (see **Climate** on page 236), but your wardrobe should be selective and lightweight. Bring cotton or linen garments, including a long-sleeved shirt, a pullover and/or jacket for the mountains, a swimsuit and good walking shoes that are not unnecessarily heavy. You can also always supplement your wardrobe with local made-to-measure items, although pure cotton is virtually impossible to find. Cheap plastic raincoats are ubiquitous, while jeans, T-shirts and trainers are easily and inexpensively purchased in the cities. The Vietnamese dress informally but keep their clothes well washed and ironed, so visitors should try to do the same: most hotels have inexpensive 24-hour laundry services.

Women travellers

Vietnam is a fairly easy country for women travellers (inasmuch as travel in Vietnam can be called easy), particularly if they stick to the main tourist circuit. Decades of strict communism have left their mark and equality is part of that system. However, as in other Asian countries, unmarried women are regarded as a strange breed, so communication is often made easier if an absent husband and children are invented. This said, the younger Vietnamese are increasingly aware of Western ways, and divorce is now common.

CONVERSION CHARTS

FROM	TO	MULTIPLY BY
Inches	Centimetres	2.54
Centimetres	Inches	0.3937
Feet	Metres	0.3048
Metres	Feet	3.2810
Yards	Metres	0.9144
Metres	Yards	1.0940
Miles	Kilometres	1.6090
Kilometres	Miles	0.6214
Acres	Hectares	0.4047
Hectares	Acres	2.4710
Gallons	Litres	4.5460
Litres	Gallons	0.2200
Ounces	Grams	28.35
Grams	Ounces	0.0353
Pounds	Grams	453.6
Grams	Pounds	0.0022
Pounds	Kilograms	0.4536
Kilograms	Pounds	2.205
Tons	Tonnes	1.0160
Tonnes	Tons	0.9842

247

MEN'S SUITS

UK	36	38	40	42	44	46	48
Rest of Europe	46	48	50	52	54	56	58
US	36	38	40	42	44	46	48

DRESS SIZES

UK	8	10	12	14	16	18
France	36	38	40	42	44	46
Italy	38	40	42	44	46	48
Rest of Europe	34	36	38	40	42	44
US	6	8	10	12	14	16

MEN'S SHIRTS

UK	14	14.5	15	15.5	16	16.5	17
Rest of Europe	36	37	38	39/40	41	42	43
US	14	14.5	15	15.5	16	16.5	17

MEN'S SHOES

UK	7	7.5	8.5	9.5	10.5	11
Rest of Europe	41	42	43	44	45	46
US	8	8.5	9.5	10.5	11.5	12

WOMEN'S SHOES

UK	4.5	5	5.5	6	6.5	7
Rest of Europe	38	38	39	39	40	41
US	6	6.5	7	7.5	8	8.5

Tourist offices

Vietnam has few tourist offices outside the country; in most cases you should contact your local Vietnamese Embassy or a travel agent specialising in the region.

Overseas Vietnamtourism offices
● **France** 4 rue Cherubini, 75002 Paris (tel: 42 86 86 37; fax: 42 60 43 32).
● **Singapore** 101 Upper Cross Street, #02-44 Peoples Park Center, Singapore 0105 (tel: 65 532 3130; fax: 65 532 2952).
● **USA** PO Box 53316, Indianapolis, IN46253-0316 (tel: 371/388 0788; fax: 371/488 5510).

Tourist offices in Vietnam
The following are government-run agencies that cater more for group travel arrangements. Independent travellers will find them of limited use except for guided tours. Apart from those listed below, each provincial capital has its own tourist office; the addresses for these are listed in side panels beside each entry in the A–Z section of this book.

Hanoi
● **Hanoi Railway Tourism Service** 104c Le Duan (tel: 04 851 0575).

● **Hanoi Youth Tourism** 14a Phan Chu Trinh, Hoan Kiem (tel: 04 826 3077; fax: 04 824 6463).
● **Hanoitourist** 18 Ly Thuong Kiet, Hoan Kiem (tel: 04 825 7886/826 6714; fax: 04 825 4209).
● **Vietnam Veterans' Tourism Service** 192 Quan Thanh (tel: 04 823 7751; fax: 04 823 7468).
● **Vietnamtourism** 5 Ba Trieu, Hoan Kiem (tel: 04 824 4131; fax: 04 824 3570). Also at 30a Ly Thuong Kiet, Hoan Kiem (tel: 04 825 5552; fax: 04 825 7583).

Hai Phong
● **Vietnamtourism** 15 Le Dai Hanh (tel: 031 842957/989; fax: 031 842674).

Ho Chi Minh City
● **Saigon Railway Tourism** 275c Pham Ngu Lao, District 1 (tel: 08 839 2031; fax: 08 843 8830).
● **Saigontourist** 39 Le Thanh Ton, District 1 (tel: 08 829 5534/ 822 5887; fax: 08 829 1026). Also at 187 Pham Ngu Lao, District 1 (tel: 08 835 4535/4542; fax: 08 835 4533).
● **Vietnamtourism** 234 Nam Ky Khoi Nghia, District 3 (tel: 08 829 0776; fax: 08 829 0775).

HOTELS AND RESTAURANTS

ACCOMMODATION

The Vietnamese hotel scene has been transformed since the early 1990s and it is now possible to sleep in relative comfort in most large towns. Government-owned hotels that once monopolised the circuit are still classic examples of socialism gone wrong: indolent employees doze in front of TVs in the lobby, and the overpriced, badly maintained rooms boast nylon curtains and decrepit plumbing. Compensation comes in the form of a thermos of hot water, doll-sized teacups, armchairs, a mosquito net, a fan and a flannel-sized towel. These state hotels also often monopolise the best locations. However, privately owned mini-hotels and guest-houses are now appearing all over the country, and in fiercely competitive towns such as Ho Chi Minh City, Hue and Nha Trang there are some excellent-value places run by helpful families.

If you plan on striking out to less-visited places you will inevitably find yourself in a nightmare budget hotel: tiles drop off the walls at night, bugs are omnipresent, electric wires meander through the shower and hygiene is distinctly lacking. When viewing rooms, always check to ensure fans, air-conditioning and lights function; maximum may mean minimum and the hot-water tap may of course run cold. Sheets may be of rayon (ask if they can be changed) and mattresses of foam.

The following hotels have been divided into three price categories:

- budget (£)
- moderate (££)
- expensive (£££)

HANOI

Army Hotel (££) 33c Pham Ngu Lao, Hoan Kiem (tel: 04 826 5541; fax: 04 825 9276). Former military guest-house south of Hoan Kiem Lake. Uninspired 1970s architecture but decent rooms, facilities and service.
Bac Do Hotel (££) 151 Yen Phu, Ho Tay (tel: 04 823 8100; fax: 04 823 8103). Forty-room modern business hotel overlooking West Lake. Bars, restaurant, garage, sauna.
Binh Minh Hotel (£) 50 Hang Be, Hoan Kiem (tel: 04 826 7356; fax: 04 824 7183). A few reasonable rooms along with the windowless variety. Phone, TV, decent bathrooms and budget prices.
Dan Chu Hotel (£££) 29 Trang Tien, Hoan Kiem (tel: 04 825 4937; fax: 04 826 6786). Formerly the institutional Hanoi Hotel; now offers 40 clean, spacious rooms, friendly and efficient service and a central location.
Especen Centre (£/££) 79e Hang Trong, Hoan Kiem (tel: 04 826 6856; fax: 04 826 9612). A reliable chain of 11 established, well-located hotels, now rather run down.

Helpful, polyglot staff, rooms usually with air-conditioning and phone. Tours, rentals.
Ho Tay Villas (££) Tay Ho (tel: 04 845 2393; fax: 04 823 2126). Former Communist Party guest-house. Well-designed, spacious villas in gardens on West Lake. Good facilities and food, efficient staff but far from centre.
Hoa Binh Hotel (£££) 27 Ly Thuong Kiet (tel: 04 825 3315; fax: 04 826 9818). Large, atmospheric old hotel with modernised colonial-style rooms. Modern annexe, roof-terrace bar, central location.
Hoa Linh Hotel (££/£££) 35 Hang Bo, Hoan Kiem (tel: 04 825 0034; fax: 04 824 3886). Good service and traditionally styled rooms in this central, rather overpriced hotel. Kitsch touches; art gallery in lobby.
Hong Ngoc (££) 34 Hang Manh, Hoan Kiem (tel: 04 828 5053; fax: 04 828 5054). A pearl of a small hotel with large well-furnished rooms in traditional style, some with antique beds. Good bathrooms with bath-tubs, air-conditioning, satellite TV, artworks, bar/restaurant and very amenable staff. Interesting location.
Metropole/Hotel Sofitel (£££) 15 Ngo Quyen, Hoan Kiem (tel: 04 826 6919; fax: 04 826 6920). Renovated turn-of-the-century landmark on east side of lake with extremely comfortable rooms and impeccable service. French restaurant, convivial bar, outdoor pool, business centre, ticketing and tours. Hanoi's only luxury hotel.
Quoc Hoa Hotel (££) 10 Bat Dan, Hoan Kiem (tel: 04 828 4528; fax: 04 826 7424). A 26-room modern hotel with wide-ranging rates. Large, well-equipped rooms with air-conditioning, fridge, TV and bath-tubs. Adjoining café/bar. Lively location.
Stars Hotel (££) 26 Bat Su (tel: 04 828 1911; fax: 04 828 1928). Highly recommended mini-hotel with excellent service, friendly staff and a central location in the old quarter.
Thang Long Hotel (£) 52 Cau Go, Hoan Kiem (tel: 04 824 5712; fax: 04 824 5502). Right in the thick of the old quarter near lake. Front rooms can be noisy, but cheaper back rooms often small and windowless. Good bathrooms, air-conditioning.
Thanh Binh Hotel (£) 81 Hang Dao, Hoan Kiem (tel: 04 824 4223; fax: 04 824 3970). Well-established hotel rising up steep backstairs, plus art-gallery entrance. Efficient, friendly staff and reasonable rooms. Tours, plus cars and motor bikes for hire.

THE NORTH
Cat Ba Island
Cat Ba Hotel (£) Cat Ba Harbour (tel: 031 888243). Government-owned hotel on quieter stretch of port. Good-sized rooms with balconies and fans. Disorganised but well-meaning staff, restaurant.

Family Hotel (£) Cat Ba Harbour (tel: 031 888231). Helpful management and good location. Small but clean rooms and bathrooms, reasonably priced.

Hoang Huong (£) Cat Ba Harbour (tel: 031 888274). New glass-fronted hotel at entrance to government-hotel compound. Well run and good views from front balconies, but light-sensitive people should go elsewhere.

Dien Bien Phu

Dien Bien Phu Mini Hotel (£) 7 Be Van Dan (tel: 023 824319). Reasonable rooms with bathrooms in a pristine white hotel. Centrally located, restaurant.

Hai Phong

Hai Au Hotel (££) Do Son beach (tel: 031 861272/861225; fax: 031 861176). Well-appointed hotel conveniently situated next door to Do Son's casino and with easy access to beach. Restaurant.

Hoa Binh Hotel (£) 104 Luong Khanh Thien (tel: 031 859029). Long a favourite with budget travellers for its reasonably priced rooms, restaurant and central location. Huge new annexe has hiked up the previously low rates.

Hong Bang Hotel (££) 64 Dien Bien Phu (tel: 031 842353; fax: 031 841044). A 28-room colonial hotel that has only maintained its façade. Uninspired rooms with TV, fridge. Restaurant, bar, sauna.

Huu Nghi (££) 62 Dien Bien Phu (tel: 031 842706/90). Once the colonial Hôtel du Commerce and clinging to this comfortable style although well renovated. Excellent restaurant, bar, air-conditioning.

Ha Long Bay

Hai Trang Hotel (£) Vuon Dao, Bai Chay (tel: 033 846094). Reasonable value in this small mini-hotel on Bai Chay's main strip. Large rooms with fan or air-conditioning.

Halong Hotel (£££) Bai Chay (tel: 033 846320; fax: 033 846318). At western end dominating the bay. Old colonial hotel now enlarged to 110 comfortable rooms, seafood restaurant.

Hoang Long (££) Bai Chay (tel: 033 846234/318). Recently modernised 56-room hotel with air-conditioning.

Queen Hotel East (£) 70 Le Thanh Tong, Hon Gai (tel: 033 826193). Eleven-room mini-hotel on eastern side of Ha Long Bay.

Suoi Mo Hotel (££) Bai Chay (tel: 033 846381; fax: 033 846729). Well-established 45-room hotel.

Van Hai Hotel (££) Bai Chay (tel: 033 846403). Right opposite the main wharf. Comfortable air-conditioned rooms with great sea views, helpful staff.

Lai Chau

Mini Hotel Lan Anh (£) Thi xa Lai Chau (tel: 023 852370). Ten-room hotel well located in centre of town, friendly owner.

Provincial Hotel (£) (tel: 023 852447). Basic facilities but there is little option.

Lao Cai

Song Hong Hotel (£) Lao Cai (tel: 020 830004/22). Located 2km from railway station right by Chinese border bridge. Large clean rooms, some with balconies and views to China. TV, phone and good bathrooms. Limited German and English.

Sa Pa

Ham Rong Hotel (£) (tel: 020 871251; fax: 020 871303). Up road behind church. Old French villa boasting spacious rooms with fireplaces. Good restaurant with snake specialities. Fills up at weekends so book ahead. Higher-than-average rates for Sa Pa.

Phuong Nam Hotel (£) (tel: 020 871286). Located on edge of village facing Phan Si Pang Mountain and overlooking valley. Fabulous views from terrace. Reasonable, basic rooms and showers (dripping plumbing) and rock-bottom prices.

Post Office Guesthouse (£) Main post office (tel: 020 871244; fax: 020 871282). Good standard of well-maintained rooms and bathrooms. Handy for postal services!

Son Ha Guesthouse (£) (tel: 020 871273). Family-owned guesthouse in solid French-style house. Rooms with private or shared bathrooms at budget prices.

Thanh Binh Hotel (£) (tel: 020 871250). Some spacious rooms with fine views at this guest-house 300m uphill from football field. Mainly shared bathrooms. Good vegetarian restaurant, limited English.

Son La

Hoa Ban Hotel (£) (tel: 022 852395). A good restaurant compensates for soulless though adequate rooms. Disco.

Son La Hotel (£) (tel: 022 852702). Close to the main bus station in the town centre. Marginally up-market compared with Son La's other offerings. State run.

Tam Dao

Tam Dao Hotel (£) (tel: 021 824234/209). Rather run down but an atmospheric hotel with sweeping views from some rooms.

THE NORTH-CENTRE
Dong Ha

Dong Ha Hotel (£) Highway 9 (tel: 053 852292). Eighteen-room modern hotel in town centre. Reasonable rooms.

Dong Truong Son Hotel (££) Km 3, Highway 9 (tel: 053 852415). Largeish hotel in rather isolated location north of town but well-kept air-conditioned rooms. Ideal if travelling by private car.

Postoffice Guesthouse (Nha Khach Buu Dien) (£) (tel: 053 852772). At southern end of town. A quiet, friendly 12-room hotel built around a courtyard.

HOTELS AND RESTAURANTS

Hue

Binh Minh Hotel (£/££) 12 Nguyen Tri Phuong (tel: 054 825526; fax: 054 828362). Wide price range varying from cheap rabbit hutches to larger rooms with balcony, TV and phone. Well located on central crossroads of east bank.

Century Riverside Inn (£££) 49 Le Loi (tel: 054 823390; fax: 054 823399). Picturesque site on Perfume River next to Huong Giang Hotel (see below). Has 138 comfortable luxury rooms and equivalent service. Restaurant, many amenities.

Dong Loi Hotel (£) 11a Pham Ngu Lao (tel: 054 822296; fax: 054 826234). On quiet central side-street one block from river. Mini-hotel with clean rooms, fan or air-conditioning. Restaurant, bicycle and motorbike rental, tours.

Duy Tan (£/££) 12 Hung Vuong (tel: 054 825001; fax: 054 826477). Large new hotel designed in colonial style dominating east bank's main crossroads. Spacious rooms, some with air-conditioning and balconies. Restaurant, tours.

Hue City Tourism Villas (££) c/o 1 Truong Dinh (tel: 054 823753/577; fax: 054 824806). Small colonial villas run by local tourist office, ideal for groups or families.

Huong Giang Hotel (£££) 51 Le Loi (tel: 054 823958; fax: 054 823102). Large modern hotel decorated in imperial style and set in gardens in prime riverside spot. Well-appointed rooms, good service, excellent restaurant. Full and half-board. Small-scale annexe in French villa style (££) is at 3 Hung Vuong (tel: 054 826070; fax: 054 826074).

Saigon Morin Hotel (££) 30 Le Loi (tel: 054 823526; fax: 054 825155). Large renovated hotel right opposite Trang Tien Bridge. Once a backpackers' favourite, now angling for the upper end of market and tour groups.

Thang Long Hotel (£) 16 Hung Vuong (tel: 054 826462/3; fax: 054 826464). New six-storey block with excellent-value rooms, some air-conditioned, some with fan. Cheap rooms with views on top floors but steep climb. Good bathrooms with tubs. Phone, restaurant, tours, bicycle rental.

Thuan Hoa Hotel (££) 7 Nguyen Tri Phuong (tel: 054 822553; fax: 054 822470). Central location for 80-room modern hotel. Air-conditioning, TV, phone, fridge, bathroom. Restaurant, coffee-shop, bar, tours and Vietnam Airlines office on premises. Soulless atmosphere.

Thuong Tu (£) 16 Dinh Tien Hoang (tel: 054 828330/1; fax: 054 828783). New hotel in atmospheric but noisy street. Up-market rooms with air-conditioning, fridge, phone, TV and real bath-tubs.

Lang Co

Lang Co Hotel (£) (tel: 054 874426). A 20-room hotel monopolising this idyllic beach, fishing village and lagoon.

Dilapidated but cheap rooms with bathrooms, good seafood restaurant.

Ninh Binh

Hoa Lu Hotel (££) Tran Hung Dao (tel: 030 871217/871807/873684; fax: 030 874126). Sprawling modern hotel with brand-new 100-room annexe on main road to Hoa Lu. Older rooms surround garden but beware of karaoke. TV and air-conditioning, massage, sauna, bar, restaurant. Overpriced.

Sao Mai (£) 30 Luong Van Tuy (tel: 030 872190). Very friendly eight-room hotel on quiet side-street. Clean rooms with TV, air-conditioning and reasonable bathrooms. Rice wine on tap, cheap bicycle and motorbike rental, excellent guide (Xuan) and good cooking by Madame Minh.

Thanh Thuy's Guesthouse (£) 128 Le Hong Phong (tel: 030 871811). Charming, simple family guest-house, recently expanded to seven rooms. Run by well-disposed young couple, Than and Thuy, always adaptable to guests' needs and budget. Cheap, good location, German and English spoken.

Thuy Anh (£/££) 55a Truong Han Sieu (tel: 030 871602; fax: 030 871200). Centrally located in side-street off Ninh Binh's main road. Very clean, modern seven-room hotel. TV, fan and excellent tiled bathrooms with bath-tubs and shower. Helpful owners.

Thanh Hoa

Sao Mai Hotel (£) Phan Chu Trinh (tel: 037 852851). Uninspired but adequate.

Thanh Hoa Tourist Hotel (£/££) 25a Quang Trung (tel: 037 852517; fax: 037 852104). Well located in centre west of Highway 1. Wide-ranging room standards and prices.

Vinh

Hong Ngoc Hotel (££) 86b Le Loi (tel: 038 841314; fax: 038 841229). Well-maintained 18-room hotel. Rooms with TV, phone, air-conditioning.

Kim Lien Hotel (££) 12 Quang Trung (tel: 038 844751; fax: 038 843699). Splurge while you can on this reasonably priced modern hotel with restaurant, massage parlour, shop and well-equipped rooms.

Thanh Lich Hotel (£) 28 Quang Trung (tel: 038 844961). Relatively new, with wide range of rooms, fan or air-conditioning.

THE SOUTH-CENTRE

Buon Ma Thuot

Cao Nguyen Hotel (££/£££) 57 Phan Chu Trinh (tel: 050 851913/4). Flashy new government-run hotel aimed at business-men. Good amenities, strict regulations, restaurant, bar. Rooms with TV, phone, air-conditioning and bath-tubs.

Tay Nguyen Hotel (£) 106 Ly Thuong Kiet (tel: 050 851009/12; fax: 050 852250). This hotel has seen better days, but offers

adequate, spacious rooms with some atmosphere. Balcony views over corrugated-iron roofs. Friendly.
White Horse/Bach Ma Hotel (££) 61/5 Hai Ba Trung (tel: 050 853963). Sparkling new hotel with well-equipped rooms, good bathrooms, TV, phone. Large restaurant and lobby area, helpful manageress.

Ca Na

Khach San Ca Na (£) Ca Na Quan, Ninh Phuoc (tel: 068 861320/1). Beachfront stilt-bungalows in stunning location south of fishing village on Highway 1. Restaurant with variable food, good service. Snorkels and masks available for exploring reef.

Da Lat

Anh Dao Hotel (££) 50–2 Hoa Binh (tel: 063 822384). Great hilltop location near market, and an up-market modern interior.
Chau Au/Europe (£) 76 Nguyen Chi Thanh (tel: 063 822870; fax: 063 824488). Well located in quiet area near centre. Decent rooms with TV and fridge.
Da Lat Palace-Sofitel (£££) 12 Tran Phu (tel: 063 825444; fax: 063 825666). Beautiful colonial building on hillside dominating lake. Recently renovated and now angling for top Asian budgets. Predictable, wide-ranging amenities.
Hang Nga Guesthouse (£/££) 3 Huynh Thuc Khang (tel: 063 822070). Not the most convenient location but certainly Da Lat's (and Vietnam's?) most eccentrically designed hotel (see panel on page 140).
Lam Son Hotel (£) 5 Hai Thuong (tel: 063 822362). Pleasant old French villa in leafy setting west of centre offering 12 comfortable rooms. Helpful management.
Palace II Hotel (££/£££) 12 Tran Hung Dao (tel: 063 822092; fax: 063 825885). Grandiose former governor-general's palace in pine forest overlooking town. Pure art deco with Vietnamese décor. Cable TV, manicured gardens, lofty reception areas. Cheaper rooms in garden annexes.
Thanh The I Hotel (£) 118 Phan Dinh Phung (tel: 063 822180). Spacious rooms, restaurant, tours. Popular with backpackers.
Truong Nguyen (£) 7a Hai Thuong (tel: 063 821772). Good mini-hotel in quiet location 10 minutes' walk from market. Clean rooms with TV, phone and some with balconies. Good breakfasts, helpful staff.
Xuan Tam (£) 25b Le Hong Phong (tel: 063 823142). Great views from site near Bao Dai's Summer Palace. Reasonable rooms and service in small family-run hotel.

Da Nang

Bach Dang Hotel (££/£££) 50 Bach Dang (tel: 051 823649; fax: 051 821659). Sprawling old favourite on waterfront. Wide range of room rates, all including buffet breakfast. Efficient and friendly. Tours, disco, shops.

Hai Au/Seagull Hotel (££) 177 Tran Phu (tel: 051 822722; fax: 051 824165). Medium-sized, central modern hotel with good-sized rooms, some with balcony. Friendly staff.
Non Nuoc Seaside Resort (££) China Beach (tel: 051 836216/7; fax: 051 836335). Three hotels form a large beach complex with extensive amenities. Reasonably well-appointed rooms, some with air-conditioning. Tours, restaurants.
Phuong Dong Hotel (££) 93 Phan Chu Trinh (tel: 051 821266; fax: 051 822854). A 36-room modern hotel in town centre with huge restaurant serving Asian and European food. Spacious rooms with air-conditioning, good views from top floors.
Tan Minh Hotel (£/££) 142 Bach Dang (tel: 051 827456; fax: 051 830172). Riverside location near market. Brand new mini-hotel with ten well-equipped rooms and bathrooms, all with air-conditioning and TV. Rooms with river views more expensive. Popular, so arrive early or book ahead.
Tan Toan (£) China Beach (tel: 051 836188). Exceptionally friendly three-room family guest-house right beside beach and close to Marble Mountains. A good alternative to frenetic Da Nang and an opportunity to get to know a Vietnamese family (former English teachers). Abundant fresh seafood, motorbike rental, transport arranged.
Vinapha (£) 80 Tran Phu (tel: 051 825072). Rather flaky but decent, airy rooms in central location. Helpful staff.

Hoi An

Hoi An Hotel (££) 6 Tran Hung Dao (tel: 051 861445; fax: 051 861636). Currently Hoi An's largest and smartest hotel, due to expand to 160 rooms and gain a swimming-pool, disco and tennis courts, so prices will rise. Some cheap barrack-like rooms with fans, others well equipped with TV, fridge, phone and breakfast. Popular with tour groups so book ahead. Restaurant, gardens, quiet location on edge of old town.
Pho Hoi/Faifo Hotel (£) 7/2 Tran Phu (tel: 051 861633; fax: 051 861382). Converted house in market area with wide range of rooms, some air-conditioned, others with fans and shared bathroom. Avoid windowless type. Efficient management, breakfast.
Phu Thinh (£) 144 Tran Phu (tel: 051 861297; fax: 051 861757). Very central location. Modern hotel fronting garden/courtyard, clean rooms though some are windowless. Air-conditioning or fan. Friendly.
Sao Bien/Seastar Hotel (£) 15 Cua Dai (tel: 051 861589; fax: 051 861382). New modern hotel on road to beach but still convenient for centre. Excellent value; very comfortable well-maintained rooms and bathrooms, small garden. Staff eager to please.

HOTELS AND RESTAURANTS

Thuy Duong I (£) 11 Le Loi (tel: 051 861574; fax: 051 861330). One of Hoi An's first mini-hotels, now in need of a facelift. Atmospheric but rooms on small side and bathrooms run down. **Thuy Duong II**, 68 Huynh Thuc Khang (tel: 051 861394) is a new annexe near bus station with a better standard but less centrally located.
Vinh Hung (£/££) 143 Tran Phu (tel: 051 861621; fax: 051 861893). Traditional old hotel in Hoi An's most interesting street. Variety of rooms, atmospheric Chinese-style lobby and bar. Pricier rooms are spacious, with air-conditioning, phone, good bathrooms and breakfast. Friendly staff.

Kon Tum
Bank Guesthouse (£) 88 Tran Phu (tel: 060 862610). Central location, air-conditioned rooms.
Dakbla Hotel (£/££) 2 Phan Dinh Phung (tel: 060 863333; fax: 060 864407). Comfortable, 43-room, air-conditioned hotel near the Dakbla river.
Quang Trung Hotel (£/££) 168 Ba Trieu (tel: 060 862249). Formerly the People's Committee guest-house, so rooms are reasonably well-appointed.

Mui Ne
Hai Duong Resort (££/£££) Km 12.5, Ham Tien, Phan Thiet (tel: 062 848401/2; fax: 062 848402). Thirteen bungalows and two villas with private terrace and air-conditioning. Facilities include a billiard table, swimming-pool, jacuzzi, private beach and watersports.

Nha Trang
Bao Dai Hotel (££/£££) Cau Da, Vinh Nguyen (tel: 058 881048/9; fax: 058 881471). Forty-eight rooms in 1920s villas scattered over beautifully landscaped hillside. Atmospheric, palatial scale, views, tennis court and great bar/restaurant. Somewhat isolated from energy of town centre.
Grand Hotel (££/£££) 44 Tran Phu (tel: 058 822445; fax: 058 825395). Nha Trang's gracious old lady could have been transported from La Croisette in Cannes. Cavernous rooms with original art deco furnishings, peeling bathrooms, all over-looking garden or sea and promenade. Very central. Lobby used as TV lounge for local youth.
Hai Yen Hotel (££/£££) 40 Tran Phu (tel: 058 822828; fax: 058 821902). Up-market 107-room modern hotel in good seafront location. Restaurant, nightclub, sauna, tours, ticketing. Service not the best.
My A (£) 9 Nguyen Thien Thuat (tel: 058 827312/3; fax: 058 824214). Ugly grey concrete block but offers decent-sized rooms with fan or air-conditioning, some with good views. Central location, restaurant. Also houses Sinh Café office for tours and tourist bus.

Rose Mini-Hotel (£) 26b Nguyen Thien Thuat (tel: 058 822778; fax: 058 823842). Small budget hotel set back from street. Rooms with air-conditioning, TV.
Vien Dong Hotel (££/£££) 1 Tran Hung Dao (tel: 058 821606/8; fax: 058 821912). Classic government-run hotel housing tourist office, prime seafront location. Four types of rooms, ample amenities such as pool and tennis courts. Transport for hire, tours.

Phan Rang
Huu Nghi Hotel (£) 354 Thong Nhat (tel: 068 822721/606). Just south of pagoda and close to bus station in town centre. Has 21 reasonably comfortable rooms, some with air-conditioning.
Ninh Chu Hotel (£/££) Khanh Hai Commune (tel: 068 873900/44; fax: 068 873023). On beach 5km south of Phan Rang. Scenic spot and adequate comfort.
Thong Nhat Hotel (££) 99 Thong Nhat (tel: 068 827201; fax: 068 822943). Recently refurbished four-storey hotel with 16 rooms. Good location.

Phan Thiet
Novotel Vinh Thuy Resort and Dunes Golf Club (£££) 1 Duc Ton Thang (tel: 062 823365/822393; fax: 062 825682). Brand new four-star 123-room hotel, with suites, two swimming-pools, private beach, sports facilities, business and conference centre, three restaurants. The 18-hole golf course was designed by Nick Faldo.
Phan Thiet Hotel (£) 276 Tran Hung Dao (tel: 062 821694/5). Well-appointed hotel in centre of Phan Thiet with range of rooms, fan or air-conditioning.

Plei Ku
Movie Star/Dien Anh Hotel (££) 6 Vo Thi Sau (tel: 059 823855). Recent addition to Plei Ku's concrete. With a name like this, dynamism is in the air. Well-appointed rooms, quiet location to west of centre.
Plei Ku Hotel (££) 124 Le Loi (tel: 059 824628). This is the headquarters of the government-run Gialai Tourism Company, but is not to everyone's taste.
Yaly Hotel (£/££) 89 Hung Vuong (tel: 059 824843/858). Convenient central location near local cafés on Highway 19. Decent rooms and bathrooms, with or without air-conditioning.

Quang Ngai
Song Tra Hotel (£/££) 2 Quang Trung (tel: 055 822665). Classic example of a government-run hotel: nonchalant staff; over-priced; dilapidated; and bug-ridden though spacious rooms, some even with nice river views. Worth negotiating. At northern end of town near turn-off to My Lai.

Quy Nhon
Bank Hotel (£) 259 Le Hong Phong (tel: 056 822779; fax: 056 821013). Overlooking Quy

Nhon's euphemistically named 'park' in town centre. Bright lobby, gloomy corridors but good-sized clean rooms, some with balconies. Lurid green paint and lurex dominate. Rooms with fan or air-conditioning, some with TV and fridge. Friendly staff.

Binh Duong Hotel (££) 493 Nguyen Hue (tel: 056 846267/355). Thirty well-equipped rooms in discreetly designed modern beachfront hotel. Air-conditioning, TV, fridge, phone. Huge restaurant.

Hai Ha Mini-Hotel (£/££) 5 Tran Binh Trong (tel: 056 821295; fax: 056 824300). Quy Nhon's first mini-hotel, in typical glass and concrete mode. Ten well-equipped rooms, two restaurants.

Quy Nhon Hotel (££) 130 Nguyen Hue (tel: 056 822401; fax: 056 821162). Beachfront location next to tourist office. Modern government hotel with 80 rooms, restaurants, tours, karaoke, souvenir shops.

Sa Huynh

Sa Huynh Hotel (£) (tel: 055 860311). Friendly beach hotel at southern end of village. Rooms with fan and cold water only, most becoming rapidly decrepit, but the scenic, outdoor location compensates.

HO CHI MINH CITY

Bach Dang Hotel (££) 33 Mac Thi Buoi, District 1 (tel: 08 825 1501; fax: 08 823 0587). New, reasonably solidly built hotel in convenient spot between riverfront and Dong Khoi. Pristine rooms with air-conditioning, bath-tub, satellite TV, phone, mini-bar. Restaurant, bar, terrace, ticketing, tours.

Bi Saigon (£/££) 185/26 and 185/16 Pham Ngu Lao, District 1 (tel: 08 836 0678/839 0979). New family-run hotel down quiet lane in backpackers' district. High-standard large rooms with phone and satellite TV. Good bathrooms, fan or air-conditioning.

Bong Sen I (££/£££) 117 Dong Khoi, District 1 (tel: 08 829 1516; fax: 08 829 8076). Popular central hotel with wide range of rates. Comfortable rooms, restaurant.

Caravelle Hotel (£££) 17–23 Lam Son, District 1 (tel: 08 829 3704/6; fax: 08 829 6767). One of Saigon's landmark hotels, with a central location in the 'golden triangle' and endless amenities. Popular with French visitors; Air France office is located here. Closed for renovation until late 1998.

Continental Hotel (£££) 132 Dong Khoi, District 1 (tel: 08 829 4456/9255; fax: 08 824 1772). A colonial classic now refurbished in luxurious style. Prime position opposite opera house. Once a Graham Greene favourite, but the watering-hole terrace has now disappeared.

Dong Du Guesthouse (£) 26 Dong Du, District 1 (tel: 08 829 6382; fax: 08 829 6377). Slightly overpriced but large clean rooms

and central location near Saigon's bars. Fan or air-conditioning. Friendly family.

Huy Hoang (££) 270 Ly Tu Trong, District 1 (tel: 08 822 4140; fax: 08 829 5120). Good rooms, excellent service, very helpful staff and central location.

New World Hotel (£££) 76 Le Lai, District 1 (tel: 08 822 8888; fax: 08 823 0710). Luxury modern hotel built by Hong Kong businessmen to top Asian standards. Expensive, but has wide-ranging facilities.

Ngoc Dang (£) 254 De Tham, District 1 (tel: 08 833 2019). Friendly, clean mini-hotel with decent rooms and rates. Fan or air-conditioning.

Orchid Hotel (££) 29a Don Dat, District 1 (tel: 08 823 1809; fax: 08 829 2245). Decent mid-range hotel in heart of nocturnal bar area. Comfortable rooms with air-conditioning. Restaurant, coffee-shop.

Que Huong/Liberty Hotel (££) 167 Hai Ba Trung, District 3 (tel: 08 829 4227; fax: 08 829 0919). Outside the main action in the quieter residential and consular district. Well-maintained 50-room hotel.

Quyen Thanh (££) 212 De Tham (tel: 08 832 2370; fax: 08 832 4946). Spiffy new hotel on crossroads in budget travellers' haven. Good-sized rooms with tiled bathrooms and balconies, all air-conditioned.

Rex Hotel (£££) 141 Nguyen Hue, District 1 (tel: 08 829 6043; fax: 08 829 6536). By far the best value of Saigon's up-market landmark hotels, in 1950s style extensively revisited with Vietnamese decoration. Unbeatable rooftop restaurant-bar, charming service. Features include individual faxes and umbrellas in each room.

Saigon Hotel (££) 45 Dong Du, District 1 (tel: 08 829 9734; fax: 08 829 1466). Established modern hotel block in excellent central location. Clean, reasonable rooms, mostly air-conditioned and with satellite TV. Breakfast included in rates. Popular, so booking is advisable.

MEKONG DELTA

Bac Lieu

Bac Lieu Hotel (£) 4 Hoang Van Thu (tel: 078 822621). A 26-room hotel with a wide range of rooms, from singles with shared toilet to air-conditioned doubles.

Ben Tre

Ben Tre Hotel (£) 8–2 Tran Quoc Tuan (tel: 075 822223). Depending on your budget, a choice of fan or air-conditioned room.

Dong Khoi Hotel (££) 16 Hai Ba Trung (tel: 075 822240). Thirty-five rooms, all of which are air-conditioned.

Hung Vuong Hotel (£) 166 Hung Vuong (tel: 075 822408). Expect to pay considerably more for rooms with air-conditioning.

Ca Mau

Bong Hong Hotel (£) 12b Quang Trung (tel: 078 831544). Classic mini-hotel with reasonable rates, but needs a facelift.

HOTELS AND RESTAURANTS

Phuong Nam Hotel (££) 92 Phan Dinh Phung (tel: 078 832129/ 831752). Large modern hotel, Ca Mau's best, with fan-cooled or air-conditioned rooms, the latter also with satellite TV and phone.

Can Tho
Hau Giang Hotel (££) 34 Nam Ky Khoi Nghia (tel: 071 821851; fax: 071 821806). Uninspired block in town centre; 36 fairly comfortable rooms with air-conditioning. **International Hotel** (££/£££) 10/12 Hai Ba Trung (tel: 071 822079; fax: 071 821039). Semi-modern hotel overlooking river. Slick service, 40 good rooms (air-conditioned or fan-cooled) but high rates. Restaurant. **Ninh Kieu** (££) 2 Hai Ba Trung (tel: 071 821171; fax: 071 821104). Large government-run hotel in walled garden at end of river promenade. Up-market prices, slow service, reasonable comfort. Floating restaurant is pleasant but food indifferent. **Tay Ho** (£) 36 Hai Ba Trung (tel: 071 823392). When top hotels are full (often the case) this is a reasonable budget stand-by. Old building at heart of riverside action. Some rooms with air-conditioning.

Cao Lanh
Song Tra Hotel (££) 178 Nguyen Hue (tel: 067 851843/852504). Large, flashy new hotel on main road. Wide range of rooms, all air-conditioned with TV, phone, fridge.

Chau Doc
Hang Chau Hotel (£/££) 32 Le Loi (tel: 076 866196/7 fax: 076 867773). Surprisingly up-market hotel in strategic river confluence site. Air-conditioned rooms with balconies, bungalows or suites. Good restaurant and friendly service. **My Loc** (£) 51b Nguyen Van Thoai (tel: 076 866167/455). Friendly, ageing hotel in town centre. Large rooms with fan or air-conditioning, restaurant. **Thanh Tra Hotel** (£) 77 Thu Khoa Nghia (tel: 076 866845). Popular new hotel just to north-west of main square. Reasonable rooms and rates, slightly dozy staff. Breakfast room/lobby in blinding neon.

Con Son Island
Phi Yen Hotel (£) 34 Ton Duc Thang (tel: 064 830168; fax: 064 830206). Offers simple rooms with fridge, hot water and fan or air-conditioning. **Sai Gon-Con Dao Resort** (££) 18–24 Ton Duc Thang (tel/fax: 064 830155). A brand new resort overlooking the beach. Five villas, each with four to six rooms with air-conditioning and hot shower or bath. Motor bikes, cars and bicycles for hire, plus restaurant with international and Vietnamese cuisine.

Ha Tien
Dong Ho Hotel (£) Tran Hau (tel: 077 852141). Hard to miss opposite toll-bridge

on main river strip. Atmospheric old building with lofty rooms, desperately needing renovation. Shared toilets in hall. Overpriced. Home to limited tourist office. **Khai Hoan Hotel** (£) 239 Phuong Thanh (tel: 077 852254). Recently built family-owned hotel in side-street off market and river strip. Decent clean rooms with fan or air-conditioning, friendly, good value.

Long Hai
Military Guesthouse (£) (tel: 064 868316). At north end of beach. Seventeen-room hotel plus beach bungalows. Reasonably well maintained.

Long Xuyen
Long Xuyen Hotel (£) 17 Nguyen Van Cung (tel: 076 841927/843394; fax: 076 842483). Good standard on main square. Rooms with fans, air-conditioning, family suites. Next door is the less salubrious **Cuu Long Hotel** (£) (tel: 076 841365), and opposite is the smarter **Thai Binh** (£) (tel: 076 841184).

My Tho
Huong Duong Hotel (£) 33 Trung Trac (tel: 073 872011; fax: 873578). Reasonably well-maintained government-run hotel. Rooms with fan or air-conditioning, friendly staff. **Rang Dong** (£) 25 30 Thang 4 (tel: 073 874400/10). New mini-hotel with spacious air-conditioned rooms, some overlooking Mekong River. Range from basic with bathroom to family suites. Helpful staff. Restaurant with Western and Chinese food.

Phu Quoc Island
Huong Bien Hotel (£) Duong Dong (tel: 077 846050/082). Phu Quoc's extremely limited accommodation makes this virtually the only choice. Three standards of simple rooms in centre of main harbour town.

Rach Gia
Nha Hang 1.5 Hotel (£) 38 Nguyen Hung Son (tel: 077 862103; fax: 077 862111). Better known as May 1st Hotel. Helpful staff but small and/or windowless rooms, fan or air-conditioning. Central location, opposite tourist office. Car and boat rental. **To Chau Hotel** (£) 4f Le Loi (tel: 077 863718; fax: 077 862111). Few façades can beat this one in the uninspiring stakes, but rooms are decent and spacious with fan or air-conditioning. Avoid noisy front. Huge restaurant at back. Bicycle and boat rental.

Soc Trang
Khanh Hung Hotel (£) 15 Tran Hung Dao (tel: 079 821026/7; fax: 079 820099). Excellent value with wide price range. Cheaper rooms on upper floors with balconies, TV, phone and fan or air-conditioning. Reasonable location south of market. Restaurant, outdoor café popular for breakfasts.

Tay Nam Hotel (£) 131–3 Nguyen Chi Thanh (tel: 079 821757/822745). Run-down government hotel with basic rooms. Not recommended unless you are desperate. Tourist office in same building.

Tay Ninh

Hoa Binh Hotel (££) 210, 30 Thang 4 (tel: 066 822345). Massive Stalinist concrete monolith but decent rooms with air-conditioning, restaurant.

Tra Vinh

Cuu Long Hotel (£) 999 Nguyen Thi Minh Khai (tel: 074 862615). Standard government hotel, limited English spoken. Located on outskirts of town.
Thanh Tra Hotel (£/££) 1 Pham Thai Buong (tel: 074 863622/1). On main street near market. Friendly staff, wide range from fan-cooled rooms to air-conditioning with all mod cons.

Vinh Long

Cuu Long Hotel B (£/££) 1 1 Thang 5 (tel: 070 823656; fax: 070 823357). The best location in Vinh Long. Spacious rooms with balconies and river views, cheaper on top floor (fan only). TV, phone. **Cuu Long A** (the original, and more expensive) is across small park on riverbank (tel: 070 822494).

Vung Tau

Grand Hotel (££) 26 Quang Trung, Bai Truoc (tel: 064 856469; fax: 064 856088). Large 76-room hotel fronting Japanese-style garden with café on Front Beach. Very reasonable rates include breakfast. Rooms with phone, satellite TV, air-conditioning. Restaurant, beauty salon, barber.
Hai Au Hotel (££) 100 Ha Long (tel: 064 856178; fax: 064 856868). Nice hillside location on corniche overlooking Front Beach. Reasonable rooms, extensive amenities, pool, restaurant. Popular with tour groups.
Royal Hotel (££/£££) 48 Quang Trung, Bai Truoc (tel: 064 859852; fax: 064 859851). Formerly the Canadian Hotel. Revamped three-storey hotel on seafront of Front Beach. Has 53 comfortable rooms with air-conditioning, phone, satellite TV. Good restaurant, pool in garden.
Thang Muoi Hotel (£/££) 4 Thuy Van, Bai Sau (tel: 064 852665; fax: 064 859876). Atmospheric old hotel set in shady gardens on Back Beach. Pool, restaurant.

ANGKOR

Cambodia international telephone code: 85
Angkor Village (££) Wat Bo Road, Sangkat 4 (Postal address: PO Box 151, Phnom Penh; tel: 023 57503; mobile tel: 015 916048). A haven of good taste. Traditional Khmer bungalows on stilts connected by plankwalks. Excellent restaurant, daily set menu. Rooms with fan or air-conditioning.

Grand Hotel d'Angkor (£££) c/o Raffles International, 11 Beach Road #06-00, Singapore 189675 (tel: 65 339 8377; fax: 65 339 1713). Fabulously renovated old colonial hotel at crossroads of Siem Reap village and road to Angkor. Over 300 rooms and villas, 24-hour butler service, and five restaurants. Pool, lush park, childminders.
Hôtel de la Paix (££) Sivutha Street, Sangkat 2 (tel: Phnom Penh 015 918771; mobile tel: 015 911131). Favourite old stand-by with straightforward air-conditioned rooms and restaurant.
Stung Siem Reap (££) Wat Promreth (tel: 015 914058). Attractively renovated colonial townhouse in centre, close to river and new market. Restaurant, reasonably priced air-conditioned rooms and helpful, intelligent staff.
Ta Prohm Hotel (£££) c/o 29 Samdech Sothearos Boulevard, Phnom Penh (tel: 015 913638/2895; tel/fax: 015 911783). Newish air-conditioned hotel in strategic riverfront position at southern end of Siem Reap near new market. Good though overpriced rooms with satellite TV.

257

RESTAURANTS

The restaurants listed below have been divided into three price categories:

- **budget** (£)
- **moderate** (££)
- **expensive** (£££)

HANOI

A Little Italian (££) 78 Tho Nhuom (tel: 04 825 8167). Predictable Italian fare but good pizzas and pasta. Popular, noisy.
Apocalypse Now (£) 338 Ba Trieu (tel: 04 821 6416). An offshoot of Saigon's original; equally noisy and crowded.
Baan Thai Restaurant (££) 3b Cha Ca (tel: 04 828 1120). Newly opened, rather soulless air-conditioned Thai restaurant, part of hotel. Popular with local expats, reasonably priced but not the best Thai cooking.
Café de Paris (££) 16 Nguyen Cong Tru (tel: 04 821 2701). Live accordion music on Wednesday and Saturday nights stresses Hanoi's Gallic past in this café.
Cha Ca La Vong (££) 14 Cha Ca (tel: 04 825 3929). Old family-run restaurant that perpetuates a tradition of fish and fresh greens cooked on a table-top hotplate. Usually packed so bookings are advisable.
Cherry Blossom Inn/Sakura (££) 16 Le Thai To (tel: 04 826 6377). Not the most authentic Japanese food but a great lakeside setting with first-floor terrace. Wide variety of international cuisine, friendly staff.
Club Opéra (£££) 59 Ly Thai To (tel: 04 826 8802). Attractive colonial building run by

the Vietnamese journalists' association. Ground floor for international cuisine and first floor for Vietnamese dishes.

Green Bamboo Café (££) 42 Nha Chung (tel: 04 826 8752). Somewhat up-market 'travellers' café' with tour desk, reading matter and reasonable Western food.

Indochine (£££) 16 Nam Ngu (tel: 04 824 6097). Hard to beat the setting, elegant service, refined cuisine and price in Hanoi.

Polite Pub (£) 5 Bao Khanh (tel: 04 825 0959). Popular expat watering-hole.

Restaurant Bistro (£££) 34 Tran Hung Dao (tel: 04 826 6136). Affordable French cuisine includes seafood, pigeon and a variety of meats. Lively, popular with French groups.

Restaurant 202 (£££) 202a Pho Hue (tel: 04 825 9487). Long-established restaurant offering traditional Vietnamese and French dishes. Nice setting, good service.

Smiling Café (£) 100 Cau Go (tel: 04 825 2750). A small corner café with good street views, serving excellent, good-value food, starting with early breakfasts at 6am. Not to be confused with upper-floor restaurant of same name a few doors away.

Sunset Pub (££) Dong Do Hotel, 31 Cao Ba (tel: 04 823 0173). Breezy rooftop gathering place for Hanoi's younger crowd: snacks, pizzas, drinks, live music.

Thit Ran (£) Thon Le Mat, Xa Viet Hung, Gia Lam, Dien Thoai (tel: 04 827 2872). Specialises in snake meat: your chosen victim is killed and prepared at your table, and the blood drunk as a pick me up.

THE NORTH-CENTRE
Hue
Am Phu (£) 35 Nguyen Thai Hoc (tel: 054 825259). An excellent address on road by stadium, one block back from Century Riverside Hotel. Delicious Hue specialities in popular canteen-style restaurant. Try the Hue spring rolls with pork or 'torn chicken'.

Song Huong (££) 3 Thang 2 Park, Le Loi (tel: 054 823738). A great location for this restaurant on stilts over river, but mediocre cuisine. Varied Western and Vietnamese dishes.

THE SOUTH-CENTRE
Da Lat
Shanghai Restaurant (£) 8 Khu Hoa Binh (tel: 063 822509). Immediately west of cinema and main square. Vietnamese, Chinese and French cuisine served 8am–10pm in lively atmosphere.

Thanh Thanh Restaurant (££) 4 Tang Bat Ho (tel: 063 821836). Popular with tour groups for its up-market setting and wide choice of Vietnamese and Western dishes.

Da Nang
Christies Harbourside (££) 9 Bach Dang (tel: 051 826645). Built on stilts over river with good views. Bar and lounge area, billiards,

restaurant. A favourite meeting place for Da Nang's expats, and run by a New Zealander. Western and Vietnamese menu.

Hoi An
Café des Amis (£) 52 Bach Dang (tel: 051 861616). Mr Kim produces one set menu (seafood and/or vegetarian) which changes daily. The very refined cuisine is served by his sons. Popularity may eventually mar the high standards.

Han Huyen (£) Bach Dang (tel: 051 861462). Hoi An's diminutive floating restaurant, just round the river bend from Japanese Bridge. Chinese-influenced cuisine plus Vietnamese specialities, such as shrimps grilled on sugar cane then rolled in rice-cakes with fresh herbs.

Restaurant Thanh (£) 76 Bach Dang. Friendly family-run restaurant in one of Hoi An's old riverside houses. Atmosphere enhanced by Chinese lanterns and candle-light. Good choice of vegetarian (including guacamole), seafood and Western dishes.

Kon Tum
Dakbla's Restaurant (£) 168 Nguyen Hue (tel: 060 862584). Small restaurant serving reasonably priced Vietnamese food. Popular with tourists.

Nha Trang
Ngoc Suong (££) 16 Tran Quang Khai (tel: 058 827030). Up-market local business-men's favourite in discreet garden one block inland from sailing club. Incredible seafood menu includes clams in alcohol, raw fish, oysters, crab, stewed jellyfish and lobster. Fish tanks hold the ultra-fresh ingredients. Roast sparrows too.

Nha Trang Sailing Club (££) 72–4 Tran Phu (tel: 058 826528; fax: 058 821906). Scenic spot in gardens opening on to beach. The lively, well-designed Australian-owned bar and restaurant attract Nha Trang's expat crowd. European food, cocktails.

Sao Bien/Seastar (£) 2b Ly Tu Trong (tel: 058 824122). Garden restaurant set back from main seafront stretch. Nothing flashy, but friendly and good-value Vietnamese seafood. Garden decorations include bonsais, TV, Santa Claus and billiards tables.

Vietnam I (£) 23 Hoang Van Thu (tel: 058 822933) and **Vietnam II** (£) 7 Hoang Van Thu (tel: 058 826588). Two holes in the wall at northern end of town. Excellent seafood, meat or vegetable dishes, efficiently served. Vietnam I is older and opens on to a street corner; Vietnam II is a modern air-conditioned dining-room.

Quy Nhon
Pacific Restaurant (£) 274 Le Hong Phong (tel: 056 823710). Bright, clean family restaurant; well-disposed owners. Seafood and meat dishes prepared in Chinese or Vietnamese style. Limited English spoken.

HO CHI MINH CITY

'A' Russian Restaurant (££) 361/8 Nguyen Dinh Chieu, District 3 (tel: 08 835 9190). Not surprisingly given Vietnam's recent history, Russian cuisine has arrived. Delicious blinis, bortsch and vodka, managed by a Russian-Vietnamese family.

Ashoka (££) 17A/10 Le Thanh Ton, District 1 (tel: 08 823 1372). Excellent aromatic Indian dishes in an appropriate décor.

Banh Xeo (£) 46a Dinh Cong Trang, District 1 (tel: 08 824 1110). Saigon's best restaurant for sampling delicious *banh xeo* (Vietnamese pancakes, stuffed with beansprouts, shrimps and pork), served with lettuce and fresh herbs, and dipped in *nuoc mam* (fish sauce).

Buffalo Blues (££) 72A Nguyen Du, District 1 (tel: 08 822 2874). The quality bar food can be washed down with draught beer. Lively, noisy, open late.

Chez Guido (££) Continental Hotel, 132 Dong Khoi (tel: 08 829 9201). Popular Italian restaurant with pasta, pizzas and more refined dishes. Rapid service.

Globo (££) 6 Nguyen Thiep, District 1 (tel: 08 822 8855). French-owned bar-restaurant with imaginative African décor. *Tapas* and Tex-Mex dishes dominate.

Kim Café (£) 272 De Tham (tel: 08 835 9859). A classic budget traveller's hang-out in the heart of the Pham Ngu Lao area. Western food, low prices, travel tips.

La Bibliothèque (£££) 84A Nguyen Du, District 1 (tel: 08 823 1438). Unusual set-up managed by Madame Dai, a former lawyer with a Parisian background, who seats customers in her antique- and tome-filled library. French and Vietnamese cuisine. Limited space so booking essential.

La Camargue (£££) 16 Cao Ba Quat, District 1 (tel: 08 824 3148). Highly recommended by Ho Chi Minh City's expat population and popular with businessmen. Chic, colonial ambience with open-air terrace. French and international cuisine.

Le Mékong (£££) 32 Vo Van Tan, District 3 (tel: 08 829 1277). *Maître d'hôtel* Mki accompanies hostess Diep on the rounds in this refined colonial villa. Delicately prepared seafood and French specialities.

Lemon Grass (££) 4 Nguyen, District 1 (tel: 08 822 0496). Good Vietnamese food; popular with young business people. Occasional live traditional music.

Liberty/Tu Do (££) 80 Dong Khoi, District 1 (tel: 08 829 9820). Popular with young, hip and monied Vietnamese who eat local, Chinese or Western food before hitting the dance floor upstairs.

Mini Japanese Restaurant (££) 50 Dong Du, District 1 (tel: 08 824 4284). Welcome relief from Ho Chi Minh City's other Japanese joints, which target businessmen's expense accounts. Red lanterns, *tatami* mats, cane furniture and walls papered with Japanese menus. Intimate, authentic and fun.

Sa Pa (££) 26 Thai Van Lung, District 1 (tel: 08 829 5754). Low ceiling fans and a long curving bar set off the unusual menu of Vietnamese and Swiss dishes.

Siren Floating Restaurant (££) Bach Dang Wharf (tel: 08 822 5402). A floating restaurant without the usual high-decibel music. Reasonable seafood while boat does its 90-minute tour.

Tib (££) 187 Hai Ba Trung, District 3 (tel: 08 829 7242). Elegant setting and extensive menu of Hue-style imperial cuisine.

Vietnam House (££) 93–5 Dong Khoi, District 1 (tel: 08 829 1623). Attractively restored and charmingly run, with Vietnamese traditions kept intact (food, musicians, waitresses' *ao dai*). Two floors include piano-bar and interconnecting dining areas.

Vy Restaurant (£££) 164 Pasteur Street, District 1 (tel: 08 829 6210). Vietnamese, Western and Chinese menus in a large colonial villa with garden patio. Piano, guitar and violin chamber music accompanies fresh seafood specialities.

MEKONG DELTA

Chau Doc

Lam Hung Ky (£) 71 Chi Lang (tel: 076 866745). Efficient Chinese-owned restaurant in market area near other similar establishments.

Hon Chong

Tan Phat Restaurant (£) (tel: 077 854404). Large breezy restaurant on stilts over water with lovely view of islands. French-speaking waiter. Fresh crab and fish from net below kitchen. Located in hamlet between cement works and main stretch of beaches, easily visible from road.

Soc Trang

Hung (£) 74–6 Mau Than 68 (tel: 079 822268). A Mekong experience not to be missed. Chinese dishes of eels, crabs, prawns, fish or snake served in large colourful canteen. Portable table-burners, itinerant fans, Chinese lanterns, photo-murals of Brooklyn Bridge, Eiffel Tower and a Swiss chalet add to ambience. Very popular with local Chinese businessmen.

ANGKOR

Bayon (£) Siem Reap. A popular courtyard restaurant which fills up rapidly, so get there early. Good Cambodian and other Asian cuisine dished up in a verdant setting. Check your bill.

Green House (£) 58 Mondol II, Sangkat 2 (tel: 015 920467). At beginning of airport road near centre. Charming little restaurant, partly open-air with endless decorative efforts. Wide-ranging menu includes Western, Thai, Chinese and Cambodian dishes, pleasantly served. Adjoining guest-house is popular and slightly up-market.

Index

Bold figures denote
the main entry of a
particular subject.

INDEX

ACKNOWLEDGEMENTS

Picture credits

The Automobile Association would like to thank the following photographers and libraries for their assistance in the preparation of this book.

AXIOM PHOTOGRAPHIC LIBRARY 21g, 28a, 28b, 29, 30b, 31a, 31b, 40, 66b, 80, 114/5, 126a, 138, 172, 216, 220/1, 222, 223, 224a, 224b, 226, 227, 228, 229, 231, 238 (J. Holmes);

BRUCE COLEMAN COLLECTION 105b (Rod Williams);

F. DUNLOP 18b, 19a, 116a, 125a, 125b, 127a, 136c, 143a, 158, 161, 178b, 207a, 214b, 218a, 218b, 219b, 225, 232a;

MARY EVANS PICTURE LIBRARY 90b, 116b;

THE RONALD GRANT ARCHIVE 166a, 166b, 167a, 167b, 167c, 167d;

HULTON GETTY 14b, 44a, 45b, 48b, 60b;

LINK PICTURE LIBRARY 32a, 32b (Shari Kessler);

MAGNUM PHOTOS 42a (Marc Riboud), 42b (Ian Berry), 42c (Marc Riboud), 44b (Don McCullin), 45a (Philip Jones Griffiths), 46/7 (Bruno Barbey), 46 (Marc Riboud), 47 (Bruno Barbey), 204a (P. J. Griffiths), 204b (P. J. Griffiths), 204c (P. J. Griffiths), 230a (P. J. Griffiths), 230b (P. J. Griffiths);

TIM PAGE PHOTOGRAPHY 108a, 108b, 109a, 109b;

TONY STONE IMAGES front cover

All remaining photographs are held in the Associaiton's own library (**AA PHOTO LIBRARY**) and were taken by **JIM HOLMES** with the exception of the following pages 192/3 (**B. DAVIES**), 208a, 208/9, 209c, 209d (**K PATERSON**), 121b (**I. MOREJOHN**), 90a, 104, 219a (**R STRANGE**).

Author's Acknowledgements

The author would like to thank the following for their help and inspiration: Patricia and Bob Greenfield, John Chalmers, Kirsten Lewis, the driver who knows every corner of the Mekong Delta, Nguyen Quynh Chuong, and the most cheerful motor bike-taxi-driver of the Centre, Than.

Contributors

Copy editor: Susi Bailey
Designer: Alan Gooch   **Verifier**: Tran Thi Hoa
Indexer: Marie Lorimer